P.F.M. FONTAINE

THE LIGHT AND THE DARK

A CULTURAL HISTORY OF DUALISM

VOLUME XIV

J.C. GIEBEN, PUBLISHER
AMSTERDAM

THE LIGHT AND THE DARK

P.F.M. FONTAINE

THE LIGHT AND THE DARK
A CULTURAL HISTORY OF DUALISM

VOLUME XIV

DUALISM IN ROMAN HISTORY V

'ENEMIES OF THE ROMAN ORDER'

J.C. GIEBEN, PUBLISHER
AMSTERDAM 1999

To my friend Dr. Joop G. Toebes,
historian, didactician,
expert in American history,
my companion on many travels

No part of this book may be translated or reproduced in any form, by print, photo microfilm, or any other means, without written permission from the publisher.

© by P.F.M. Fontaine / ISBN 90 5063 148 7 / Printed in The Netherlands

"For all things are called
light and darkness"

Parmenides

CONTENTS

Preface — XIII

Manual — XXI

I DUALISM IN THE PHILOSOPHY OF LATE ANTIQUITY — 1

PART I ROMAN EPICUREANISM — 1

1. A flash-back — 1
2. Lucretius — 2
   a. The contingency of the atoms — 2
   b. No place for the traditional gods — 3
   c. Was Lucretius a religious person? — 3
   d. Dualism in Lucretius — 4
   e. What made Epicureanism attractive — 5

PART II THE ROMAN STOICS — 6

1. Seneca, his life — 6
2. The Stoic — 7
3. Psychological dualism — 7
4. Materialism — 8
5. Seneca's religion — 8
6. Seneca a dualist? — 10
7. Epictetus and his works — 12
8. A pre-Christian? — 12
9. Soul and body — 13
10. A philosopher on the imperial throne — 14
11. What Roman Stoics have in common — 16

PART III ROMAN NEOPYTHAGOREANISM — 16

1. The eclipse of the original Pythagoreanism — 16
2. The revival of Pythagoreanism in the last century B.C. — 17
3. The mystical urge — 18
4. Pythagoreanism in Rome — 18
5. Pythagoreanism and Neopythagoreanism — 19
6. Numenius the Neopythagorean — 20
   a. Who was Numenius? — 20
   b. Numenius a dualist? — 20
   c. The origin of Numenius' dualism — 22

		d. The First God and the Demiurge	22
		e. The world souls	24
		f. The two souls in the human person	24
	PART IV MIDDLE PLATONISM		25
1.	Plato's heritage		25
2.	Antiochus of Ascalon		26
3.	Albinus and Alcinous: two persons or one?		27
4.	Alcinous and his 'didaskalikos'		27
		a. The man and his handbook	27
		b. Alcinous' theory of the soul	28
		c. Alcinous' conception of man	29
		d. Alcinous' idea of philosophy	30
5.	Plutarch: historian, essayist, moralist, philosopher		30
		a. The man and his work	30
		b. Plutarch's attitude towards Rome	31
		c. Plutarch on women	31
		d. Plutarch's conception of God	32
		e. The One and the Many	33
		f. Metaphysical dualism	33
		g. The transcendent god	35
		h. Plutarch's dualism	35
		j. The world soul	37
		k. The human soul as a construct	38
		l. The soul as a mixture	39
		m. Conclusion	41
6.	Atticus, the purifier of Platonism		41
		a. The man and his philosophical position	41
		b. The composite soul	42
		c. Atticus on matter	42
		d. The work of creation	43
		e. Pre-cosmic dualism	43
		f. The impossible feat of no mean philosopher	44
	PART V NEOPLATONISM		45
1.	Plotinus		45
		a. The man and his work	45
		b. The man object of his philosophy	46
		c. Plotinus hard to comprehend	47
		d. Plotinus the thinker	47
		e. A metaphysician or a religious thinker?	48
		f. The role of desire	48
		g. The lure of beauty	49
		h. What the soul should really desire	50
		j. The nature of Plotinus' god	51
		k. The three principles: on the road to the cosmos	52

		l.	Is the soul the source of generation?	56
		m.	Separation in the soul	58
		n.	Dualistic elements in the human person	59
		o.	Matter	60
		p.	The place and the function of the soul	63
		q.	Kosmos and kosmoi	64
		r.	The ultimate fate of man	65
		s.	Conclusion	67
2.	Porphyry			70
		a.	The man and his work	70
		b.	The main aim of philosophy and how to attain it	71
		c.	The need of ascetism	72
		d.	Far from the maddening crowd	73
		e.	Body and soul	73
3.	Iamblichus			74
		a.	The man and his work	74
		b.	The ineffable	75
		c.	The Intelligible	75
		d.	Two spiritual worlds and the World Soul	76
		e.	Terrestrial souls	77
		f.	'Funktionslust'	77
		g.	The physical world	78
		h.	Iamblichus' psychology	79
		j.	Conclusion	79
4.	Proclus			80
		a.	The man and his work	80
		b.	Proclus the mystic	81
		c.	Eternity and time	81
		d.	The One and the Many	83
		e.	Can the One be known?	83
		f.	Proclus' monism	84
		g.	The essential problem	85
		h.	Being	86
		j.	The chain of being	86
		k.	The One and the Many once again: the role of the henads	89
		l.	Syrianus' view of Monas and Duas, Peras and Apeiron	91
		m.	Proclus on these problems	92
		n.	The offspring of the henads	93
		o.	The sphere of the soul	94
		p.	Nature	94
		q.	Demiurgic functions	95
		r.	The soul's descent	96
		s.	The question of Evil	97
		t.	The return of the soul	97
		u.	Conclusion	97
Notes to Chapter I				98

II   DUALISM IN THE NEW RELIGIONS OF LATE ANTIQUITY   121

   Introductory   121

   PART I '... KOMMT DER NEUE GOTT GEGANGEN': DIONYSUS-BACCHUS 124

1. Dionysus and the Greek religious establishment   124
   a. A wild and elusive god   124
   b. The Dionysiac cult in the Hellenistic orient   126
   c. The religious crisis of the end of the fourth century   127
2. Dionysus comes to Rome   128
3. The affair of 186 B.C.   129
   a. The authorities investigating   129
   b. Why Livius wrote as he did   130
   c. Action against the Bacchics   130
   d. What the authorities feared   131
   e. Dualistic oppositions   132
4. The survival of Dionysus-Bacchus   132

   PART II   ISIS   133

1. The lure of the Orient   133
2. The home of the Isis cult   134
3. The myth of Isis and Osiris   134
   a. The original version of the myth   134
   b. Plutarch's version   135
4. Isis' entry into Rome   136
5. The offensive against Isis   137
6. The triumph of Isis   138
7. The interior life of the Isis cult   139
8. The great prize   141
9. How not to be an ass   142

   PART III   MITHRAS   143

1. The home of Mithras   143
2. Mithras as an Iranian godhead   144
3. Mithraic legends   144
4. The functions of Mithras   145
   a. Mithras as a protective deity   145
   b. The cosmological Mithras   145
5. The westward journey of the Mithras cult   146
6. Devotees of Mithras   147
7. A male cult   148
8. Was the Roman Mithras the Mithras of Iran?   148
9. The foreign god   149
10. Initiation   150
11. Mithraic ritual   151

12.	The sanctuaries	152
13.	Mithraic dualism	153

PART IV 'ENEMIES OF THE ROMAN ORDER' — 154

1.	Roman order	154
2.	Imperfections of the Roman order	154
3.	The philosophers as disturbers of the Roman order	155
4.	The new religions	157
	a. Judaism	157
	b. Christianity	157
	c. The mystery religions	158
Notes to Chapter II		159

III ATTITUDES TO THE BODY AND SEXUALITY IN THE GRAECO-ROMAN WORLD — 167

PART I ON NATURALNESS — 167

1.	Now natural is the human body?	167
2.	Dressing and undressing	168
3.	Is sexuality natural?	169
4.	The man-woman relationship as the test-case	170

PART II PAGAN ATTITUDES — 171

1.	A macho society	171
2.	Not a secularized state	171
3.	'Horror materiae'	172
4.	Highs and lows	173
5.	The austerity of the Roman Republic	174
6.	Mutations in the basic attitude	174
7.	'Benevolent dualism'	175
8.	Sexual norms	176
9.	Superiority and inferiority	177
10.	What the learned thought of it	179
11.	A dualistic attitude	181

PART III CHRISTIAN ATTITUDES — 181

1.	The Jewish heritage	181
2.	The New Testament	182
	a. In the Gospels	182
	b. In the Letters of Paul	183
3.	The practice of the early Church	186
	a. The danger of 'over-spiritualising'	186
	b. The status of the widows	187
	c. Female celibacy	187

4.	Men, women, and the priesthood	189
	a. Why women were not permitted to the priesthood	189
	b. Why priests are not allowed to marry	192
	c. Married and unmarried clerics	194
	d. The development of the obligation of celibacy	195
	e. The custom of the Eastern Church	197
5.	The early Fathers on body, sex, and marriage	197
6.	'The devil's gateway'?	198
7.	Other opinions	201
8.	What about the vox populi?	202
9.	In defense of matrimony	202
10.	Origen's sombre views	204
11.	The pastoral care of John Chrysostom	205
12.	Jerome the moralist	208
13.	A defender of marriage	210
14.	Augustine the good pastor	211
	a. A man of a radical nature	211
	b. Was Augustine a dualist?	211
	c. Was Augustine sex-obsessed?	213
	d. Augustine as an almost married man	213
	e. The break	214
	f. Augustine's basic position on sex, women, and the body	215
	g. The effects of the Fall	215
	h. Saint Augustine speaking to married couples	216
	j. Augustine woman-unfriendly?	218
	k. In defence of women	219
	l. An assessment of Augustine's attitude	220
15.	An overall assessment	225
	Notes to Chapter III	228
IV	CHRISTIANITY AND CLASSICAL CULTURE: REJECTION OR ACCEPTANCE?	239
1.	An issue that hung in the balance	239
2.	The great flourishing of Roman culture	240
3.	What to start with?	240
4.	The Christians and the pagan Empire	241
5.	The Christians and military service	242
6.	First contacts between pagan and Christian culture	246
7.	Opponents of classical culture	247
8.	The true philosophy	248
9.	Evidence of a change to the positive	249
10.	Between two worlds	250
11.	The problem of Augustine	252
12.	Conquest or fusion?	252
13.	Was the Christian attitude to classical culture dualistic?	255
14.	The chasm remains	256
	Notes to Chapter IV	257

PREFACE

When people inquire, 'what is dualism?', my usual answer is, 'it is about unbridgeable oppositions'. When they ask me for an example, my tag is, 'Hitler and the Jews'. Yet there is more to it than this. In this volume, as in all others, I have employed the formula that I for the first time presented in Volume I (p. 263), way back in 1986. We are justified of speaking about dualism, if there are two systems or concepts or principles or groups of people or even worlds that are utterly opposed and cannot be reduced to one another. They exist alongside each other; in some cases they are not even dependent on each other, without any intermediate terms. One of the two is always thought to be of a much higher quality than the other, so much so that one term is always seen as distinctly inferior, fit to be neglected, repudiated, or even destroyed. I refer those readers who want to be more extensively informed to the Prefaces of Vols. I, VI, IX, XI, and XIII, to the Afterword of Vol. I, and to Vol. IV, Ch. IV, § 4.

Since I want my intentions to be correctly understood, a few points should be paid heed to. First of all, I have repeatedly argued that Zoroastrian dualism is not the source and fountain-head from which all dualisms have flown. Dualism is an anthropological phenonemon that we may find everywhere where people act and think, discuss and argue. The second point is that the term 'dualism' should not be restricted to the fields of the history of religion and of philosophy. That would mean a deplorable impoverishment and rob us of many possiblities of understanding the history of Antiquity, and of all history, indeed.

A third point is that we should not dub every opposition dualistic. Sometimes people inquire, 'what if there intermediate terms?' I always consequently answer, 'then there is no dualism'. If we would call every opposition that exists, however unimportant or innocent, dualistic, the term would lose its significance entirely. Nevertheless, many people keep mixing terms like 'dual, duality, dualism' as if they were identical. An example of this I found in the work of the French poet and essayst Michel Leiris.

I ploughed my way through the countless literary utterances of this author with the help of a book by Guy Poitry, *Michel Leiris, Dualisme et totalité* (Presses Universitaires de Mirail, 1995). Leiris finds that the universe in which we live is dominated by disorder; it is the ultimate aim of artistic activity to combat this disorder. What he everywhere detects is the dualistic model; his aim is to get beyond it. Leiris uses the terms 'dualistic' and 'duality' as if they were synonyms and opposes them to 'totality'. By the combination 'duality/dualism' he understands the presence of two elements that are opposed and antagonistic. Totality, by way of contrast, signifies the reunification of what was partial, of distinct objects, so that they become a whole that transcends them in a unity. What Leiris wants to tell us in this way is that all distinctions, of whichever kind, can be dissolved into a unity. From his viewpoint, it is only consequent that he characterizes the play (his word) between duality and totality as an oscillating movement. All of the time totality exerts itself to abolish duality, even to negate it, but succeeds in this only momentarily.

Leiris then presents some ideas that are very dear to many western intellectuals and artists. To him the West is the region of the insupportable duality (with which he means dualism) of body and soul, and of matter and spirit. Africa and the East are the countries of the totality. Nowhere does it become more evident how loosely he is using the terms 'duality' and 'dualism'. Did Leiris realize that he was creating a dualistic opposition, namely that between West and East? He travelled in China, to him the country of the perfect harmony between the three realms of nature; even in Mao's China of 1955 he did not detect a flaw in this harmony. Contrasts there were, indeed, but by the concerted action of *Yin* and *Yang* they were fused in the totality of the universe.

Duality, thought Leiris (again meaning dualism), is the very condition of individual existence. Being born already signifies separating oneself from the All, in order to take one's place in a universe where division reigns and splinters. In all earnest he believed, with a gullibility that is characteristic of so many westerners, that the sacred festivals of the ancient Chinese ended in mass copulations making everybody one with his or her partner and with the All. The poet had found his Chinese inspiration in a performance by Beijing Opera in Paris; it became an overwhelming experience of totality for him. This sentiment was fortified when he was in China itself. In the autumn of 1955 he witnessed an enormous march-past on the Square of the Heavenly Peace in Beijing, which was, according to him, a mirror in which the population could contemplate itself. "Chinese life finds itself completely integrated in it." The innocent man obviously did not know that there is nothing spontaneous in such a spectacle. Leiris's historical vision was astonishingly wide. "A single thread unites the earliest time with the present, from the *Sinanthropus pekinensis* to Comrade Mao Zhdong."

But his belief in the blessings of the East was severely shocked by the Soviet interventions in Poland and Hungary in 1956, and later also by China's occupation of Tibet in 1959. He was so deeply disappointed that he attempted suicide in 1957. Things also went wrong in his personal life. He became estranged from his wife Louise to whom he had already been married for thirty years. He found her stiff and petty-bourgeois, although she successfully ran a modern art gallery, a profitable affair since it had the monopoly in the sale of Picassos. It was the profits from these that enabled Leiris to live as he liked, for he himself did not earn much. He began a liaison with another woman, which he kept hidden from Louise.

He found proof of a general bipolarity everywhere, above all in Paris. The French capital had, he thought, two *côtés*, separated by the Seine. The *rive droite* was mundane, the realm of contract and objectivity; the *rive gauche* was leftist and populist, the realm of liberty, of the 'I'. He traced this opposition even in the street pattern of Paris. On the *rive droite* streets are straight, as if drawn by a ruler; on the *rive gauche* the streets are tortuous, and their pattern is confused. The same *côtés* Leiris also discovered in

XVI

Kumasi, the ancient royal city of the Ashantis in Ghana, and in the Chinese capital Beijing (this in spite of the fact that totality was supposed to reign in China). It is always so, in his view, that the social 'I' is to be found on the *rive droite*, but the 'profound I' on the *rive gauche*.

Leiris characterized the two *côtés* by means of the following oppositions, always going from left (favourable) to right (unfavourable), and back : feminine-masculine; child-adult; nostalgia-courage; past-present and future; poetry-political action; non-committal preferences-morality; desire-creed; imagination-reason; love-constraint; sentiment-idea; beauty-truth; aesthetic-ethics; play-direction; pleasure-duty; eroticism-comradeship; frivolity-rigour; fragility-force (or stability); instants-eternity. Very revealing stuff for a clever psychiatrist! Dualism, often disguised as 'duality', is far from dead!

For the benefit of the overburdened reader I have added a thematic Manual, where he or she can find the field(s) of interest with which he or she is occupied, with an indication of the Volumes and Chapters where they can be found.

An additional note. Somewhat to my dismay I discovered only a short while ago that there is a book with almost the same title as mine, one that precedes my book in time. It is a two-volumed work by an Austrian scholar, Karl R.H. Frick, *Licht und Finsternis* (Graz, Austria, 1975 and 1978). Now that I have it in hand, I see that Dr. Frick's focus of interest differs from mine, his being not dualism, but theosophy and freemasonry. This work is in fact a sequel to an earlier work by his hand, namely *Die Erleuchteten. Gnostisch-theosophische und alchemistisch-rosenkreuzerische Geheimgesellschaften bis zum Ende des 18. Jahrhunderts - Ein Beitrag zur Geistesgeschichte der Neuzeit.* (Graz, Austria, 1973). What Frick's work is about appears from the subtitle of Volume II : *Gnostisch-theosophische und freimaurerisch-okkulte Geheimgesellschaften bis an die Wende zum 20. Jahrhundert. Wege in die Gegenwart;* it is a book of 582 pages. The much less voluminous Volume I (343 pages), subtitled *Ursprünge und Anfänge*, is an introduction to Volume

II. My initial dismay changed into gratitude, when I discovered that this volume contains a mass of extremely valuable material, which will be of great use to me in the preparation of a volume on the continuation of the Gnosis during the Middle Ages.

As always I have to thank several people for their highly appreciated assistance. Dr. Jo Swabe corrected the English of the whole text, carefully and courteously. Then there is my daughter Dr. Resianne Smidt van Gelder-Fontaine, who miraculously found the time to read and comment upon the chapters of this volume. Then comes my wife who, painstakingly as ever, corrected the one but last version on typing errors. As always, I want to stress that I am the one who is to blame, if there is anything wrong with the scholarship, the English or the typography and lay-out. Mr. Gieben, my publisher, gladly accepted my text and saw to it that it became a book. This is the last volume about Antiquity. I am grateful that it has been possible for me to come thus far. Since I am seventy-seven now, I dare not promise that I will be able to cover also the Middle Ages. Anyhow, Vol. XV, about Byzantine history 470-632 and the Islam 570-732, is well under way.

Piet F.M. Fontaine
Amsterdam NL

MANUAL

This manual is designed for those readers who do not want to read the whole work, but, instead, want to see what is said in it about the subject(s) they are interested in.

I   ON DUALISM AS SUCH

       Prefaces of Vols. I, VI, IX,
       Vol. IV, Ch. IV.4

II   PERIODS AND CIVILIZATIONS

       1. Greece
           Vol. I   Archaic and early classical periods
           Vol. II and III   Fifth and fourth centuries B.C.
           Vol. VI   The Hellenistic world
       2. Egypt
           Vol. IV, Ch. I
       3. Mesopotamia and Anatolia
           Vol. IV, Ch. III
       4. Israel
           Vol. IV, Ch. II
       5. Iran
           Vol. IV, Ch. IV, Vol. V, Ch. I
       6. India
           Vol. V, Ch. II
       7. China
           Vol. V, Ch. III
       8. Roman history
           Vols. X, XI,
           XII, Ch. I,
           XIII

III   POLITICAL HISTORY

       1. Greece
           Vol. II
           Vol. VI, Chs. I and II

2. Rome
   Vol. X
   Vol. XI, Chs. I, II, III, IV
3. Egypt
   Vol. IV, Ch. I.1-4
4. Mesopotamia and Anatolia
   Vol. IV, Ch. III.1-9.
5. Israel
   Vol. IV, Ch. II.14
   Vol. VI, Ch. II.11
6. Iran
   Vol. IV, Ch. IV.1-3
   Vol. V, Ch. I.1-3
7. India
   Vol. V, Ch. II.1-11
8. China
   Vol. V, Ch. III.1-5

IV SOCIAL HISTORY

1. Greece
   Vol. II, Ch. III.3
   Vol. II, Ch. IV.4
2. India
   Vol. V, Ch. II.13-15
Since esoteric religious movements are socially distinct from the rest of the population, we may subsume these too under this heading :
3. The Pythagoreans
   Vol. I, Ch. I
4. Eleusinian mysteries and Orphics
   Vol. I, Ch. IV
5. Yoga
   Vol. V, Ch. II.21
6. Jainism
   Vol. V, Ch. II.22
7. Dao
   Vol. V, Ch. III.25
8. The Essenes
   Vol. VIII, Ch. V
9. Almost all Gnostic movements
   Vol. VII, Ch. III, Vols. VIII and IX
10. The subjected peoples of the Roman Empire
    Vol. XI, Ch. IV
11. The Jews of the Roman Empire
    Vol. XI, Ch. V
12. The Greeks of the Roman Empire
    Vol. XI, Ch. VI
13. The Roman Empire and the Christian Church
    Vol. XII, Ch. I

V   HISTORY OF RELIGIONS

1. Pythagoreanism
   Vol. I, Ch. I
2. The Olympian religion
   Vol. I, Ch. IV.1-8
3. The Eleusinian mysteries
   Vol. I, Ch. IV.8
4. The cult of Dionysus
   Vol. I, Ch. IV.9
5. Orphism
   Vol. I, Ch. IV.10
6. Greek shamanism
   Vol. I, Ch. IV.11
7. Egyptian religion
   Vol. IV, Ch. I.5-7
8. The religion of Israel
   Vol. IV, Ch. II
   Vol. VII, Ch. VI
9. Religions of the Middle East
   Vol. IV, Ch. III.10
10. Iranian religion
    Vol. IV, Ch. IV.4-12
    Vol. V, Ch. I.4-5
11. Mazdakism
    Vol. V, Ch. I, Appendix
12. The New Testament
    Vol. VII, Ch. IV
13. The Essenes
    Vol. VII, Ch. V
14. Hermetism
    Vol. VIII, Ch. II
15. The Veda
    Vol. V, Ch. II.17
16. Brahmanism
    Vol. V, Ch. II.18-19
17. Hinduism
    Vol. V, Ch. II.20
18. Yoga
    Vol. V, Ch. II.21
19. Jainism
    Vol. V, Ch. II.22
20. Buddhism
    Vol. V. Ch. II.23
21. Confucianism
    Vol. V, CH. III.16-21, 23-24
22. Mohism
    Vol. V, Ch. III.22
23. Daoism

XXII

            Vol. V, Ch. III.25
      24. The Gnosis
            Vol. VI, Ch.IV
            Vol. VII, Chs. I-III
            Vol. VIII, Chs. III-IX
            Vol. IX
      25. The Christian Church and the Jews
            Vol. XII, Ch. II
      26. The Christian Church and Judaizing
            Vol. XII, Ch. III
      27. Christian theology in the first centuries
            Vol. XIII

VI   PHILOSOPHY

      1. Pythagoreanism
         Vol. I, Ch. I
      2. Ionic and Eleatic philosophy
         Vol. I, Ch. II
      3. Sophists and Socrates
         Vol. III, Ch. II
      4. Plato and Aristotle
         Vol. III, Ch. III
      5. Hellenistic philosophy
         Vol. VI, Ch. III
      6. Indian philosophy
         Vol. V, Ch. II.16
      7. Chinese philosophy
         Vol. V, Ch. III.15
      8. The philosophy of Philo
         Vol. VIII, Ch. I

VII   LITERATURE

      1. Greek epics and lyrics
         Vol. I, Ch. III
      2. Greek tragedy and comedy
         Vol. III, Ch. I

VIII   HISTORIOGRAPHY

      1. Greek historiography
         Vol. III, Ch. III.1
      2. Old Testament
         Vol. IV, Ch. II.1-6
      3. New Testament
         Vol. VII, Ch. IV.1-2.

CHAPTER I

DUALISM IN THE PHILOSOPHY
OF LATE ANTIQUITY

PART I ROMAN EPICUREANISM

1. A flash-back

In Chapter III of Volume VI of this series, where I described Hellenistic philosophy, I ended my disquisition with the work of Posidonius (135-51 B.C.), a great polyhistor. We must now flash-back, first to Epicureanism, later to the Stoa, in order to find the origins of Roman and Late Hellenistic thinking. Epicureanism [1] is named after the Greek scholar Epicurus (341-270 B.C.) who founded a famous school in Athens. Just as the Stoa thinkers, Epicurus wanted to teach people how to live rather than how to think. There is a dominantly practical side to both philosophical schools. Epicureanism was in fact a guide to a blissfull life, based on the premise that living happily and as carefree as possible could be learned by using philosophical and scholarly methods. Epicureanism became highly popular since many people in the last centuries before Christ felt thrown back upon themselves and desired to be taught how to live a quiet life in the turmoil of events.

It is not surprising that Epicureanism found its way to Rome in the course of the second century B.C. There are two reasons for this. The first is that the Romans who, as an eminently practical people, were not much given to abstract speculating [2], had a predilection for the schools of Epicurus and the Stoa. The other reason is that, what with the increasing confusion in their public life, resulting in the civil wars of the last century B.C., the Romans also needed a guide to the blissful life [3].

2. Lucretius

a. The contingency of the atoms

It was above all Titus Lucretius Carus (ca. 96-55 B.C.) who, with his didactic poem De rerum natura, made Epicureanism popular in Rome. Lucretius, of whom no other works are known, is not considered a philosopher by some modern scholars, because he wrote in poetry. But it is a fact that, philosopher or not, he was the very first author to present philosophical opinion to his countrymen in their own Latin tongue. And since he was a great poet, he did so in an attractive form. The system that he presented to the Romans was a materialistic one, as may be concluded already from the title of his poem, 'On the nature of things'. We learn through sensations, the poem says; impressions come to us by way of the senses. This does not mean that the senses constitute an infallible tribunal; man can certainly err in his judgments. Our method of judging will mislead us more easily than the impression conveyed to us by the senses.

Lucretius' materialism may also be called 'atomism'. He subscribed to the doctrine of Democritus, the father of all atomic theories [4], who said that the world is a configuration of atoms that are moving about in empty space. Since atoms, small though they are, have a certain weight, their natural tendency is to fall downward, 'like raindrops through the profound void', as Lucretius wrote [5]. But if they were all falling down in straight, parallel lines, they could never hook on to each other, and "thus nature never would have produced anything" [6]. The poet-philosopher had, therefore, to postulate a slight deviation in the course of the atoms - the so-called 'clinamen' - so that they could collide, stick to each other, and form configurations [7].

The consequence is that, in the course of the atoms, there is room for a certain contingency; it is in this contingency that the origin of free will is to be found. Not everything and everyone is subject to the inexorable course of nature. Human beings are capable of changing this course.

b. No place for the traditional gods

A consequence of Lucretius' atomism is that the cosmos is neither divine nor immortal in his view. With this perspective he deviates considerably from traditional opinion in Antiquity. What about the gods? His materialism did not turn him into an atheist. To him, like to most educated Romans of his time, religion was essentially a public affair, a state religion that made the citizens fulfil certain obligations towards the gods and duly perform certain rituals. Lucretius' gods, however, were not so much the divinities of the Graeco-Roman pantheon but rather luminous beings who lived somewhere beyond this visible world. His real goddess was probably Nature whom he almost personified and deified; she is the source of all that is good and true [8].

For Lucretius Nature - with a capital N - takes for him the place of the traditional gods who do not interest him. Here he is of an opinion different from that of his venerated master Epicurus who believed in the existence of the Olympian divinities, although he objected to the excesses and superstitions of the popular cult [9]. But Lucretius was a declared enemy of the state religion. Philosophy, the power of the mind, can triumph over religion under the weight of which man lies crushed. [10] Now she (religion) is "in her turn cast down and trampled under foot, whilst we by the victory are raised to heaven" [11]. This serves her right, for religion brings forth 'criminal and impious deeds' [12]; she is 'potent in persuading to evil acts' [13]. Was he the first in history to express this opinion that is so popular nowadays?

c. Was Lucretius an irreligious person?

But does this mean that Lucretius was an a-religious person? Not at all! He proclaims that the victory of philosophy transports man to heaven, the place where the luminous beings dwell who are his gods. We saw how he deifies Nature, the creative force that "makes all things and increases and nourishes them" [14]. And since he obviously needs some personal god, he deifies Epicurus who "was a god ..., a god who first discovered that reasoned plan of life that is called Wisdom" [15]; "he was wont to discourse often in godlike fashion" [16]. Perhaps even Lucretius himself is entitled to a measure of divinity; anyhow, he unambiguously states that one who is capable of "building a song worthy of the majesty of nature ... cannot be counted among the sons of mortal men" [17]. Dualistic distinctions were becoming apparent, between religion, especially in the shape of the traditional cult, state religion, and popular beliefs, and the religion of Nature, and also between the philosopher and ordinary people. The true Epicurean goes to heaven the delights of which the poet pictures in glowing terms [18]. But the life of the 'stulti', the stupid, the unknowing, will be 'a hell on earth' [19].

d. Dualism in Lucretius

This leads us to the question whether Lucretius' poetic philosophy, or philosophical poetry, is of a dualistic nature. At first sight there seems to be an unbridgeable chasm between his materialism and metaphysics. He does not acknowledge a supernatural world in the ordinary sense of the word. Everything consists of atoms, even the mind, even spirit, even the gods; every configuration of atoms is destined to dissolve into separate atoms. But when all is said and done, his materialism is not of the most pedestrian sort. We have already seen that something makes the atoms deviate from their downward course so that they are able to coagulate into configurations. There is a touch of finalism in this, although the poet does not explain the origin of this force.

I spoke of 'poetic philosophy' on purpose. There is myth in his poem; it is not the sheerest scientism. Without this mythical element it would not have become a real poem. His work opens with a wonderful evocation of the goddess Venus, 'darling of men and gods' [20]. But we would be wrong to think here of the Olympian goddess : "the figure of Venus is reinterpretated by Lucretius; what is superficially mythological is turned into a myth in which Lucretius really believes, the myth of Nature" [21]. "You alone govern the nature of things", the rerum natura [22]. As Erick Ackermann states, there is in Lucretius no clear demarcation line between pure myth and pure logos; "they interlock without necessarily contradicting each other" [23].

However, that there is a mythological side to Lucretius' materialism does not make it any less materialistic. No materialistic-atomistic system has room for a genuine spiritual world. Highly important existential questions are never answered. What brings about the mass of atoms? What makes the atoms move? To what purpose do they move? There is no creator, no divine lawgiver, no unmoved mover. In Vol. VI I wrote that atomistic theory, according to which the world is a product of chance and devoid of any divine design, runs counter to the basic Hellenic belief that the universe is a *cosmos*, a well-ordered whole, and that it is purposeful and meaningful. I spoke there of the dualistic opposition between this Hellenic concept and atomistic doctrine [24].

e. What made Epicureanism attractive

With regard to Epicureanism I wrote that educated Greeks, dissatisfied with the real or supposed superstitions of the Olympian religion, tried to find solace in an utterly non-religious, purely 'natural' system. And I added that this not only estranged them from the broad mass of the Hellenic population, but also undermined the position of orthodoxy still further [25].

These remarks also apply to Roman Epicureanism as represented by Lucretius. A modern author calls the diffusion of this doctrine in Roman circles 'grandiose' [26]. There were many popularizers of Greek thought active in the last century B.C. who, more or less aptly (less, found Cicero [27]), transposed the technical terms of Hellenic philosophy into Latin. "There is a multitude of such men", sighs Cicero, meaning Epicureans, "the ignorant let themselves seduce [28]; ... Italy is full of them" [29]. It did not please him at all. "I don't know how it came about, but the least competent but most influential judge, the populace, is with them [the Epicureans]" [30]. Epicurus was to him "the man who destroyed the foundations of religion, and overthrew ... the temples and altars of the immortal gods" [31]. It was, among other things, to stem such fatal tendencies that he wrote his book 'On the nature of the gods'. What people found so attractive in Epicureanism was that "it confirmed the rights of reason in a world dominated by irrationalism and arbitrariness" [32]. However, the undermining of orthodoxy would not go unpunished; it left a void that would be filled, and not by philosophy.

PART II THE ROMAN STOICS

The history of philosophy in the Roman Empire, insofar as the treatises were written by Romans and not by Greeks, in Latin or sometimes in Greek, is not studded with great names. An exception should perhaps be made for Cicero (106-43 B.C.) who, however, is remembered as the great master of Latin prose rather than as an original philosophical mind. As a philosopher he was tributary to such worthies of the Middle Stoa as Panaetius [33] and Posidonius [34] whom he heard in Rhodes. When Cicero spoke of moral duties or peace of mind, he did so as a Stoic. But he is mainly significant through the influence that his elegant prose had on his contemporaries and on later great minds like Augustine and Boethius [35]. Apart from Cicero, there were popularizers and minor authors, but the first name of importance was that of Seneca.

1. Seneca, his life

Lucius Annaeus Seneca (ca. 4 B.C.-A.D. 65) was a Spaniard from Cordoba, born into a family of Roman knights. Early in his life, he went to Rome where he received the traditional training in rhetorics and philosophy. He fulfilled several public functions and gained a reputation as a rhetor. As the tutor of young Nero he was for a time one of the most powerful men of the Empire and became extremely rich. Later in his life he was mainly active as the author of nine tragedies and some philosophical works. In A.D. 65 fate overtook him. Nero, now Emperor, suspected him of being a party to a plot against him; obeying a command by his former pupil, he had to cut his veins.

2. The Stoic

As a philosopher Seneca was a Stoic, and this brings us back to the school of the Stoa of which I wrote in Volume VI [36]. There I described it as a practical movement that left many important metaphysical questions unanswered. As such, combined with its stress upon a high morality, it appealed to the eminently practical mind of the Romans. Seneca, wrote Copleston, "emphasizes the practical side of philosophy, ethics ... He does not seek intellectual knowledge for its own sake, but pursues philosophy as a means to the acquirement of virtue. Philosophy is necessary, but it is to be pursued with a practical end in view" [37].

3. Psychological dualism

Seneca, says Pohlenz, was a man full of contradictions; no wonder then that in his work he shows a predilection for antitheses [38]. We find in him that same ambiguous attitude towards the body, that psychological dualism, that is so conspicuous in Plato [39]. In Seneca it will have been an important determining factor that he was a man with a sickly constitution : "Yesterday I shared my day with illness" [40]. Body and soul cohabit uncomfortably and unwillingly. "The soul sighs under a heavy load, burning to deploy herself and return to those essences from where she emanated. What is our body? A weight on the soul to torment her. It oppresses her, it overwhelms her, it keeps her in chains" [41]. And elsewhere : "The body is not a fixed abode, but an inn, a haunt for one day, to be left at the moment one discovers being a nuisance to the inn-keeper". He then goes on to describe in some detail the ailments that beset him from head to toe [42]. This is vintage dualism. [43]

Is there a way out? There is, it is the way of philosophy. "Philosophy has appeared and it is she who causes the soul to respire of the things of nature and to transport her from what is terrestrial to what is divine." This is the freedom of the soul; this is her upward flight. "From time to time she escapes from her prison and recreates herself enjoying heaven" [44]. Plato would have applauded this!

4. Materialism

Discussing the older Stoa, I wrote that it was a materialistic system, since its primary principle, its archê, is a physical or corporeal element. But not everything found a place in their physical universe. There is an infinite void, the *apeiron*, that is not part of the cosmos. And neither Place (topos) or Time are of a physical nature. I therefore concluded that there is an unbridgeable opposition between the fundamental materialism of Stoic philosophy and the equally fundamental assumption that incorporeal elements exist [45].

Seneca too could not avoid this dilemma. "We Stoics acknowledge ... in nature two generating principles of all that exist : cause and matter." With this statement he adheres to the opinion of the older Stoa. His problem is that matter is of itself motionless; in consequence, it cannot generate anything. Matter "lies down inertly, as something that is ready for everything, but hesitates [i.e. to do something], if nobody causes it to move." To escape from this quandary, Seneca needs an incentive to motion, a cause. "This cause, that is, reason (ratio), gives form to matter and makes it turn as it wills, using it for all kinds of works. Two things are needed : one that causes everything to originate, and one from which everything comes. The first is the cause, the other matter" [46]. It is stated here in the plainest possible terms that there are two first principles.

The question now is what exactly Seneca means by his 'cause', the ratio. Is it Plato's summum bonum? Or Aristotle's 'unmoved mover'? "What we are looking for is a first and general cause; it must necessarily be simple, for matter too is simple ... This cause is creative reason, it is God" [47].

5. Seneca's religion

It must be pointed out that in Seneca's philosophy God did not create matter. This makes it clear that Seneca's godhead is not the God of Jews and Christians. But he also takes his distance from the Roman *pantheon* and the public cult, although he did not openly reject it; as an imperial official (he has been quaestor, senator, and consul), he could hardly do so. He is quite tolerant. If the people want to call God 'Juppiter', so be it.

Seneca, states Giuseppe Scarpat, "wrote not much on theology, but in a very clear way, and we believe to be able to say that he was even profoundly religious, but not according to the official religion that was sometimes criticized and condemned by him ... and sometimes seen as a traditional and useful instrument of the state" [48]. How deeply religious was he really? He castigates Epicurus for acknowledging an impassible God, uninterested in mankind, "beyond the reach and sight of mortals ..., dwelling alone, without a living creature ..., having no ear for our prayers and no concern for us," a God "who is surrounded by a fast and impassible wall" [49].

On the other hand, theology is to him a branch of philosophy; in this discipline there is "that branch which deals with man and that which deals with the gods ... One teaches us what ought to be done on earth, the other what is done in heaven." There seems to be a supernatural look to this, but Seneca needs no supernatural being in order to reveal the things of heaven to him. His teacher is nature. He claims to be able to look further than 'what is obvious to everybody'; he has 'penetrated its mysteries'. And what did he learn? He learned "what the stuff of the universe is, who its author or custodian is, what God is." Is his God really different from nature? It seems not, for he asks himself "whether he (the godhead) is a part of the universe or (whether he) is the universe" [50].

His answer to this question is unequivocal. "There is no Nature without God, nor God without Nature, but both are the same thing; they differ only in their function." And somewhat further on : "Speak of Nature, Fate, Fortune, but all these are names of the same God who uses his power in several ways" [51]. But is God really identical with Nature? Doubt sets in when we hear him ask : "What is God?" and answer : "The mind of the universe" and that God "maintains his own work both from within and without" [52]. If he is 'without' (the universe), he is not wholly identical to it.

Trying to have the best of two worlds, Seneca proves unable to cope with the logical dilemma pantheism presents : either God and Nature fuse together entirely, but then there is no sense in speaking of 'God', or they do not, but in that case there is no pantheism. His idea of God is rather vague. I therefore do not understand why Pohlenz, the greatest expert on the Stoa, says that Seneca thought 'monotheistically'. In almost the same breath this scholar states that in Seneca's philosophy "God remains a corporeal pneuma" (isn't this a contradictio in adiecto?); he adds that the ancient thinker stays perfectly Stoic in that "he rocks the monistic fundament of the world picture just as little as the immanence of the deity" [53]. If he is correct in this, Seneca did not think 'monotheistically' [54].

I do not feel that Seneca was a religious man; what was important to him was not religion but philosophy. Philosophizing is the authentic task of mankind [55]. Philosophy is the true magistra vitae. "Let the philosopher know where he must go, from where he comes, what is the good for him, what the bad, what he must seek or avoid, what is that *ratio* that is able to discern between what we should strive after or fly, what alleviates the insane impulses of desire and bridles its wildness" [56].

6. Seneca a dualist?

Was Seneca a dualist? I do not follow Copleston when he says that Seneca "in practice certainly tends to regard God as transcending matter;" he dubs this 'metaphysical dualism' [57]. Knowledgeable though this author is, I feel that his use of the term 'dualism' is here not correct. In Seneca's philosophy (we should not call it 'theology') there is no room for a divine being who is utterly opposed to creation; that alone may be called 'metaphysical dualism'. But let us look in another direction. There can be no doubt that to Seneca man is a free being responsible for his life and deeds. "Set yourself free for your own sake," this is the very first thing that he writes to his penfriend Lucilius [58] The proper task of man is to educate himself; the instrument at his disposition is the will. "What do you (Lucilius) need in order to become good? To will it!" [59] Will is more necessary than knowledge. And where does will lead us? To 'virtus', to virtue, that is, to simplicity, fidelity, civic sense, thrift, frugality, all of them old Roman virtues.

All this may give us the impression that in Seneca's vision man is free to dispose of his own life. But then there is Fortune, there is Fate, the old spectre that continued to haunt the ancient world, the idea that there existed a merciless and inexorable entity to which all and everything were subjected. "What function do expiatory and propitiating sacrifices have if the fates are immutable? ... The fates pursue their rights imperturbably ... The fates do not know how to be turned by pity or by favour. Once started upon an irrevocable course, they flow on in accordance with a unalterable plan ... The eternal sequence of events causes the order of fate to roll on" [60]. What must be man's attitude with regard to Fate? "It is to this law that our souls must adjust themselves; this they should follow, this they should obey. Whatever happens, assume that it was bound to happen, and do not be willing to rail at nature" [61]. "Let Fate find us ready and alert. Here is your great soul : the man who has given himself over to Fate" [62].

Of course, Seneca was aware that this objection would be made : "So nothing is left to our free will and all control of action is handed over to Fate?" In a passage of the 'Natural questions' he promised his readers to explain "how something (sic) may exist in man's choice, while Fate remains undiminished" [63]. But he never did so explicitly, since he did not know how to escape from this dualism of Fate and freedom. The nearest he comes to it is in a letter to Lucilius where he seems to be discussing with himself. "How can philosophy help me, if Fate exists? Of what avail is philosophy, if God rules the universe? Of what avail is it, if Chance [casus] governs everything?" It becomes apparent here that, in Seneca's view, the universe and God and Fatum are all one. And what is his answer? There is no real answer. "We must be philosophers ... Philosophy must be our defence" [64]. It sounds rather helpless.

This is dualism, but of which kind? It is surely not metaphysical, since Seneca does not really acknowledge a supernatural, metaphysical world. Perhaps it would be best to dub it 'existential dualism'.

7. Epictetus and his works

The philosopher Epictetus (who taught and wrote in Greek) was, although he later rose to great fame, of humble origin. He was born around A.D. 50 in the Phrygian town of Hieropolis as the son of a slave woman and became a slave himself. He was lame, the result of ill treatment by one of his masters, it was said. Later he became the house slave of Nero's private secretary. This master allowed him to follow lessons in philosophy. Freed later, he began to teach. But in A.D. 89 the Emperor Domitian banned all philosophers from Rome, and so he went to Nicopolis in the Epirus where he founded a much frequented philosophical school. He was a friendly and likeable man who practised a very austere way of living; he never married. He died around 135, about eighty years old.

His lessons were called 'diatribes' (discourses); his pupil Flavius Arrianus published a collection of them in eight books, four of which have come down to us. After his master's death he published a sort of summary of his philosophical teachings, called the *Enchiridion*; both this book and the Diatribes are very probably based on shorthand notes the editor made during the lessons. *Enchiridion* is often translated with 'manual' or 'handbook'. It is, however, not meant to be a standard work or book of reference, but as something to have 'ready at hand', in order to consult it every now and then. And consulted it was, even to the present day! It influenced the Emperors Hadrian and Marcus Aurelius, several of the Church Fathers, monks' orders of the Middle Ages, Pascal and philosophers like Descartes and Kant, and rulers like Frederick the Great. Copleston even mentions that the director of a Swiss psychiatric clinic gave the *Enchiridion* to his mentally disturbed patients and found that it had a favourable influence on their health [65].

8. A pre-Christian?

Epictetus was above all a practical philosopher, not given to abstract speculations; what he wants is to help people to live the good life, a life in accordance with the will of the godhead, a thoroughly virtuous life. Many later admirers saw in him a sort of pre-Christian, because he is always speaking of conforming to the will of God, permanently stresses the excellence of virtue, and advocates a quiet, frugal, and even ascetic way of life - the last element being especially attractive to monks. Such enthusiasts overlook the fact that their idol, being a Stoic, was also a monist, that is, that he knew only the natural, the *diesseitige* world. There is not a trace of a supernatural world or of a transcendental godhead in his philosophy.

The German scholar Adolf Bonhöffer lists all the New Testament terms that indicate the existence of a supernatural world and that fail in Epictetus. [66] Epictetus' God is identical to the world, with the cosmos. Being obedient to God means submitting to the natural course of events. However, when he speaks of purity, goodness, and holiness of God, there is a theistic ring to it that seduced later Christian thinkers. This philosopher is also saddled with the pantheistic dilemma, although he would not have been conscious of it. [67]

9. Soul and body

A consequence of Stoic monism is that the 'pneuma' - mind, spirit, or Logos - is material. This pneuma is at the same time a cause, namely the universal cause of everything; the Stoics calls this the 'hêgemonikon', the leading principle. Every human being participates in this pneuma; it helps him or her to understand oneself as he or she really is and to bring a person's life to a higher level. We should, therefore, expect, that the human soul and the human body form a unity, but in Epictetus this is not the case. Already in the very first phrases of the Enchiridion the author makes an important distinction, not free of dualism. "Some things are under our control, while others are not under our control. Under our control our conception, choice, desire, aversion, and, in a word, everything that is our own doing. Not under our control are our body, property, office, and, in a word, everything that is not our own doing." The dualistic character shines through in what follows. "The things under our control are by nature free, unhindered, unimpeded, while the things not under our control are weak, servile, subject to hindrance, and not our own" [68]. Special attention should be paid to that 'our own' and 'not our own'. Epictetus considers as the body something alien, something foreign to a human being. It is the things that are under our control - in short, thinking - that alone bring freedom and happiness [69].

Epictetus is a determined opponent of the Epicurean idea that the body is a source of pleasure and happiness. He would equally not say, along with Paul, that the body is the temple of the Spirit [70], since this would conflict with his monistic materialism. Although he does not advocate the neglect of the body [71], it is something of an inferior order to him. "You are in a bad way? What does that mean? That you are close to a separation of the soul from the body. What, then, is terrifying about that?" [72] "From now on my mind is the material with which I have to work, as the carpenter has his timbers, the shoemaker his hides ... My paltry body is nothing to me; the parts of it are nothing to me" [73]. This is a revealing passage, and not only because of the contempt for the body that it shows. As the philosophical materialist he is, Epictetus calls 'mind' (dianoia) 'matter' (hulê).

Further contempt for the body is displayed in the following quotations. "You are looking for serenity and happiness in the wrong place, (for) ... it does not reside in the body" [74]. "How can anything that pertains to the body be unhampered? And how can that which is lifeless, earth, or clay be great or precious?" [75] "You ought to treat your whole body like a poor loaded-down donkey" [76]. Elsewhere he dubs the body 'a little portion of paltry flesh' [77]. There is more in this line, but this is enough to show that in Epictetus there is working a body-soul dualism; the two parts of the human being are of a different quality and do no cohabit harmoniously. This is the same 'horror materiae', the same aversion to what is corporeal that we come across so frequently in late-Roman authors. But it is astonishing to find it in the work of a philosopher who professes to be a materialist. There certainly is an inconsistency in this!

10. A philosopher on the imperial throne

The Emperor Marcus Aurelius (161-180) was a philosopher on the imperial throne; as a thinker, he was a Stoic, a great admirer of Epictetus. Alongside his administrative duties and the military campaigns he led he found occasion to note down philosophical musings (in Greek) that are commonly called 'meditations', but the original title of this work was 'Marcus Aurelius the Emperor to himself'. It is, in fact, a collection of aphorisms. He too is not a thinker given to abstractions. He hoped to help himself forward with a practical morality and perhaps also his fellow-men. The great teacher in life is philosophy. "All the things of the body are as a river, and the things of the soul are as a dream and a vapour ... What then can help us on our way? One thing and one alone - Philosophy" [78].

What does philosophy teach us? The main thing is that the universe is a whole. "Cease not to think of the cosmos as one living Being, possessed of a single substance and a single soul, ... and how it does all things by a single impulse" [79]. He shows himself a true monist by exclaiming : "All that is in tune with you, oh universe, is in tune with me ... All things come from you, subsist in you, go back to you" [80]. We should keep in mind that to Marcus Aurelius too God, nature, and the universe are one and the same thing.

However, the body does not fully share in this harmony. He calls it a sheath from which the soul will emerge at the hour of death [81]. The soul is 'overlaid' with the body [82]; he even speaks of man as 'a little soul bearing up a corpse' [83]. The body is inferior; it is 'the baser and mortal partner' and has 'gross notions' [84]. The 'sensations of the flesh' stand in the way of thought [85]. Evidence enough to show that the body-soul dualism is also present in Marcus Aurelius' writings. He thus did not remain wholly true to Stoic monism. According to him, man is composed of three parts : body, the pneumatic element, and mind (nous). The real self is only to be found in the nous [86]. As Pohlenz remarks, this tripartition is 'unstoical'; the Stoa knew only a division into two [87].

Body and pneuma (the seat of the images and drives) are material. But what about the mind? The Emperor is not outspoken with regard to the question of whether it is material or immaterial. Its being material would fit into the line of Stoic materialism. On the other hand, he employs expressions that have a distinctly spiritual ring. Zeus (with whom he does not mean the Homeric Olympian ruler) has given to every human being a 'genius' (a 'daimoon'), a particle of himself to serve as man's captain and guide; this particle is nothing more than each human being's intelligence (nous) and reason (logos) [88]. This 'logos' is the leading part in man, the 'hêgemonikon', that "which in you is divine" [89]. It should be served truly [90], for it is 'the very deity enthroned in you' [91]. What is evident here is that body and pneuma on the one hand and nous/logos on the other have separate origins and are distinct from each other.

11. What Roman Stoics have in common

The three Roman Stoics we have discussed, Seneca, Epictetus, and Marcus Aurelius, different as they are in many respects, have one thing in common : the body-soul dualism. The dualism in their way of thinking may suprise us, for they were all monistic materialists. Fundamentally, it seems, they cannot be dualists, since, according to their line of thinking, spirit or mind is just as material as the body, although of a much finer texture than the coarser stuff of which the body is made. But, as I argued in earlier volumes [92], it would be superficial to view dualism as the exact opposite of monism; both are from the same stock. Monism tries to reduce everything to the same denominator, either spirit or matter. In both cases the excluded one keeps knocking on the back-door, for it is hardly conceivable that it would be possible to turn all matter into spirit or the reverse. This is an opportunity for dualism, because an unwelcome guest appears on the scene. This is what happens to our three philosophers who are obviously at a loss what to do with the mind or spirit.

PART III ROMAN NEOPYTHAGOREANISM

1. The eclipse of the original Pythagoreanism

Pythagoreanism was influential in the Greek world of the sixth and fifth centuries B.C., not the least because Plato was tributary to it in some important respects [93]; it should be remarked that this Pythagoreanism was thoroughly dualistic in its doctrine and practice, so much so that I opened this whole series with a description of it [94], in order to make it serve, so to speak, as an introduction to or a model of all the dualisms that were to follow. During the fourth century B.C. it disappeared from the philosophical scene, but not completely, since traces of it are discernible in later times. Mention is sometimes made of people who were living according to Pythagorean precepts. There existed 'Pythagorean mysteries', in southern Italy for instance, the mother country of the sect, that were barely distinguishable from the Orphic mysteries with which they had much in common [95].

2. The revival of Pythagoreanism in the last century B.C.

Pythagorean philosophy enjoyed a marked revival in the last century B.C. A role in this revival was played by Alexander Polyhistor. This man was a Greek, born in Milete around 110 B.C. Taken prisoner during one of the Mithridatic Wars, he came to Rome as a slave where he became the teacher of a wealthy Roman. In 81 B.C. he was set free and probably even acquired Roman citizenship. He stayed in Rome as a professor of philosophy and wrote about twenty-five books on the most different subjects, one of them being a book on Pythagoras and his doctrine. He died around 40 B.C. [96]. The book in question has been lost, but Diogenes Laertius presents us with a long excerpt from it [97].

It is not impossible that it was Polyhistor's book that introduced the Roman intelligentsia to Pythagoreanism; Zeller calls it 'the oldest document known to us of Neopythagorean philosophy' [98]. Pythagoreanism soon became popular. There was a marked religious side to it, with a strong tendency towards mysticism; there was something mysterious in it, what with its theory of numbers that presented itself as an explanation of how the universe is ordered. Its approach of the godhead was far more personal than that of the official Roman cult. All this made it attractive to a wide public that could find no real satisfaction in traditional Roman religion.

3. The mystical urge

This inclination towards mystical religion is exemplified in the life of Apollonius of Tyana, the 'Pythagorean', or perhaps rather in the legends told about him. It is hard to state with reasonable exactitude what is authentically 'Apollonian' in the accounts and what is free interpretation by other authors. There is very little that is really reliable in his biography. He came from Tyana in Cappadocia (the heartland of Asia Minor that had a reputation for magic and sorcery) and his life spanned the first century A.D.; he died during the reign of the Emperor Nerva (96-98). Our only source for his life is Philostratus who describes him as a wandering sage living ascetically, who visited many countries including India; he is said to have performed miracles [99]. But Philostratus' relation is generally considered untrustworthy [100]. No writings of the sage are extant; a number of letters are ascribed to him, in all probability incorrectly.

It seems that this Apollonius played a considerable part in the popularizing of Pythagoreanism, the more so because he modelled himself on the venerated master. Pythagoras was, he found, divine and possessed a deep insight into supernatural matters. If we may believe Philostratus on this point, Apollonius was no admirer of a philosophy that accords with (human) nature, a philosophy, that is, that is based on the natural capacities of the thinking person; one should rather get one's insights from 'a secret intercourse with the gods' [101]. Apollonius even became a cult figure. The Emperor Caracalla who "delighted in magicians and jugglers ... erected a shrine to him" [102]. Another Emperor, Severus Alexander, had in his private chapel statues of 'certain holy souls, among them Apollonius, and further of Christ, Abraham, Orpheus, and others of this same character' [103].

4. Pythagoreanism in Rome

A learned Roman of the first century B.C., Publius Nigidius Figulus, is known to have been a Pythagorean; he was a friend of Cicero, a grammarian and a theologian. Since he had been a supporter of Pompey, he was forced into exile in Caesar's days, where he died in 45 B.C. Cicero reports that he had a conversation with Nigidius in Cilicia in 51 B.C.; he mentions him as renovator of Pythagorean philosophy that, he says, "flourished some centuries ago in Italy and Sicily but has now become extinct somehow" [104]. Elsewhere this same author writes that many people came together with Nigidius [105]. On the basis of fragments, we may assume that he was an 'anchorman' in Rome with regard to the revival of Pythagoreanism.

However, Zeller does not believe that Rome was the place where the Pythagorean doctrine came to life again. He mentions that in the first century A.D., according to Seneca, "that famous school of Pythagoras ... has not found a teacher" [106]. What this means is that there was no Pythagorean academy in Rome, but not that there were no Pythagoreans. Zeller finds Rome, with regard to scholarship, not important enough to become the cradle of Pythagoreanism. In his opinion it was instead in Alexandria that it began its second lease of life [107].

5. Pythagoreanism and Neopythagoreanism

For some time we have only the names of people who called themselves Pythagoreans, and not Neopythagoreans, because they were convinced that they were referring to the original teaching of the master [108]. This is, however, far from being the case. Their Pythagoreanism was a Neopythagoreanism because it was at the same time eclectic and syncretistic; there was Pythagorean doctrine in it, but it also borrowed from Plato, Aristotle, and the Stoa [109]. Furthermore, it was by no means so that there would have been only one Neopythagorean school; Sextus Empiricus informs us that there were several. "There were Neopythagoreans who had everything start from one point; this point produces the line, and from the line comes the plane. And when the plane 'moves towards depth', we have three dimensions" [110]. Since everything comes from a Monad (the one point), we clearly have a monistic system here, in a geometrical garb.

Sextus feels that this system is close to the original one, since he mentions later Pythagoreans with a deviating system. "For these latter formed the numbers (in Pythagoreanism the numbers stand for substances - F.) from two principles, the One and the Infinite Dyad", while "the former (the above mentioned) build up all of them from a single point" [111]. This evidently refers to a dualistic system. "For with the name of unity (the Monad, the One - F.) will be indicated the fundament of all that is good, of all that is perfection and order, of all that is permanent and unchangeable Being, and with that of duality (= the Infinite Dyad - F.) the fundament of all that is imperfection and evil, of all disorderliness and change. The first is identified with the godhead, with spirit, with Form, the other with matter, as the source of all evil" [112].

6. Numenius the Neopythagorean

a. Who was Numenius?

Numenius is usually described as a Neopythagorean [113], but sometimes as a Neoplatonist [114]. It must be stated at the outset of these sections that it is not always easy to distinguish between Neopythagoreanism and Neoplatonism. This is no wonder since Plato himself, highly original though he was, was influenced by Pythagoreanism so that many Pythagorean elements found their way into his doctrine. Of the philosopher Numenius' life we know precious little; he lived in the second century A.D. and was born in Apameia (now Qal 'at el Moudiq) in Syria [115], that much is certain. None of his philosophical works is extant; we have no more than quotations from other authors [116]. His principal works were 'On the Good' and 'On the infidelity of the Academy with regard to Plato'. It is sometimes thought he had a Jewish background [117]. It is impossible to verify whether this is really so, but he demonstrates an acquaintance with the Old Testament [118] and a predilection for things oriental [119].

b. Numenius a dualist?

Was Numenius an out and out dualist [120]? He is reported to have found that "all incarnations are evil" [121]. This denotes a deeply pessimistic view of the world, but not necessarily dualistic; such an opinion is, however, much closer to the Gnosis than to Judaism. But he reveals himself as an ontological and cosmological dualist in a long fragment preserved by Calcidius [122]. He rejects the opinion of that Neopythagorean school I already mentioned, namely that all that is originates from the Monad (the monistic system) [123]. Numenius points out that the Master himself clearly distinguished two principles, the first being God who is the Monad, the other Matter which is the Dyad, the duality. That Matter and duality could proceed from God is hard to believe, even for people of a feeble mind, he says. Like God, Matter has no origin; it is just as ancient as God himself. The two principles have eternally existed side by side. Matter is of itself formless, but God the Demiurge has conditioned it.

What is good in the material world is the form that has been given to it by God. But Matter itself is fluid and without quality and the source of evil. Since the cosmos is made of Matter, it is shaped of something that is bad. It has, so to speak, a father and a mother. The father is God who extends his Providence to the world; the mother is Matter by which all that is evil is caused. If things go wrong in the world, it is not the fault of Providence, but of the confused instability of Matter. For the structure of the cosmos is a composition of the persuasive power of God and submission to necessity.

Karin Alt, in her fine study on the dualism of the Neopythagorean and Neoplatonic philosophers [124], concludes that this is not only cosmological but by the same token ethical dualism : God and Matter, good and bad. God is Providence and he cares for the world, but he is incapable of eliminating the fatal necessity of Matter [125]. Of course, Matter, bad as it is, "opposes itself to Providence and attacks its plans; the depth of Matter produces its blind and confused temerity ... But when Matter has received its adornment, it becomes the mother of the corporeal and generated gods. Its fate is propitious". This may suggest that this is a case of the good principle triumphing over the bad one, so that the dualistic opposition is done away with. But Numenius adds cautiously : "Not wholly, however, because its original vice could not be eliminated entirely" [126]. Since the opposition of God and matter is of an ontological nature, and since the qualitative difference is essential to it, the defects of Matter cannot be removed without destroying it. "God embellished Matter by his magnificent power and corrected its defaults in every manner, without killing them, out of fear that material nature would totally perish" [127]. Could it be stated more clearly that Matter is fundamentally and irremediably evil?

c. The origin of Numenius' dualism

As usual scholarly opinions differ, not with regard to the question of whether Numenian cosmology was dualistic - it undoubtedly is -, but how dualistic it was, and where this dualism came from. Again as usual, the thoughts of one or another scholar go in the direction of Persia. According to Dillon, Numenius comes close to "the old Pythagorean position'. But even in old Pythagoreanism "the Dyad is really a passive principle and subordinate to the Monad". I do not understand what this means. Less still do I understand his conclusion that, in consequence, "Numenius' radical dualism must be seen as influenced by Persian ideas" [128]. There is not the slightest indication that either Pythagoras or Numenius knew anything of Persian theology.

Karin Alt, for one, does not believe in this Persian connection. However, she herself is speaking here of 'integrated dualism'; she does so because the divine principle remains the sovereign one, although tension certainly exists between God and Matter. I find this confusing, for 'integrated dualism' contains a contradictio in adiecto. Dualism and integration never go together, since dualism is without exception always about holding apart, opposing, not fitting together, being fundamentally different.

d. The First God and the Demiurge

As a good Greek philosopher Numenius cannot do without Being, without 'to on'. Matter, continuously moving and changing as it is, cannot stand for Being, for this is eternal, incorporeal, and immovable, as a real 'on' should be [129]. This 'on' must keep that moving mass of Matter together [130]. However, Numenius' God, who is Being, is not the creator. This is an ontological impossibility, for God - the First God, says Numenius - is 'haplous' = simple, in the sense of 'undivided', 'dwelling in himself ..., entirely concentrated in himself. Because he is indivisble, he cannot make something that is divisible [131]. This God is the Supreme King who is 'argos' = 'a-ergos', doing nothing [132]. Once again we meet here that 'horror materiae' that is so frequent in the authors of this century.

The First God is father to the Demiurge who is the Second God [133]. Whereas the Supreme God is Being, the Second God is responsible for Becoming [134]. The Demiurge is related to the supreme one as the farmer is to his gardener. From the First God comes the seed that is present in the souls of all those who participate in him; the Demiurge cultivates these [135]. The First God and the Demiurge have different functions : the one occupies himself with intelligibles, the other with intelligibles and sensibles [136]. The term 'Demiurge' may make us think of the Demiurge of the Gnostics who is usually evil-intentioned. But in Numenius this is not so; he says expressly that the First God is the Good in itself, and the Second God is good because he is the imitator of the First [137]. "He (the Demiurge) regulates the harmony in Matter and governs it by means of the Ideas, looking on God" [138].

However, whereas the First God is undivided, a perfect unity, there is duality in the Demiurge. Numenius compares him to a navigator who steers his ship across the sea; he has his eyes on the signs of heaven in order to determine his course and at the same time on the sea to avoid steering his ship into the rocks. Just so the Demiurge is looking at God and at Matter simultaneously [139]. This causes the Second God to be moving, while the supreme God is stable [140]. It brings the Demiurge dangerously close to Matter. "(The Demiurge) is not really attached to the Intelligible (= the First God) in which case he would be sufficient to himself; instead, he is looking at Matter and, as a result, he is occupying himself with it and forgets himself. He enters into contact with the sensible ..., because his desire goes out to Matter." And what is the consequence? "Associating himself with Matter, which is dual in one substance, he is torn into two by it" [141]. Matter is obviously a kind of whirlpool into which everything that ventures near it is engulfed. Dillon remarks rightly that "it would be going too far, however, to take Numenius' Demiurge as being in any sense an evil principle, despite the dangers of his position" [142].

e. The world souls

In the long fragment taken from Calcidius' 'In Timaeum' it is said that "Numenius praises Plato for professing two world souls, the one extremely beneficious, the other malign" [143]. In the same text the philosopher unequivocally states that the malign world soul is matter. But who or what is the beneficious world soul? Numenius nowhere says that it is God [144]; actually he says nothing about it at all [145]. When speaking of God, he does not use the term 'world soul' ('anima mundi' in Calcidius' Latin), but 'nous' = mind, or intellect. He does so in several places, even calling God 'the First Intellect', identical with Being and the Supreme Good [146]. God sends his Intellect downward "through the spheres for all those who are destined to participate in it" [147]. He makes the Second God share in it, and then also the Third God (the cosmos) which utilizes it 'in a discursive way', i.e. operative, creating forms [148].

f. The two souls in the human person

Far more important than the idea of there being two world souls, of which we hear precious little, is Numenius' doctrine of the two souls in the human person. There can be no doubt that, according to him, man has two souls, a rational ('logikos') and an irrational ('alogos') one [149]. Karin Alt does not think that there is an analogy to the two world souls in this [150]. I agree with her opinion since we know far too little of the two world souls to conclude that there is a dualistic opposition between them. The two human souls cohabit uncomfortably : "they are opposed for battle" [151].

Where does the irrational soul come from? It originates outside the body and gets its evil character from matter [152]; "even before entering the body it is filled with evil" [153]. This may suggest that the irrational human soul forms part of the malign world soul [154]. The rational or spiritual soul is called 'nous' or 'psuchê'; it is immaterial, incorporeal, and without dimensions [155]. It is because of these qualities that the rational soul can hold together the always changing and moving elements of the body. "Everything is in need of something that binds it together; this (namely movement and change) would go on forever, if it did not come into contact with something incorporeal" [156]. Where does the rational soul come from? It "has as its authors reason and God" [157].

Numenius' doctrine of the human soul(s) is squarely dualistic. The rational and the irrational soul have different origins and are qualitatively distinct; although they meet in the human person, they remain apart and do not fuse into a unity. To be incorporated is, in Numenius' view, the ultimate misfortune.

PART IV MIDDLE PLATONISM

1. Plato's heritage

The most important and influential thinker of Antiquity was Plato; I do not think anybody will contradict this statement. Since Plato was a thoroughgoing dualist [158], it will be necessary to study the vicissitudes of his heritage. I have done this (partly) already in earlier volumes, for instance, where I discussed Plato's influence on philosophers like Philo [159]. Platonism did not experience the long eclipse Pythagoreanism had to undergo; there was always some school of it. In Athens Plato's own foundation, the Academy, continued to flourish as a philosophical institute of prime importance, surviving all vicissitudes, even its destruction by Sulla in 87 B.C., until it was finally closed on Justinian's orders in A.D. 529. In the history of Platonism in Antiquity five stages are distinguished, all of them connected with a phase in the existence in the Academy, and each with its own principal representative. It is usual to speak of Platonic philosophy during the first and second centuries A.D. as 'Middle Platonism', while the last great flourishing period, inaugurated by Plotinus in the third century goes under the name of 'Neoplatonism'.

2. Antiochus of Ascalon

To connect the older Platonism with the later one, it is best to start with Antiochus of Ascalon (ca.120-68 B.C.), with all the more reason because he was 'a person of standing and distinction' in the Academy, "which", wrote Cicero, "after having been almost abandoned is now being revived" [160]. Antiochus is considered to be the founder of the Fifth Academy which was more 'Platonic' than its predecessors. We would not know him if Cicero had not heard him, his 'guide and teacher', lecturing in Athens during the winter of 79/78 B.C. [161], for every sentence the man wrote is lost. He was born around 120 B.C. in Ascalon (in what is now the Gaza-strip, no longer existing) and went as a young man to Athens where he later became the head of the Academy. Later still the Roman general Lucullus became his patron whom he followed into the second Mithridatic War in 73 B.C. He died in 68 or 67 B.C. Cicero describes him as the only authority on Platonism he could find in Athens [162]. A modern specialist on Middle Platonism, however, says that he was "not really a first-rate philosopher nor can he be said the immediate founder of Middle Platonism. He was too firmly wedded to Stoic physics for that" [163].

The great problem that Antiochus poses is whether or not he was a dualist. He was said to be a Platonist [164]. But if he was a Platonist, one might expect that he was a dualist. But in the surviving fragments little evidence on dualism is to be found [165]. This may be ascribed to the paucity of the fragments; we have no records of direct speech. In particular, he cannot be placed within the typical Platonic soul-body dualism.

The nearest approach to dualism is in his physics, expounded in Cicero's 'Academica posteriora' by a certain Varro, who speaks of Platonists among whom he reckons Antiochus. The substratum of everything is, according to the Platonists as Varro explains, matter ('hulê') which is absolutely formless and possesses no quality whatsoever. It is entirely passive so that everything imaginable can be done with it, in a negative as well in a positive way. It can be endlessly transformed and divided into parts; it can also be used as the raw material from which all things can be modelled. It is difficult to define the exact state of matter since it is in constant flux.

But there is also a principle that is immutable and eternal and that can never perish. This is the 'ratio perfecta', Perfect Reason, also known as the World Soul and Perfect Intelligence and Wisdom; the Platonists - I am still quoting Cicero - call it 'God'. This force or principle, which is immanent in the cosmos, shapes the things that possess quality, the things that have a form the totality of which constitutes the organic whole of the world, the cosmos. God governs all this, especially the celestial bodies [166]. It is quite remarkable that the Platonic Demiurge is not mentioned in this context [167]. What a pity that Cicero does not tell us more! Perhaps he was more interested in transforming Antiochus into an authentic Stoic [168] than in giving us more a clearer picture of his real mind [169].

3. Albinus and Alcinous : two persons or one?

For ages two Middle Platonists, Albinus and Alcinous, lived peacefully side by side, as two different persons. But in 1879 the German scholar Freudenthal [170] wrote a study in which he set out to prove that these two philosophers were in reality one and the same person, or rather, that there had never been an Alcinous (who, in any case, has always been a rather mysterious figure). As a result, Alcinous' name disappeared from the scholarly discussion. This eclipse lasted for more than a century, until the Canadian scholar Whittaker brought him back into the picture [171]. However, the last shadow of doubt has not yet been removed [172].

4. Alcinous and his 'Didaskalikos'

a. The man and his handbook

We know almost nothing of Alcinous except that he lived during the second century A.D. and that he wrote a handbook on Platonism called the 'Didaskalikos' [173]. Or rather should we say that he was its compiler, for many influences came together in it [174]. As a handbook, it played a role in the transmission of Platonism from the earlier to the later centuries A.D. If Alcinous' work was the bridge between earlier Platonism and the great Platonist thinkers of Late Antiquity, it might be expected that he was a thorough dualist. But it would be difficult to maintain that he was one, or that he was a dualist in all the branches of Late Platonic philosophy. Karin Alt says that many of his theses differ from those of other Platonists, in particular Plutarch, and asks whether this might be a reaction or even a polemic against certain philosophical positions [175].

b. Alcinous' theory of the soul

There is no dualism in his cosmology and metaphysics. "A force directed against God cannot be detected; the divine ordering (of the cosmos - F.) does not meet with any resistance ... The problem of evil is clearly eliminated in the Didaskalikos, and the word 'kakon' does not occur (i.e. on the sections on cosmology - F.) ... For an introduction into Plato's philosophy this is really astonishing" [176].

It is somewhat different with regard to his theory of the soul. In accordance with Plato's teaching Alcinous holds the soul to be something composite, consisting of three parts : the rational part (which is the leading one) and the part that is the seat of the passions, which in its turn is subdivided into the irascible and concupiscent parts [177]. This is in fact a bifurcation into two. The Demiurge of the universe, says Alcinous, sends the souls down to the earth [178]. The gods - not be confused with the Demiurge - fashion the human person out of the four elements, and then they place the principal part of the soul, the rational part, in the head [179]. This part is destined to rule. The other parts of the soul are joined to the first one but are located further down, the irascible near the heart, and the concupiscent in the region of the navel [180]. This is sheer Platonism, with the consequence that there is more than a whiff of dualism to it. Soul and body are of different origin; the body is placed under the mastery of the rational soul. The two non-rational parts of the soul are obviously of a lesser quality than the rational one. It is more telling still that the higher and lower parts of the soul are in conflict with each other [181]; the passions cause mental troubles [182].

The rational soul is innately endowed with a life-giving faculty, and "that which is capable of giving life is not susceptible to dying". Therefore, the soul is immortal and indestructible; it is essentially incorporeal and immovable. It is intelligible, invisible, and one; it is not composite, insoluble, and indivisible. The body, by contrast, is observable, visible, divisible, and composed of multiple parts. When the soul is confronted by the body, it is troubled and becomes dizzy, but when it has to do with the intelligible, it remains calm and undisturbed. Alcinous' conclusion is that the rational soul is divine, whereas, by implication, the body is not [183].

c. Alcinous' conception of man

Alcinous' conception of man is not as pessimistic as it is, for instance, in the Gnosis. Human persons are the only living beings who possess an immortal soul; they are, therefore, kindred to the gods. Just as Plato, this author describes the metempsychosis, i.e. the transmigration of souls. People should master their passions; "those who allow themselves to be dominated by injustice will be reborn, in a second existence, as women, and, when they do not succeed in amending themselves, once again, and then definitely, as animals" [184]. Here this philosopher is just as hostile towards women as was his master.

Alcinous is, however, not wholly negative with regard to the body; to him, as it is the case in Plato, a philosopher is not necessarily not a 'philosomatos', no lover of the body. According to him, there exists a certain relationship between body and soul [185]. What this relationship entails depends entirely on the meaning of the very rare Greek word used here, 'oikeiotês'. Louis translates this with 'une certaine affinité', Alt with 'gehören zu einander', which is stronger than 'affinity' [186], while Liddell-Jones has s.v. 'appropiative', which, in my opinion is less positive. I feel that we should opt for a less positive rendering of this term, because Alcinous adds that the affinity between soul and body is like that of fire and bitumen (asphaltos).

Does this express reciprocal fondness? A Wahlverwandtschaft? The author compares the soul to fire and the body to bitumen; this comparison has a rather negative connotation. This impression is strengthened by another communication of Alcinous, namely that souls pass into the bodies of human beings and animals, among other reasons because they love bodies too much; here the word 'philosomatia' is employed but in a negative sense [187]. I therefore ask myself whether it is really correct when Alt says, that "Alcinous turned out to be a thinker who is foreign to the dualistic tendencies of that period and attempts to close off himself against them" [188].

d. Alcinous' idea of philosophy

Alcinous is without any doubt a dualist when he is speaking about philosophizing. "Philosophy is striving after wisdom, or the liberation of the soul and its turning away from the body, directing us towards what is intelligible and to what truly exists" [189]. He begins his disquisition with this important statement, adding that this is the doctrine of Plato. In this context it should be stressed that the souls of wisdom-loving people ascend directly to the realm of the gods without taking their bodies with them. Alt thinks that Alcinous is not really interested in the way such souls exist after death, but she concludes that he is a dualist with regard to his conception of the soul [190].

5. Plutarch : historian, essayist, moralist, philosopher

a. The man and his work

Plutarch is usually seen is a typical representative of what is called Middle Platonism. This famous and prolific author was a Greek, born in Chaeronea around A.D. 45, who spent most of his life in his native town. He also travelled and was for some time a teacher in Rome. It is not certain that he fulfilled an imperial office, but in any case he was a priest of the temple in

Delphi for three decades. Plutarch was married and had five children two of which died in a tender age. He died around A.D. 120.

The catalogue of his works mentions two hundred and twenty-seven books; of these an astonishing one hundred and nine are extant. They contain treatises on the art of rhetorics and on ethics and behaviour, on philosophy, on antiquarian subjects and on history, the famous 'Parallel Lives'; many of his treatises are in the form of dialogue [191].

b. Plutarch's attitude towards Rome

We shall come to know Plutarch as a dualist but in one particular respect he was not : in his attitude towards Rome, the Romans, and the Roman Empire. He is occasionally critical of Roman customs; he abhors, for instance, the gladiatoral games. But C.P. Jones, who studied Plutarch's relationship with Rome, says that his "attitude to Rome is in a sense both Greek and Roman : Greek, in that he saw himself as a Greek by birth and language, Roman, in that his interests and sympathies are bound up with the Empire" [192].

c. Plutarch on women

The picture Plutarch presents of Athenian women in his 'Parallel Lives' reflects what I wrote on their status in Vol. II [193]. This ancient author restricts himself to the women of high society. They have no freedom at all and pass from the hands of their father (or their brothers or even the state) to those of their husbands. Their contours remain vague; hardly any names are mentioned. These women lived behind the walls of their houses and did not appear in public. By way of contrast, loose-living women and their liaisons are often mentioned. "It seems as if Athens were peopled by hetaeres!". They are much more in view than the respectable house-wives. The great exception in Greece was Sparta where the women were the equals of men, courageous, temerarious, and forceful as they were.

In his judgment on the female sex Plutarch reveals himself to be a Greek traditionalist. He has no eye for the beauty and charms of women, although he sometimes mentions that some woman or other is beautiful. But in the case of two of the most renowned beauties of Antiquity, Aspasia and Cleopatra, he praises only their intellectual capacities. He fears the traps amorous females may set for unwary men and does not believe in marriages based on love.

On the whole his attitude towards women is disparaging. The best they can do is to remain devoted to their husbands. And of course, they should be blamelessly virtuous. In order for a marriage to be happy, it should be arranged. He abhors homosexuality, although attachments of this kind were not generally disapproved of in Greek society, at least not for younger men. But to be enamoured with your own wife he does not see as something virile. In Volume II I characterized the relation of men and women in Greek society - men here, women there - as dualistic [194]. With his ideas on women Plutarch fits neatly into this tradition [195].

d. Plutarch's conception of God

"Plutarch aimed a purer conception of God", wrote Copleston [196]. And Julien Riès said that "Plutarch searched in the diverse doctrines the elements that best answered the aspirations of an élite : a new face of the godhead, a higher moral elevation, a personal piety which effectuated the encounter of the soul with the godhead, that might even lead him to a mystical ideal" [197]. Giving a new face to the godhead meant presenting God as abstract and impersonal as possible - an evident reaction against ordinary Greek anthropomorphism. To Plutarch God is the Supreme Being, 'to ontoos on', the Real Being [198] - a term suggesting that other forms of existence are situated lower in the ontological order. This Supreme Being is "eternal, without beginning and without end, to which no length of time brings change". For time is movement and change, 'a receptacle, as it were, of birth and decay'; terms like 'afterwards' and 'before', 'shall be' and 'has been' "are of themselves a confession of Not Being" [199] - which relegates history to the category of Not Being. We are close to Parmenides' dualism here, that of Being and Seeming.

"But God IS ... and only when Being is after his pattern it is in reality Being" [200].

e. The One and the Many

Plutarch then conjures up the old spectre of the One and the Many. "The Deity is not many", he says. To be many means, even for human beings, to be "composed of hundreds of different factors ..., a heterogeneous collection combined in a haphazard way". The conclusion will not surprise us : to be Many is equivalent to not being. Being is unity and unity is Being. "Divergence from unity, because of its differing from Being, deviates into the creation of that which has no Being." Plutarch gives the highest Being the name of 'Apollo' which, in his peculiar etymology, signifies 'a-polloon' = denying the Many and abjuring multiplicity. Only that which is "one and uncombined (is) imperishable and pure" [201]. We have quite a number of dualistic oppositions here : God and man, the One and the Many, unity and multiplicity, purity and impurity.

f. Metaphysical dualism

How thoroughly dualistic Plutarch's metaphysical position is appears from a passage in another work [202]. He is speaking here of 'numbers' by which he obviously means 'first principles', the 'archai' of Greek philosophy. He calls them 'archai' indeed and elsewhere 'those numbers which come at the very first'. It begins with the number 'one'; the second is 'the Infinite Dyad', the 'indeterminate duality'. This Dyad is also called 'infinity'; it is the 'element underlying all formlessness and disarrangement'. Is this radical dualism? The dualism of two utterly opposed first principles having nothing to do with each other and constantly in conflict? Not really, because the Dyad is subjected to and ruled over by the One. "The nature of the number One limits and arrests what is void and irrational and indeterminate in infinity, gives it shape, and renders it in some way tolerant and receptive of definition". Plutarch is moving here within the orbit of Pythagoreanism.

In his most famous work, the treatise 'On Isis and Osiris', he is an especially outspoken metaphysical dualist [203]. Let me first of all relate the Egyptian Osiris-myth, without getting bogged down with the many modifications it has undergone throughout the course of time. Osiris was a (legendary) king in Egypt, a good king. He was fought, defeated, and killed by his evil brother Seth (Typhon, in Plutarch's version). Some versions say that Osiris' body was cut into fourteen parts, each of which was buried in a different region; other versions maintain that the corpse was laid into a coffin and thrown into the Nile. The coffin washed ashore near Byblos in Fenicia. His grieving sister Isis travelled through the country seeking her dead brother. She either assembled the fourteen parts and reconstituted the body, or else the coffin was brought back to her. However, the corpse was not really a corpse, for there was still a vital force in it. So, when Isis laid herself on her brother's body, she conceived and bore a child called Horus. The revitalized Osiris became the king of the dead in the underworld, while Horus grew up and became the avenger of his father by killing Seth-Typhon [204]. There are dualistic elements in this saga that were used and moulded into some sort of system by Plutarch [205].

We find in this treatise a crucial passage expressing that 'horror materiae' which we encounter so often in the authors of Late Antiquity, whether pagan or Christian. The text speaks here of Osiris who, in this context, is the godhead par excellence. This god "is far removed from the earth, uncontaminated and unpolluted and pure from all matter that is subject to destruction and death". That a supreme godhead should be immaterial is not exceptional, for this equally applies to the Jewish-Christian God. The point is that contact with matter would defile him. Plutarch distances himself from the majority of people who think that Osiris, "as god of the dead, truly dwells in the earth and beneath the earth". But no! he is instead 'far removed from the earth'. In other words, Osiris is a transcendent god, but not an immanent one, like the Jewish-Christian supreme godhead who is at once Creator and Providence.

g. The transcendent god

The transcendence of Plutarch's god is so absolute that it is almost impossible to approach him. "For the souls of men here, which are compassed about by bodies and emotions, there is no association with this god." Once again it is stressed how great a hindrance the human body, with its passions, is. There is only one way that can bring one nearer to the god, but this is not the way of liturgy, prayer, sacrifice, or mortification. People "may attain a dim vision of his presence by means of the apperception which philosophy affords." Yet another dualistic opposition becomes visible here : that of those who philosophize and those who do not; the latter category will remain completely unaware of the real nature of the godhead.

But even philosophy affords only 'a dim vision'. It is only after death that full vision is possible; it needs no argument that the body will have to be left behind. "When these souls are set free and migrate into the realm of the invisible and the unseen, the dispassionate and the pure, then this god becomes their leader and king, since it is on him that they are bound to be dependent in their insatiate contemplation and yearning for that beauty which is for men unutterable and indescribable" [206].

h. Plutarch's dualism

It will be evident that Plutarch's supreme godhead can never be a creator. Creational activity would bring him into contact with matter and, far worse, with evil, which is unthinkable. He had, in consequence, to postulate an intermediary entity who could be charged with the work of creation. There is perhaps, as Deuse explains, a certain development in Plutarch's thinking on this point, from De Iside to De procreatione (which is his Timaeus-commentary) [207], but in both interpretations we find the same dualistic concept : "the principle of the Good, the godhead or the Nous, stands opposite the principle of Evil" [208].

Speaking of Plutarch's dualism, we will do well to ask what its origin may be. In several places of the earlier volumes I contested the view that all dualism is derived from the dualism of the ancient Iranian religion of Zoroaster. But in Plutarch's case it may be assumed that there was a real connection [209]. He quotes 'the great majority of the wisest of men" who believe that there are two gods, one of the Good and one of Evil, who are rivals; among those 'wisest of men' he specifically mentions 'Zoroaster the sage (Magus)'. He then presents a description of the Zoroastrian religion [210].

Plutarch explains his own specific problem in the following terms. "The fact is that it is impossible for anything bad to be engendered where God is the creator of all, or anything good where God is the creator of nothing" [211]. If we assume that God is the sole ruler of the universe, then the existence of evil is unexplainable and even impossible. But there is evil! Plutarch is thus forced to postulate two principles, two 'archai', as we saw before. "There is not one Reason (Logos) which rules and guides it (the universe) ... In this life of ours (there are) many experiences in which good and bad are commingled." He then concludes that there are two principles, "two opposed archai and two antagonistic forces, one of which guides us along a straight course to the right, while the other turns us aside and backwards". The 'right' must be understood in the Pythagorean sense as the region of the good [212].

This mingling makes our lives complex, 'and the universe too'. But here Plutarch takes several steps backwards. He does not mean the whole universe, he says; he makes the well-known dualistic division of the cosmos into a supralunar and a sublunar part. The sublunar region, "the terrestrial universe, including its moon as well, is irregular and variable and subject to all manner of changes" [213] which is tantamount to stating that it is inferior. We have before us here 'a definitive statement of Plutarch's dualism' [214].

According to Plutarch's metaphysics Evil is an independent element; it is neither God nor matter. He argues that the evil principle is acknowledged by all kinds of people and is given different names : Ahriman, Typhon, Duality (in Pythagoras), War (in Heraclitus), Difference ('thateron' in Plato), and Privation (in Aristotle) [215].

j. The world soul

Following Plato, he does not locate Evil in matter nor does he see this as its cause. "By Plato matter is said always to be amorphous and shapeless and devoid of all quality and potency of its own" [216]. Matter is passive and motionless, 'of itself inert and without propensity' [217]. He agrees with Plato that the cause of Evil must be put 'at the farthest remove from God' [218]. It was not the supreme godhead who aroused matter from torpor ...; (he) did not impart to nature the origins of change and of modifications ... The cause of Evil is the motion that moves matter and becomes divisible in the case of bodies, a motion that is disorderly and irrational." This motor must of course be found outside matter that cannot move itself; "soul is cause and principle of motion", and this soul is "contrary and averse to the one who is beneficent" [219].

With this 'soul', as will be understood, is not meant the human soul but the world soul instead. The relation of the supreme godhead and the world soul is dualistic. He is quoting Plato when he calls this soul an 'ugly and maleficent infinitude ... and largely refractory and recalcitrant to God' [220] (Plato called this evil principle 'anankê' = necessity). 'Refractory' is Cherniss's rendering (in the Loeb Classical edition) of 'dusmachousan'. Alt remarks that the world soul's resistance will hardly bring it success, for the verb 'dusmachein' means fighting a hopeless battle [221].

Plutarch is actually postulating a third archê between God and matter; it is, by definition, a pre-cosmic principle [222]. His explanation of the ontological status of this archê, the world soul, is not free from inconsistencies. It is an independent principle but at the same time it is part of the godhead. Or rather, it becomes part of it. "There are two constituent parts of the universe, body (= matter) and soul. The former God did not beget the body ... The soul, however, when it has partaken of intelligence and reason and concord is not merely a work but also a part of God and has come to be not by his agency but both from him as source and out of his agency" [223]. Thus it became the world soul [224].

It seems as though this soul was 'adopted' by the godhead, but Plutarch nowhere explains how it originated. Like matter, it is obviously eternal. The original situation of both world soul and matter is disorderliness : "What preceded the generation of the universe was disorder" [225]. But the godhead "took over both the principles, the former vague and obscure (= the soul) and the latter confused and stupid (= matter) and both of them indefinite and without their appropriate perfection, and he ordered and arrayed and fitted them together" [226]. Whoever might think now that the originally recalcitrant world soul was tamed and made obedient would be wrong, for it remained what is was : the principle of Evil. Its handling by the godhead did not overcome the metaphysical dualism [227]. There is, however, in Plutarch no wholesale rejection of the cosmos as evil.

k. The human soul as a construct

In Plutarch the human soul is a construct of two parts. In one of his treatises he used a mythical story in order to explain this. There was a man in the town of Soli who led the life of a profligate, 'abstaining from no shameful act', and gaining in this way 'a prodigious reputation for knavery'. Then he made a fall from a height and ended up in a coma; in this state he had what would be today called 'a near death experience'. Part of his soul, the intelligent part, left his body, while the other part stayed behind in it, 'like an anchor', evidently to enable the thinking part to return. His intelligent soul now travelled through space, among the stars, and observed what was happening to the souls dwelling there and how they all had different fates. After three days this soul-part came back to his body and he awoke from his coma. This experience caused him conduct a honest life ever after [228].

What Plutarch is describing here is in fact a shamanistic experience. In Vol. I I explained how shamans, seemingly lying unconscious, felt how their spirit left their bodies and saw strange and uncommon things [229]. I called this a (temporary) dualistic split of body and soul. The peculiar element in Plutarch's tale is that there is not only a dualistic division of soul and body but even one in the soul itself.

In his long dialogue 'Concerning the face which appears in the orb of the moon', Plutarch takes a more stringently dualistic stand still. He castigates those people who hold man to be composed of two parts, body and soul, as though the soul were part of the body. It is equally wrong to see mind (nous) as part of the soul (psuchê), for "in the same degree as soul is superior to body so is mind better and more divine than soul" [230]. Curiously enough a human being does not die once but twice. The first death liberates the soul from the body; the second sets the mind free. The first death is a swift and violent occurence; the second is a slow and painful process. The souls of the unjust will be punished, but even the souls of the good are to be purified 'from the pollutions of the body as from an evil odour' [231].

This is the sheerest dualism, but Karin Alt says that it is primarily of an ontological nature and that this becomes evident in the cosmological field. The soul is not the seat of evil; at least, this is not said in as many words. There is no talk in Plutarch of an irrational opposition of the soul to the body. But still less it should be supposed that the soul could be attained by evil [232]. Separated from the body as well as from the mind, the soul will linger on for some time in the lunar region. The souls of those who have led a philosophical life will wither away quietly [233].

1. The soul as a mixture

"The soul", says Plutarch, "is a mixed and intermediate thing ..., a compound and blend of the things above and below" [234]. It serves as the connecting link between mind and body; it "receives the impression of its shape through being moulded by the mind and moulding the body in its turn and enfolding it on all sides" [235]. This means that there is no soul-body dualism in a human person as long as he or she wanders the earth. But there is a latent dualism that breaks through as soon as a person has died. Then the elements of which a human being consists are disconnected. The bodies of the dead and their souls are 'resolved into the moon' [236]. What remains is the nous, the mind, because it is 'impassible' and 'sovereign' [237]. The nous is imperishable and far superior to both soul and body; it is our 'self', our identity, "that with which we reason and understand" [238].

The position taken by Plutarch in yet another treatise is somewhat different. It is impossible to say whether this is the result of a development or of a change in his way of thinking. It is a hopeless task to establish the exact order of his dialogues, and perhaps he was not always consistent in his philosophy. In the dialogue in question, 'On the sign of Socrates', the position of the soul as an intermediate link between mind and body is far less secure. On the one hand, explains Plutarch, the soul partakes of the mind; 'none is irrational or unintelligent". But another part of the soul associates with the body. "The portion of the soul that mingles with flesh and passions suffers alteration and becomes irrational in the pleasures and pains it undergoes." There are souls that "sink entirely into the body". Others are almost wholly submerged but part of them, 'what is purest in them', is not dragged down but remains afloat, 'like a buoy' [239].

We are here much nearer closer to a mind-body dualism in man, with the soul, no longer a connecting link, in an awkward position. There is obviously not much soul left. This impression is strengthened when we read that the part that is submerged in the body is called soul. It would be entirely wrong, however, to think, as 'the multitude' does, that it is something within our- selves. "But those who conceive the matter rightly called it a daimoon, as being external" [240]. What is essential is not the soul but the nous, here called a 'daimoon' which is not an integral part of the human person. To be exact, Plutarch does not say that the daimoon is external, but that it is 'hoos ektos', as though external [241]. We should not imagine that the human person is here and the daimoon somewhere else. Elsewhere Plutarch dubs it an 'oikeios daimoon', an indwelling daimoon [242].

The strained relation of the daimoon with what 'the multitude' calls the ordinary human person is exemplified by Plutarch when he, reminiscent of Plato, compares the daimoon to a charioteer driving horses. Some souls "are docile to the rein and obedient to their daimoon"; they are 'the race of diviners and of men inspired' [243]. But souls like these are obviously a minority. There are so many more who are 'constantly deviating in all directions from a straight course' and are 'contending with a character refractory and unruly from lack of training' [244]; with this 'training' a philosophical education is of course meant.

m. Conclusion

Although Plutarch leaves some points unexplained and although his theory - or theories - are not perfectly consistent, one thing is certain - so much we may agree with Karin Alt -, his interpretation of the human soul is dualistic. That what he calls 'nous' or 'daimoon' is the essential part of man, whereas soul and body are far inferior to it. In the struggle between 'above' and 'below' the soul is constantly at risk [245]. That soul and body are opposed will not surprise us; we find this in many other authors also. What distinguishes Plutarch from other thinkers is that he makes such a sharp distinction between mind and soul. "Never before had such an unequivocal distinction of them as separate entities been made" [246].

6. Atticus, the purifier of Platonism

a. The man and his philosophical position

We know next to nothing of the life of the philosopher Atticus; of his works little but fragments remain. He was active in Athens around 176-180. His main claim to fame is that he was a staunch opponent of Aristotelian philosophy; he found Platonism, as he knew, it tainted by it and attempted to purge it of Aristotelianism.

Atticus divided the realm of philosophy into three parts : ethics, physics, and logic [247]. With 'physics' metaphysics is meant. A problem is that our knowledge of his metaphysics is third-hand; we know it from Porphyry, but Porphyry learned it from Proclus. It is often thought that Atticus follows Plutarchs' metaphysical doctrine closely, but the question is whether Plutarch's irrational world soul and the nous are also present in Atticus' teaching.

b. The composite soul

Atticus argued that there is a pre-existent irrational (alogos) soul or substance and also a divine soul or substance. He does not speak of a 'nous'. The difference between the two souls is that the divine soul is indivisible, i.e. one, but the irrational soul is divisible [248]. Together they form the rational (logikos) soul of which the divine part is the substrate and the other the form. The soul is, therefore, a composite of two differing parts, one engendered and the other unengendered.

c. Atticus on matter

Just like Plutarch, Atticus assumes that matter was pre-existent to the cosmos. This matter moved in a disorderly way [249]. It has no cause and is uncreated, that is, self-existent [250]; nothing and nobody brought it forth [251]. Matter, therefore, exists independently of any higher power. Its movement is caused by a maleficent soul [252]; obviously, this soul is the source of all evil. What Atticus says must in all probability be interpreted in a dualistic fashion. "Matter, moved by an uncreated, irrational, and maleficent soul, is swung to and fro without order and regularity; chronologically, matter exists before what is perceptible, irrationality before reason, disorderliness before order" [253]. This does not mean that time did not yet exist. It existed, because there was movement, and where there is movement, there is time. But, since movement was disorderly, time was also disorderly [254].

It will be evident that, before the cosmos was created, two entities, the godhead and matter - if chaotic movement may be called an entity -, totally different in everything, stood opposite each other. Atticus' cosmology, therefore, begins with a situation of radical dualism. This dualism becomes all the more stringent since, according to Atticus, the godhead was 'absent' for a time [255].

d. The work of creation

At first, Atticus' godhead exists without undertaking any act of creation. But then he appears on the scene and the work of creation begins. This happened at a given moment in time [256]. Then Time - with a capital letter - began, Time in the sense of 'the number of the movement of the universe' [257], ordered and regulated time, that is, chronology. The creator of the world, the Demiurge, is according to Atticus identical with the Good. He is no Gnostic; his Demiurge is not an evil being who creates a world out of sheer malevolence. "Just as a cabinet maker does in all his works of joinery, although making them all different according to a different pattern, here a foot-stool, there a bed, just so God too, because he is good, makes all things similar to himself, making them all good, using the designs which give them their individuality and so realizes their substances one by one according to exemplary causes" [258]. It is interesting to see how Atticus postulates an 'analogy of being' avant la lettre (of the Schoolmen), because all created things bear a similarity to their creator.

We are, however, justified in asking why the Demiurge chose a particular moment for beginning his creational activity. Atticus' answer to this question is not really satisfying [259]. The Demiurge waited to intervene until matter had become better disposed or more suitable, that is less disorderly. Speaking in his own words (in Proclus), the philosopher said that "Matter acquired a disposition to receive the plan of the Demiurge; this is exactly what the Demiurge looked for, this disposition". Matter obviously made an end of disorder herself. "But how", asked the astonished Proclus, and do we ask with him, "did Matter now become something ordered?". This question is not answered [260].

e. Pre-cosmic dualism

A final point must be made. Thus far we have seen that the world soul is a mixture of rational and irrational elements. This pre-cosmic dualism is also found within the cosmos itself. The mode of origination of each individual human soul, that is a compound of rational (divine) and irrational parts, resembles closely that of the cosmos. "There is only one manner of joining all the souls to the bodies; in an identical way, at every incorporation of souls, they (Atticus and other Platonists) make exist first the irrational soul which is disorderly and immersed in matter, and when this soul is well-ordered, they make it join the rational soul" [261]. Once again, how disorder changes into order is not explained . That the irrational part of the world soul did not depart entirely from the scene after it had come into contact with rationality becomes apparent from the fact that the disorderliness of the individual soul has to be tamed, every time a human being comes into existence. This means that disorder and irrationality are continuously active in the cosmos as well as in human beings [262].

f. The impossible feat of no mean philosopher

Atticus was no mean philosopher. Proclus quoted him quite a number of times, in a negative sense, since he did not agree with him. But he would not have taken the trouble of refuting Atticus time and again, if he had not found him important enough to mention. How then and why did a strange anomaly creep into his doctrine - that of a Demiurge who orders something, that has already ordered itself, Matter? Why was Atticus, whose analytical powers were so acute, suddenly so unthinking? It looks to me like an incomprehensible blunder of a great chess master. Why did the Demiurge not do the ordering himself? Was he powerless to do so? I do not preclude the possibility that he felt at a loss with disorderliness. It is possible that we here once again meet that 'horror materiae' already mentioned more than once in this volume. In order to create, the Demiurge had to come into contact with matter. That was bad enough in itself. But bothering himself with chaotic matter was something inconceivable. He could only do something with a matter that knew how to behave and that did not confront him with insuperable difficulties.

The fundamental explanation, however, is in my opinion to be found in this that Atticus wanted to perform an impossible feat, namely that of turning a thoroughly dualistic system into a non-dualistic one. He starts from the radical dualism of the divine and the irrational, of the godhead and matter, of order and disorder. But then there occurs that unexplainable and unexplained event, that of chaotic Matter ordering itself and making itself amenable to the creational intentions of the Demiurge. Obviously - perhaps in the last resort? on second thoughts? subconsciously? - Atticus did not want his doctrine to be basically dualistic. For this reason he performed this curious trick. But the dualism that was chased out of the front door reentered subreptitiously through the back-door. The trick had to be repeated at the creation of every individual human soul. In order to present a doctrine free of all sorts of dualism, Atticus should have started from different premises.

PART V NEOPLATONISM

1. Plotinus

a. The man and his work

The greatest philosopher of Late Antiquity, the founder of the School of Neoplatonism, was Plotinus [263]. In which town exactly he was born is not known, but in any case it was somewhere in Egypt; this must have been around 205. This does not necessarily mean that he was an ethnic Egyptian, but if he was one, he was hellenized. He was already twenty-eight when he became interested in philosophy. The city par excellence to study it was, of course, Alexandria. However, the teachers there disappointed him. But then later he came to be taught by Ammonias Saccas whose teaching suited him perfectly. We don't know much of this professor, but it is interesting to know that Origen was another student of his. For eleven years Plotinus remained with Ammonias in the Egyptian capital.

Since some elements of Iranian and Indian wisdom had seeped through to Alexandria, Plotinus, wanting to learn more of it on the spot, joined the army of the Emperor Gordianus III who was campaigning in the East. This undertaking ended disastrously [264]. The Emperor was murdered in Persia in 244, and Plotinus, for some unknown reason, fled to Antioch from where he travelled on to Rome. For the next twenty-five years he lived in the imperial capital. He opened a school of philosophy there and had much success in the higher echelons of Roman society. It was only in 253 that he began to write. An attempt to found a Platonic community in the vicinity of the city was unfruitful. When he died in 270, he was not in Rome, but at the estate of a friend near Minturnae (not far from the present Minturno). He died alone, assisted only by a physician, because he was suffering of an infectious disease, probably leprosy.

Plotinus himself appointed his pupil Porphyry as his literary executor. During the last sixteen years of his life he had written a substantial amount. Porphyry arranged the treatises into six sections each comprising nine essays, the famous 'Enneads', fifty-four in all [265]. Plotinus wrote only about philosophical subjects. There is not the slightest doubt about the authenticity of his texts.

b. The main object of his philosophy

I feel it would be useful to state from the outset what the main object of Plotinus' philosophy was before we start looking for the dualistic elements in it [266]. With regard to this philosopher's place in the history of thinking, it is certainly correct to speak, along with Armstrong, of 'the great final rethinking and development of Hellenic Platonism which began with Plotinus' [267]. What Plotinus really strove for was complete unification with the godhead; his main aim was, therefore, of a mystical nature. Remaining immersed in the sensible world would make the ascent impossible; one had to leave all that is finite behind, even the world of ordinary consciousness.

This implied that he distinguished a higher, purely spiritual world, far above the home of the phenomena. As Zeller writes, Plotinus was so firmly convinced of this distinction that he did not even take the trouble to prove it. Likewise he did not prove the reality of the suprasensual realm. Philosophy does not start with the study of our visible and observable world but with the contemplation of the higher regions. Only when we have dwelled long enough in these regions may we return to our world here to investigate and study it.

Philosophy's main object, however, is to teach man how to raise himself to the transcendental world.

Plotinus is often considered a mystic for whom, in the last resort, philosophy has to cede its place to experiences of an ecstatic character. As Copleston expressed it, "in Plotinian Neo-Platonism philosophy tends to pass into religion" [268]. This scholar situates Plotinus in the line of Pythagoreanism, Platonism, and Orphism in which 'otherworldliness' plays such a great role. The tendency towards intellectual ascent and the desire of salvation through assimilation to and knowledge of God reaches its most complete expression in Plotinus' system [269].

c. Plotinus hard to comprehend

Although there are several books and articles on Plotinus' mysticism, this element is not to everybody's taste. His writings are frequently considered obscure and incomprehensible [270]. This was already so in Antiquity. Porphyry, his first biographer, wrote that in his own time people found him 'a big driveller' and that he was a plagiarist, making a show by copying from Numenius. But even this admiring student of him had to admit that "he was not quick to make clear to anybody the compelling coherence of his discourse". Porphyry himself had experienced something of this sort when he first heard the Master; he had urged him to bring more system in his doctrine [271]. Arnou, a modern admirer, finds that Plotinus, just like Plato, argued in an intuitive way, rather than syllogistically; he did not so much want to prove but more to demonstrate, 'putting everything at its place in the universal hierarchy' [272].

d. Plotinus the thinker

In describing Plotinus as a 'mystic', as somebody who is easily transported by an elevated religious sentiment, we should not forget that he was a 'thinker' in the most literal sense of the word. He gave the impression that he did hardly anything else than think. "He was wholly concerned with thought ...

He worked out his train of thought from beginning to end in his own mind. And then, when he wrote it down, since he had set it all to order in his mind, he wrote as continuously as if he was copying from a book".

But Porphyry adds that the Master "paid no attention to spelling" [273]. He mispronounced and misspelled certain words in a curious way [274]. "Even when he was talking to someone, engaged in continuous conversation, he kept to his train of thought ... In this way he was present at once to himself and to others, and he never relaxed his self-turned attention, except in sleep", and his sleep he reduced as much as possible [275]. In short, "he never, while awake, relaxed his intent concentration upon the intellect" [276].

e. A metaphysician or a religious thinker?

Although he was gentle and honest and by no means a-social - he had to care for many persons under age [277] -, the overall impression is that of a very reticent man who did not love to speak about himself; he did not even allow his portrait to be made [278]. His thinking was straightforward and he did not admit to doubt. His sentences abound with 'it must, it is necessary, reason forces us' [279]. His propositions are no matter for discussion. This absence of doubt is the main reason why Arnou is not prepared to call Plotinus a mystic but prefers the epither of 'metaphysician' [280].

However, he may certainly be dubbed a religious person. The subjective basis of his life and work is the desire of God. How important this is for him appears already from the number of words he uses for it : 'ephesis' = aiming at, appealing to, 'orexis' = longing, yearning, 'pothos' = desire, 'hormê' = striving forward, onrush, 'boulêsis' = willing, wishing, 'epithumia' = desire, urge, and above all, of course, 'eroos' = love tout court. Desiring is common to everyone, says Plotinus; he calls it 'pangs' or 'travail' [281].

f. The role of desire

People would not desire, have desires, if there were not something to strive for, something that is desirable, that is good to have. "It is not the striving that constitutes the good but the good calls out the striving" [282]. It is evident that Plotinus does not start from what is natural, namely that we all have our desires, but from something that is metaphysical and supernatural, the Good. Since the soul is aware that it is lacking something - something that is not to be found in this natural world -, it strives upwards, to that what is best, towards the Good [283].

An objection could be raised that this upward striving becomes a circular movement. "The primal nature and the appetition of the Good, which is the appetition of unity, lead back to what is authentically one; every form of Being is urged in a movement towards its own reality. For the good to every nature possessing unity is to be self-belonging, to be itself, and that means to be a unity" [284]. Is this striving after the Good nothing then but a stage in the process of self-realization? Is this not fundamentally egocentric?

g. The lure of Beauty

Plotinus does not deny that desire may pull us in the wrong direction. He speaks of the love of Beauty with which he means 'the charms of this world'; some people "struggle venomously for Beauty". But Beauty is something secondary, and those who give priority to it are also secondary. "The Good has no need of the Beautiful" - of the charms of this world -, "while the Beautiful does not need the Good ... Beauty is all violence and stupefaction; its pleasure is spoiled with pain, and it even draws the thoughtless away from the Good". This makes it sufficiently clear that the concept of 'the Good' is identical to other-worldliness.

That the desire of the Good is really impersonal and not self-centered is proved by Plotinus' opposition of Beauty and the Good, Beauty to be understood as the natural world and the Good as the supernatural realm. "The perception of Beauty and the awe and the stirring of passion towards it are for those already knowing and awakened. But the Good ... is inherently present even to those asleep ... (It) is always with them though in their drowse they are not aware of it" [285]. The philosopher is here alluding to two layers of consciousness that are different and opposed : an ordinary and superficial one that is no less superficial because it is 'awake', and a deep and fundamental layer where we perceive the Good.

Beauty is only casual; "anyone that takes this kind of thing for the Good goes empty, carrying away nothing but an emotion which the Good might have produced ... The Good, worthy of the name, can be no such tasting of the casual". This opposition, such as it described here in Plotinian terms, smacks of dualism, but it is not absolute. For would we strive for what is worthless and painful, if it did not suggest to us the Good, however wrongly? "All the striving, all the pain show that to everyone something is a good" [286].

h. What the soul should really desire

It is perfectly true that the soul, in loving the Good, discovers itself, but this does not mean that it is self-seeking. It is not able even to begin the upward surge without a prompting from above. Before this impulse comes to it, it "lies supine, cold to all". Nothing stirs it. All "beauty is dead until it takes the light of the Good ... But when there enters into her a glow from the divine, she gathers strength, awakens, spreads her wings, and however urged by her nearer environing, speeds her buoyant way elsewhere, to something greater than her memory ..., taking that outflow from the divine; with a Bacchic passion, goaded by these goads, she becomes love" [287].

What then is it that the soul desires so much, whether or not it is aware of it? Plotinus uses lofty expressions to answer this question : 'the wellspring of life, wellspring also of the intellect, the beginning of Being, fount of the Good, root of the soul'. "Of all these the soul is pregnant when she has been filled with God ... The soul in her nature loves God and longs to be at one with him in the noble love of a daughter for a father." But just as a daughter may leave her father for another love, the natural love can go astray. Some day, however, it will realize that "our love here is perishable, hurtful, that our loving is of mimicries and turns awry, because all was a mistake. Our good was not here; this is not what we sought". Something different from natural life is necessary. "The soul takes another life as she draws nearer and nearer to God and gains participation in him ... We must put aside all else and rest in this alone ..., with all the earthly environment done away, in haste to be free, impatient of any bond holding us to the baser, so that with all our being we may cling to this" [288]. It remains to be seen yet whether this union with God implies a dualistic separation from all else. What will occupy us for the moment is the nature of Plotinus' God.

j. The nature of Plotinus' God

First of all, it is important to know that to Plotinus God is the One, the principle that is absolutely simple and unique. He is alone because logically there cannot be two Ones. "Untouched by multiplicity, the One will be wholly self-sufficient, an absolute First. It is above all reasoning and knowledge; nothing can be predicated of it, except that it transcends Being [289]. Even "if we define it as the Good and the wholly simplex, we will, no doubt, be telling the truth, but we will not give any certain and lucid account of it ... This Entity transcends all of the intellectual nature". It is that which is 'above everything' [290].

The One is not something that exists; it is prior to all existents [291]. It is limitless [292]. He is not a 'chance product' but 'the principle of all' [293], and therefore it is "of a higher quality than anything that follows it". He is utterly ineffable, for we cannot, we may not predicate anything of him [294]. We must not say, he is 'thus', but also not, he is 'not-thus'. Every predication would limit it; it has no defined form. "The One, therefore, is beyond all things that are 'thus' [295]. Plotinus makes his One so absolutely undetermined and devoid of quality that he (or it) does not even know itself. He is "before all understanding and before all movement. For what would he understand? Himself? But this would imply a previous ignorance" [296]. And proceeding from ignorance to self-awareness would mean (intellectual) movement which is impossible, because the One is motionless [297]. Standing before the indefinable, you may name any of these sequents but you must say 'this is none of them'. At most he is to be conceived of as the total power towards things, supremely self-concentred [298]. Once again the question arises : does this supreme godhead, indefinable, ineffable, not find himself at an immense, unbridgeable distance from the cosmos and mankind?

The divine, says Plotinus, is 'pure' [299]. Since God is identical to the intelligible. He has no contact with the sensible, that is, with matter [300]. In his writings we do not find the bawdy stories the Greeks told about the love-life of their gods and goddesses nor the sexual imagery that is so characteristic of Gnostic mythology. The philosopher acknowledges a twofold Aphrodite. "There is the heavenly Aphrodite, daughter of Ouranos or Heaven; and there is the other, daughter of Zeus and Dione. This is the Aphrodite who presides over earthly unions; the higher was not born of a mother and has no part in marriages, for in Heaven there is no marrying" [301]. And he goes on to say that this heavenly Aphrodite "is no other than the Intellectual Principle" and "must be the soul at its divinest : unmingled as the immediate emanation of the unmingled (i.e. with matter) ..., so unreservedly an authentic being as to have no part with matter" [302]. We have a clear distinction here of Above and Below, of the Pure and the not-so-Pure, of a higher and a lower kind of Love, of the mixed and the unmixed, of Soul (at its divinest) and Matter.

k. The three principles : on the road to the cosmos

Plotinus' God, in his utter aloofness, in his complete ineffability, does not resemble the Jewish-Christian God. In yet another respect he is different from him : he is no Creator. Since the God of Judaism and Christianity created the multiple world directly, and since Plotinus did not deny the reality of this world (as Parmenides did), the question is how, in his vision, the many-splendoured cosmos arose. The idea that the Plotinian God would create is almost a blasphemy, for every creational act would mean a diminishing of God. His being active would mean that he is both changing and absolutely unchangeable [303].

It is tempting to use the term 'emanation' here. Philip Merlan describes 'emanationism' by saying that it "explains the origin and structure of reality by postulating a perfect and transcendent principle from which everything is derived by a process called emanation ... which is comparable to an efflux or radiation. Emanation is timeless and thus can be called a process only figuratively. It leaves its source undiminished, so that the source remains transcendent; but as the process continues, each of its products is less perfect." This description seems to fit Plotinus' concept like a glove, and indeed, this same scholar states that "the philosophy (of emanation) first appears in full clarity in the system of Plotinus" [304].

But one should err with caution! Not everyone agrees with this. Zeller, for one, argues that, in the strictest sense, there can be no emanation in Plotinus' system since absolutely nothing can go forth from the supreme godhead; he cannot communicate his being but he can communicate his power. For this reason Zeller would prefer to speak of 'dynamic pantheism' [305]. To some commentators Plotinus' philosophy is emanationist, to others it is not. Arnou thinks it is not emanationist but neither is it pantheistic; he prefers to call it 'Plotinism' [306] which is tantamount to saying that it is sui generis. One thing is certain in the diversity of opinions : Plotinus is not a creationist and is worlds apart from the biblical story in Genesis 1.

The philosopher speaks metaphorically of the way multiple things proceed from the One. He speaks of a first principle, itself "unmoved, while all circles around it, as a circumference round a centre from which all the radii proceed" [307]. The image of the rays returns elsewhere when souls are described as rays; "the source (the One) remains self-locked and these (the rays) are flung forth to impinge upon particular living things" [308]. A favourite image of his is "the sun, central to the light which streams from it, and yet is not linked to it, or at least is always about it, irremovably; try all you will to separate the light from the sun, or the sun from its light, for ever the light is in the sun" [309].

As Dodds expressed it, "all the forms and phases of Existence flow from the Divinity" - by a process which may be called Emanation, Procession, or Irradiation - "and all strive to return thither and remain there. This Divinity is a graded Triad" [310]. This divine Triad consists of three principles [311] with the first of which we are already sufficiently acquainted. It is the One, the Good, that is absolutely transcendent, infinite, and unconditioned. Dodds calls it 'the ineffable Supra-Existence' [312].

The second of the 'archai' that make up the Divine Triad is Nous. This is 'mind, divine thought, divine intelligence, intellection'; Mackenna translates it inelegantly with 'the intellectual-principle'. Dodds suggested that it should be translated sometimes with 'spirit' or 'supreme soul' [313]. Does Nous have its origin in the One? Not in the ordinary sense, since every bringing forth would imply movement in the One which would be inconceivable. "What happened, then?", is Plotinus' question. "It must be a circumradiation, produced from the Supreme but from the Supreme unaltering, and may be compared to the brilliant light encircling the sun and ceaselessly generated from that unchanging substance" [314]. But is this a satisfying answer?

The philosopher employs a very curious term when he speaks of the way Nous proceeds from the One. "It is a principle that in some measure has <u>dared</u> (tolmêsas) secession" [315]. The Moroccan scholar Naguib Baladi remarks that this term - daring, audacity - seems to refer 'from the very origin (of all that is - F.) to a separation, a distancing, a being something else and a difference that are irreducible, a primary breach'. If this is correct, are we then not speaking of dualism? Baladi adds that this creates a problem since it jeopardizes Plotinus' fundamental idea of a regular outflowing from the One, of automatic emanation. How, he asks, can the presence of the One, his immanence, in all that is, be reconciled with the otherness, the refractoriness of the emanations [316]? There is no answer to this question, I fear. It is a quandary that Plotinus himself creates. More than once I have argued in this series that monism and dualism come from the same stock. The philosopher who attempts to bring everything into a monistic system is asking for dualism. Unable as he is to cope with otherness and difference, he remains saddled with loose ends.

Another problem is that Nous is an offspring of the One, a 'genomenon', something that has been generated, "because there is a certain necessity that the First should have its offspring" [317]. But an offspring "is always minor"; Nous "must be the second of all existences, for it is that which sees the One on which alone it leans, while the First has no need whatsoever of it" [318]. Whereas the One has no need of Nous, Nous needs the One. This suggests that there is a difference in quality between the first and the second principles

[319]. On the other hand, Plotinus describes the Nous as 'the image of the One'. The One "in its self-quest has vision : this very seeing is the Nous". Here the philosopher seems to deny that there is some degree of difference; there is no 'divisibility' in the ordinary sense of the word [320].

There is, however, a very sound reason why Plotinus is not really interested in the fact that he is creating very complex problems. The reason for this is that his subjective urge, his 'desire', is directed towards God whom he, as an objective thinker, has declared to be unknowable, indefinable, ineffable. How, then, to approach him? It is for this approach that he so desperately needs a second principle; with the first alone he would be nowhere. In the Nous we have at least an image of God, just "as the sun's rays tell us of the sun" [321]. We are not able to look straight into the sun, but we can see and admire its light [322].

There is a second good reason why there is a Nous. The One is so absolutely one that it cannot contain the multiple world, not even the manifold intelligibles. This last category is contained in the Nous. This is possible because the second archê, as an offspring, cannot be wholly perfect and, in consequence, also not wholly one. This opens the possibility that there is multiplicity in it. And indeed, "the Nous is all Being (= all that exists) in one total ... The Nous holds many branches and items of knowledge simultaneously" [323]. Speaking from a Platonic perspective, we can say that the Nous is the treasure-house of the Ideas. And the Ideas are legio. Thus, together with the Nous, Plotinus introduces the concept of multiplicity and with this a bridge to the reality of the cosmos.

He saves the connection of the Nous, which is a 'not-one', with the One by stating that it is, indeed, a multiplicity, "but a multiplicity that is striving towards unity, that is to a one-that-is-many. All that is not-one is conserved by virtue of the One, and from this derives its characteristic nature ... Multiplicity is at the same time an all-embracing unity" [324]. In this way Plotinus denies that the distinction of the One and the Many would be of a dualistic nature.

Since the Nous, as not being perfect, admits movement, it can be productive; it may bring forth. What it engenders is the third principle. This is the Soul, with a capital, the 'All-Soul', the 'Soul of the All' [325]. It cannot be denied that we have now come one step nearer to the cosmos. A first step has already been taken when Plotinus introduces the concept of the 'kosmos noêtos', the 'intelligible universe' [326]. A further step is taken when the cosmos is described as 'a living thing, capable of including every form of life', but its "source is traced back to the Nous; it follows that the all-embracing archetype (of all existents) is in the Nous" [327]. However, where in the Nous unity is greater than multiplicity, in the Soul we see the reverse. Since as the third principle it is still less perfect, here multiplicity takes pride of place.

As yet we have not met any overt dualism, and certainly not one of a radical sort, that of two utterly opposed first principles, two inimical 'archai'. But it must make us think that Plotinus interposes so many intermediate stages between the One and the cosmos, between the godhead and the physical world, between divinity and physicality, between the infinite and indetermined and the finite and definite. It is as though he wants to avoid all direct contact between his God and matter; the One is not allowed to perform creational acts. He does not mean that the One and the world have to remain absolutely separate, but all the same the connecting cord is stretched to its breaking point.

1. Is the soul the source of generation?

"The Nous is forever repugnant to distinction and to partition. (But) the Soul ... has a nature lending itself to divisional existence." Do we here find the source of generation, of movement and change? Plotinus is not wholly comfortable with this development. Division and secession are not properties of the whole soul. It has "phases above and below, (one) that is attached to the supreme and (one that) reaches down to this sphere (the cosmos), like a radius from a centre". There is, so to speak, a contemplative part in the soul, looking upwards, and a generating part, looking downwards [328]. Are there, then, in fact two souls? No, there is only one. "Entering this realm (the cosmos), it possesses still the vision inherent to that superior phase in virtue of which it unchangingly maintains its integral nature. Even here (i.e. when entering the cosmos) it is not exclusively the partible soul; it is still the impartible as well."

Plotinus stretches his logical capacities and our power of understanding to the limit by attempting to explain that the soul is whole and split at the same time. "Undivided as giving itself to the entire body, a whole to a whole, it is divided as being effective in every part" [329]. Somewhat further on, he openly admits that there is no solution to this problem. "If the soul is a perfect unity ..., if it continually eludes all touch of multiplicity and divisibility, then ... it will stand as a circle-centre to every object, remote on the circumference, so that nothing at all can be ensouled". There is, therefore, no escape : "soul is, in the degree indicated, one and many, parted and impartible."

In a desperate attempt to save his system Plotinus brushes aside one of the main tenets of plain logics : that A is not B. Here A indeed = B. "We cannot question the possibility of a thing being at once a unity and multi-present since to deny this would be to abolish the principle which sustains and administers the universe : there must be a kind (= the World-Soul) which encircles and supports all with wisdom, a principle which is multiple since existence is multiple, and yet is one soul always since a container must be a unity", in short, a 'multiple unity' [330].

To Plotinus this means that all individual humans souls form part of the All-Soul; because they have a single common origin, they can communicate with another. They "are held together at the source ... (and) issue from the unity while still constituting, within certain limits, an association". But this throws up a new problem. Do individual souls belong to the All-Soul rather than to the bodies they inhabit? Once again, a split becomes visible. The individual souls "do not belong unreservedly to any particular being". There is no organic unity between soul and body : "they meet, so to speak, fringe to fringe" [331].

What is behind Plotinus' sometimes opaque way of arguing is that he is resolutely rejecting the Gnostic position that there would exist a principle of Evil that generated the cosmos; he even devoted one of his treatises to the refutation of this opinion [332]. On the other hand, as I said, he does not want to bring his supreme One into contact with matter. There is, therefore, no creation. Even his second principle, the Nous, is too sublime for this. And the third, the All-Soul, has to be one and multiple at the same time in order to form the link with the human souls. "The Supreme is exclusively one; bodies are exclusively many; the soul is ... one and many" [333].

m. Separation in the soul

We know that in orthodox Platonism the soul consists of three parts, and in Middle Platonism of two parts, one higher, one lower, one superior, one inferior, one rational, one irrational and passionate. In Plotinus' Neoplatonism neither tripartition nor bipartition are strongly stressed, although terms referring to either of them are not entirely absent [334]. There is, however, in his doctrine also a separation in the soul of what is spiritual and what is irrational. The division in the All-Soul into what is looking upwards and what is looking downwards is repeated in the individual soul. The superior part of the soul does even more than looking upward, for it remains in the higher sphere of the Nous which means that it is not entirely at home in the body.

"The soul has not sunk entire; something of it is continually in the Nous." It is quite possible that a person is not at all aware of this lofty part of his being; one may be "blind to what the upper part of the soul holds in contemplation ... Every soul has something of the lower on the body side and something of the higher on the part of the Nous" [335]. And because of this 'higher side' "each of us is an intellectual (noêtos) cosmos" [336]. Once again to the long chain connecting the One with the body and matter a link has been added.

By inserting so many intermediate phases the philosopher tries to avoid giving the impression that he would be a (Gnostic) dualist. All the same the bipartition in the soul is so marked that there seem to be two souls, each with a different origin. He says repeatedly that we are 'ditton' = double, twofold [337].

n. Dualistic elements in the human person

Dualism begins to rear its head when we hear that man consists of a brute part, the beast in us, and a part that transcends it. "The beast is the body which has been given life ... The true man is the other, going pure of the body" [338]. The body tries to drag down the inferior part of the soul. There is a celestial order which is from God; both the All-Soul and (the higher part of) our human souls belong to this order. And there is a terrestrial order, that of physicality, not created directly by the Supreme one but by 'divine beings in the heavens'. Here lies the origin of the inferior soul that associates itself with the body [339].

Even man as such, according to his mode of existence, consists in fact, when we stop speaking of the soul and its parts, of two beings. Consider the following curious passage. "Before we had our becoming here (i.e. in the terrestrial order), we existed there (i.e. in the celestial order), being other than now, some of us being gods; we were pure souls ..., members of the Nous, not fenced off, not cut away, integral to that All. Even now, it is true, we are not put apart (i.e. from the Nous, because the higher part of our souls links us to it). But upon that (blissful situation) primal man has intruded, a man seeking to come into being and finding us there ... This other has wound itself about us, foisting himself upon that man which each of us was at first ... Now we have lost that first simplicity. We are become the dual thing, sometimes no more than that later foisting (i.e. no better than that lower creature that crept upon us), with the primal (superior) nature dormant and in a sense no longer present" [340]. Man is likened here to a tree overgrown with lianas and almost strangled by them.

Karin Alt concludes that Plotinus does not differ greatly from other Platonists in that he posits two essentially distinct realms of the soul that oppress each other. The spiritual part has the primacy; it runs the risk of 'sinking down' into the lower realm of the soul; it has, therefore, the task of mastering the inferior forces. The two realms of the soul have different origins. "The existence of the incarnated soul is full of risks; it is a temptation and a challenge for it, a problem that has always again to be mastered" [341].

The dualism that is inherent to the human soul is brought out very clearly by Plotinus in the following terms. "This is the evil of man. Man includes an inner rabble - pleasure, desires, fears - , and these become masters when man, the manifold, gives them play. But one who has reduced this rabble and gone back to the Man he was (= 'the true man'), lives up to that and is that man again, so that what he allows the body is allowed as to something separate" [342]. The soul-body antagonism was certainly no abstract problem for Plotinus [343]. The very first thing Porphyry has to say of his master was that he "seemed ashamed of being in the body" [344]; he ate very little food and restricted his periods of sleep to the utmost [345].

o. Matter

Speaking of the body, we will also have to mention Matter. Plotinus devotes one of his essays to it [346]. Although he accepts its reality somewhat reluctantly, he does not deny that Matter exists. But it is something 'indetermined and void of shape' so that it cannot be found in the sphere of the Supreme where "there can be nothing that lacks determination". The question is, therefore : where does it come from [347]? In the last resort it is an emanation of the One, but the lowest one. "It forms the lowest stage of the universe and is the antithesis of the One" [348]. So, although Plotinus does not admit to a Gnostic separation of the cosmos into two opposed halves, there is in his doctrine a constant deterioration of the quality of the emanations. There is discussion among the scholars of whether there is general emanation in the Enneads, which would include Matter, or that Matter is ungenerated [349]. For our viewpoint it does not really make a difference.

The change from the One to the last emanation could not be more radical. Matter, as being in the Nadir, has no identity; "it is all things in turn, a new entity in each separate case, so that nothing is permanent and one thing ceaselesly pushes another out of being" [350]. We are worlds apart from the permanence and the absolute identity of the One [351]. Plotinus is forced to accept the existence of Matter by the observable fact that, while bodies pass away, new bodies are engendered all the time; so there must be some substratum from which they are formed, a substratum that is different from themselves [352]. This substratum is Matter.

We should not, however, think of Matter as something physical. "Since it is without quality, it is incorporeal; bodiliness would be a quality". To make clear what he means Plotinus uses a comparison. "Clay ... is matter to the potter, but is not Matter pure and simple. Nothing of this sort (i.e. specific kinds of matter) are our object; we are seeking the stuff which underlies all alike. We must therefore refuse it all that we find in things of sense (i.e. in material objects) ... It cannot be a compound, it must be a simplex, one distinct thing in its nature; only so can it be void of all quality" [353]. There seems to be a curious similarity between the One and Matter, although they could not be further apart on the continuum. Both are simplex and qualityless; nothing can be predicated of either of them. It is as though Plotinus, though he nowhere says so, posits Matter as a counter-god.

I said that Plotinian Matter comes very close to non-being. Plotinus' Matter is non-being, indeed. "Matter has no reality and is not capable of being affected ... (It) is not Soul; it is not Intellect; it is not Life; it is no Ideal-Principle, no Reason-Principle; it is no limit or bound, for it is mere indetermination; it is not a power ... It lives on the farther side of all these categories and so has no title to the name of Being. It will be more plausibly called a non-being, ... a veritable Non-Being" [354].

The philosopher uses very harsh words for Matter, as if he fiercely hates it. "Its very utterance is a lie. It pretends to be great and it is little, to be more and it is less; and the existence with it masks itself is no existence, but a passing trick making trickery of all that seems to be present in it, phantasms within a phantasm. It is like a mirror showing things as in itself while they are really elsewhere, filled in appearance but in reality empty, containing nothing, pretending everything" [355]. But is it possible to philosophize about a 'non-existent', a 'negation', a 'privation' ('sterêsis') [356]? Plotinus does not deny that this constitutes a problem.

"How do you form the concept of any absence of quality?" Since the mind is conscious of objects that possess shape and size and colour and other qualities, it may also have an awareness of that which is its (i.e. the mind's) counterpart, Matter. The mind knows "a whole which includes two components : it has a clear knowledge of the overlie (the Ideas) but only a dim awareness of the shapeless which is not an Ideal-Principle ... What is left from the process of abstraction (is) this, the dim; it (the mind) knows dimly, it knows darkly; this it knows in a sort of non-knowing" [357]. This seems like a clumsy attempt to avoid a radical dualism within Plotinian ontology so that there will not be, as I said before, two independent principles; he keeps Matter in his system by the narrowest of margins.

It is true, for "Plotinus the Matter of this lower world derives from the higher principles, and so, ultimately, from the Good" [358]. All the same, there is a sharp separation of the Good and Matter, so that a 'hylic' (= material) element is introduced into the realm of the Intelligible, albeit intellectually discernible however so vaguely. This makes Armstrong speak of 'dyadic' [359]. This 'dyadic' character of Plotinian ontology is clearly obvious when the philosopher speaks of the origin of Evil to which he devotes one of his treatises [360]. He distances himself from Iranian dualism by categorically stating that no separate Principle of Evil exists that would be anterior to Matter [361].

Equally, we should not think of all that is wrong as a manifestation of the radically evil. "What falls short of the Good is not Evil"; when there are moral shortcomings, we must only speak of 'non-Goodness'. The source of Evil is also not we ourselves; "we are not evil in ourselves; Evil was before we came to be". With this statement Plotinus rejects the explanation given in Genesis 3 (if he knew t) that man himself is the cause of Evil [362].

Plotinus postulates that the existence of the Good requires the existence of Evil. "As there is Good, the Absolute, ..., so there must be Absolute Evil." As the true dualist he is, Plotinus cannot manage without stark oppositions. Evil is not an essence, "cannot have a place among Beings or in the Beyond-Being (= God); (it is) situate(d) in the realm of Non-Being". It is 'Undermination-Absolute, some Absolute Formlessness' [363]. It is an 'absolute lack' [364].

The direction in which we are heading should be obvious : the real source of Evil is Matter which is Non-Being itself and "has no trace of good by any title of its own but ... takes order and grace from some principle outside itself, ... the authentic essence of Evil - in so far as Evil can have an authentic Being", thus Plotinus hastens to correct himself. In Matter "Reason recognizes the Primal Evil, Evil Absolute" [365]. "There is no escape : the cause of Evil is Matter" [366]; Matter is 'to prooton kakon', the Primal Evil [367]. Just as the Good is working downwards, Evil extends its influence upwards. "Evil can enter into other things" [368]. Insofar as the human body partakes of Matter, it is 'an evil thing' [369]; we should, however, not necessarily think that bodies are evil in themselves.

p. The place and the function of the soul

And what about the soul? The soul is the lowest emanation of the supernatural principle; it is the element which descends into the sensible world; it stands, as it were, on the frontier between two worlds. "As a whole it is partly in a body and partly above; it has plunged from among the primals and entered this sphere of tertiaries." The function of the soul is to bring order to the cosmos. "The Nous ... operates throughout the Soul to flood the universe with beauty and penetrant order" [370]. But because the soul belongs with one part to the higher world and with another to the lower, it is perfectly possible - and this happens indeed -, that the forces of the lower world, even Evil, find their way, via the body, to the inferior regions of the soul. "This is the fall of the soul, this entry into Matter : thence its weakness. Not all the faculties of its being retain free way, for Matter hinders their manifestation; it encroaches upon the soul's territory, and thus, as it were, crushes the soul back ... Thus the cause, at once, of the weakness of Soul and of all its evil is Matter" [371].

q. Kosmos and kosmoi

One would expect that to Plotinus the cosmos would be utterly bad, just as it is in the view of the Gnostics. But this is not the case. "There is no Platonist", writes Armstrong, "who more passionately insists on and defends the divine goodness and holiness of the material cosmos" [372]. "This universe exists by him" - by the supreme God, that is - "and looks to him ... and tells of him to men, all alike revealing the plan of will of the Supreme". People who refuse to accept this are called 'imbecils' by Plotinus [373]. He even speaks of the earth as having a vegetal soul, since it brings forth vegetals. And it must also be animated since it produces animals. And because it is animated, it is a part of the living All so that, in consequence, it must have a nous "by which it holds rank as a god" [374], albeit a lesser god than the Supreme one. The conclusion is that "the All must, in every detail and experience, be an expression of the Supreme" [375].

Must we now jump at the conclusion that Plotinus is no dualist after all? That would be somewhat rash. The Supreme one is not immanent in the cosmos. "All that is Nous will rest eternally above, and could never fall from its sphere"; it is "poised entire into its own high place". As we saw, the Divine Intellect can only communicate itself to our sphere 'through the channel of the soul'. But what we also saw is that the soul is twofold; there is "one phase, the World Soul, maintaining the unvarying march (of the cosmic circuit), the other (the soul of the invididual) adapting itself to times and seasons" [376], the one invariable, the other constantly changing.

Bipartitions occur everywhere throughout the Enneads. There are, for instance, two 'kosmoi'. There is an ideal cosmos of which the Nous is the archetype and model, so that it is 'authentic and primal'; it has 'no spatial distinction and none of the feebleness of division' and is, therefore, 'one and complete' [377]. Another, lower cosmos is derived from it which is 'no longer a true unity'. "It is multiple, divided into various elements ... No longer is the concord unbroken; hostility has entered as the result of difference and distance; imperfection has inevitably introduced discord ... (It) has not come into being as the result of a judgment (i.e. by the divine Nous - F.) establishing its desirability, but by the sheer necessity of a secondary kind." As a consequence the cosmos is a mixture - of harmonious and disharmonious elements : "inevitably there are formed groups concordant and helpful in contrast with groups discordant and combative; sometimes of choice and sometimes incidentally, the parts maltreat each other; engendering proceeds by destruction" [378]. It is as though Plotinus is explaining the origin of dualism in his own way.

Yet another Plotinian opinion must be taken into consideration. In his system there exists a gliding scale, starting with 'the Good', which is 'good unmixed'; next comes the mingling of Good and Bad (in the human person, for instance), then the 'rather Bad than Good', and finally 'the utterly Bad' [379]. In view of all this, we may well ask whether Plotinus really believes his cosmos to be as beautiful as he thinks it is. He admits that there are 'two extremes' in it, namely 'Matter and the Divine Reason', and we know that these are radical opposites. The philosopher attempts to save the wholeness of his construction, that is, to safeguard it from being considered dualistic, by positing the soul as 'its governing principle ... presiding over the conjunction of the two (Matter and Reason)' [380]. And indeed, where there is an intermediary link there is no dualism. But Plotinus seems to forget that the soul also is twofold and consists of higher and lower parts that do not fit together harmoniously.

r. The ultimate fate of man

What will be the ultimate fate of man? As a true esoteric philosopher of the line of Pythagoras and Plato, Plotinus divides the human race into three groups of unequal size. The greatest group is that of the 'mere populace'; he uses the denigrating Greek word 'ochlos' here. These people are only fit 'to provide necessities for the better sort'; this is an echo of the ancient master-slave mentality. Then there are those "who are reminiscent of virtue and therefore not without touch with (the) good"; one might call them the candidates for whom there is still hope. Finally, there is a, in all probability, small group of 'spoudaioi', which means the active, the zealous. 'Spoudaioi' are earnest and devoted people, sages who are intent on the highest good; they are not greatly interested in worldly things [381].

The outlook for those of the 'mere populace' is bleak. Being uninterested in the life of the spirit, they are constantly weighed down by the burden they carry, unable to lift themselves up because of their heaviness and forgetfulness. They cannot acquire eternal bliss but will pass on from body to body, bodies that are 'progressively more earthly' [382]. It is, however, possible that in the long run a human soul is purified and then travels upwards to the higher spheres [383].

One need not ask in which group Plotinus himself belongs. He tells us that he often had mystical experiences. "Many times it has happened : lifted out of the body into myself; become external to all other things and self-centered; beholding a marvellous beauty; then, more than ever, assured of community with the loftiest order; enacting the noblest life, acquiring identity with the divine" [384]. It is important to note that the philosopher had no need of the body in this experience; leaving the body means 'going into oneself'. The body is seen as different from and alien to the true self. This is a telling difference to the mystical experience that the apostle Paul had; he says that he did not know whether it happened 'in the body' or 'outside the body' [385].

We should, however, not think of the ascent into higher spheres as something that comes about as the result of a sudden impulse or an inner illumination. The condition is that one must live a virtuous life, assiduously practising the four Greek cardinal virtues, Prudence, Fortitude, Wisdom, and Rectitude, the civic virtues [386]. It is highly important for an aspirant to higher things that he or she is lord and master over the impulses of the body; only so one can lead a purified life. Secondly, it is imperious to become indifferent to all other things. "We must withdraw from all what is extern, pointed wholly inwards; not leaning to the outer; all things ignored, first in their relation to us and later in the very idea." Turning inwards does not mean being preoccupied with oneself. Quite the contrary! "The self should be put out of the mind in the contemplation of the Supreme" [387]. The means for achieving this is 'method and discipline' with which is meant philosophy and science. By assiduously practising dialectics one can "give up one's touring of the realm of sense and settle down in the intellectual cosmos (kosmos noêtos) ..., abandoning all the realm of deceit and falsity" [388]. One who practises the civic virtues leads the human life of a good man, but who applies oneself wholeheartedly to the study of philosophy leaves this beneath him and "will take up instead another life, that of the gods" [389].

But the study of philosophy is not the final aim. It brings the soul to unity with the Nous. This, however, is not yet the highest since the Nous itself is an emanation from the godhead, the Supreme One. The ultimate stage of the ascent is the mystical union with the highest God. "The man is changed, no longer himself nor self-belonging; he is merged with the Supreme, sunken into it, one with it [390] ... Here is living, the true; that of today, all living apart from him, is but a shadow, a mimicrry. Life in the Supreme is the native activity of the intellect ... This state is its first and final, because from God it comes; its good lies there, and once turned to God again, it is what it was. Life here, with the things of earth, is a sinking, a defect, a failing of the wing" [391]. The person who may experience this transport is wholly transfigured, for he has become God himself without mingling with anything else; "no movement now, no passion, no outlooking desire, nothing within him or without inducing any diversity ... Caught away, filled with God, he has in perfect stillness acquired isolation; all the being calmed, he turns neither to this side or to that, not even inwards to himself" [392].

It is true that, while we are still in the body, this state of ecstatic rapture will remain something momentary. We will fall back again. But it is always possible to make the journey anew : through the virtues and through the study of philosophy to the Nous, and through its wisdom to the Supreme. And after death it will be definite for those, the happy few, who are ready to go this road, the way that leads to 'the term of all journeying' [393].

s. Conclusion

We have now followed Plotinus on his long journey, starting with the subjective impulse of his desire for God, and after having reached the Supreme, returning with him through the Emanations, Nous and Soul, to the lowest level, that of Matter, here detecting at last the origin of Evil. We then followed Evil upon its upward course, penetrating as it does into Matter and into the physical order and establishing itself in the lower parts of the soul. The climactic question, dominating the whole thought of Plotinus, was how a human person can free him- or herself from Evil, from matter, from the bonds of the body, and surge upwards until the soul becomes utterly one with the supreme godhead. It is true what Copleston says that "in Plotinian Neo-Platonism philosophy tends to pass into religion - at least, it points beyond itself : speculation does not set up itself as the ultimate goal to be achieved" [394].

Insofar as it is a religion, Plotinian Neoplatonism is a religion of redemption. As such it offers a third way, after the Gnosis and Christianity, both them also religions of redemption. In the last centuries of Antiquity Neoplatonism exercized a powerful appeal on many intellectuals who were looking for a satisfying form of personal spirituality and above all for salvation, people to whom the Gnosis was too fantastic and Christianity too absurd. But this appeal remained restricted, because Plotinian philosophy is rather abstract and difficult to understand.

We have already seen that Plotinus was an opponent of the Gnosis. His main difference to it is that, whereas the Gnostic requires a special kind of Knowledge to be saved, there is nothing of this in Plotinus. Another difference is that Plotinus does not share the utter contempt of the Gnosis for the cosmos. But it is a curious anomaly in his work, namely that, whereas in his view the cosmos is beautiful, he despises Matter and sees it as the origin of Evil. There is, indeed, in Plotinus no evil-intentioned Demiurge who would be responsible for the creation of a bad world. But Evil is obviously a principle in his own right, meeting the Good half-way in the human person. This opposition of Good and Evil is without any doubt of a dualistic nature.

Another point of contact with the Gnosis is Plotinus' subdivision of humanity into two groups, the smaller one of those striving upward and the much larger one of the massa damnata. Just as the Gnosis does not tell us why some chosen people receive that specific Knowledge and the great majority not, so Plotinus does not explain why a few of us may see the light, while most others must dwell in darkness.

Perhaps Plotinus' moving description of the flight of the soul towards the highest bliss will strike some readers as something very much akin to Christian ideas of redemption and eternal happiness. But this would be a superficial and deceptive impression. For if redemption and salvation exist in Plotinian thought, there is no Redeemer, no Saviour. Whereas Christians are redeemed by the merits won by Jesus Christ through his death on the cross, according to Plotinus salvation is the effect of one's personal efforts in the moral sphere. Christian salvation means breaking the bonds of sin, of original sin and of personal sinfulness. Plotinian salvation means being freed from the things of this earth, from the senses, from the passions, and above all from the body. For the body will not accompany one on the flight upwards. There is such a distinction between the higher and the lower worlds that we must necessarily call it dualistic.

What is surely not Christian is that body and soul do not form an organic unity. The superior part is the soul that dwells uncomfortably in the body, the inferior part. The soul-body dualism that is so characteristic of Platonism in all its stages is found also in Plotinus. There is even a dualistic division within the human soul, for part of it seems to exist outside the body or independently of it, in order to remain pure and not contaminated by Matter, while, in the body, another part comes into contact with Matter and in consequence with Evil and is defiled by it, creating the necessity of purification [395].

The dualistic nature of Plotinus' thinking [396] about the essence and destiny of man is most clearly expressed at the end of the Enneads where he speaks of the 'essential man'. This 'essential man' is obviously someone very different from the ordinary human person, someone we are not but should become. As the result of a converse, a transition, "the essential man outgrows being (existence) and becomes identical with the Transcendent of Being (= the highest godhead) ... When the soul begins to mount, it comes not to something alien but to its very self; then detached (namely from the earth, from the body), it is nothing but itself; self-gathered, it is not in the order of being; it is in the Supreme" [397].

2. Porphyry

a. The man and his work

Porphyry is the best-known disciple of Plotinus, although he does not enjoy the reputation of being an original and independent thinker. His fame is rather that of being a polymath and a transmitter of Neoplatonist thought [398]. He was born in 234 in Tyre or perhaps somewhere in Palestine; his birth-name was Malchus which he changed for the more Greek-sounding one of 'Porphyrios'. He studied philosophy at Athens with Longinus and later he proceeded to Rome where he met Plotinus whose disciple, editor, and biographer he became. His stay in Rome lasted from 263 to 268. When he was thirty-four years old, he began to suffer from a psychic depression; on Plotinus' advice he departed for Lilybaeum in Sicily. Later in his life he returned to Rome where he became the principal of a philosophical school. He was already an old man when he married a widow called Marcella, a mother of seven children; he had no children of his own with her. He died, about seventy years of age, in the period 301-305.

Porphyry was a prolific writer. Nine of his own works have been handed down to us in a complete form; among those are the Life of Plotinus, a biography of Pythagoras, a treatise on vegetarianism (of which he was an adherent), and some philosophical commentaries on Aristotle and Plotinus. Some other books are entirely lost and of still others only fragments remain. In all sixty-six titles are known.

One ancient author, Socrates, a Christian historian, wrote that Porphyry had once been a Christian, but that he had apostatized because he had been insulted or attacked by some Christians in Caesarea in Palestine [399]. He himself nowhere alludes to a Christian past. However this may be, he was an inveterate enemy of the Christian religion which he found stupid, illogical, and devoid of sense. He expounded this opinion at length in fifteen books against the Christians, written during his stay in Sicily. They were burnt by imperial decree in 448, but fragments of them are still extant.

b. The main aim of philosophy and how to attain it

As may be expected, Porphyry nowhere distances himself from his venerated master at whose feet he had sat for five years and with whom he remained in contact as long as Plotinus lived. For him also the main aim of philosophy is to enable the soul to ascend to God and to be thereby redeemed. But he had its own doctrine of virtue. There are four classes of them constituting the ladder along which the soul can climb on its way to God. The first class is that of the 'civic virtues', the 'arêtai politikai' : wisdom, courage (with which to combat the passions), prudence, and justice. These virtues are needed to keep the passions and the tendency to disorderliness under control.

With the 'political' virtues we still stay with our feet on the earth, or rather within the walls of the polis, for their aim is to ensure an exemplary intercourse with the co-citizens. But we are already preparing for an upward flight with the practice of the 'cathartic' virtues, the purifying ones. Their aim is to distance us from what is bodily and terrestrial; they lead to a state of 'apatheia' which literally means 'not suffering', but which, in this context, may be best rendered with 'being unaffected by' or 'indifferent to', namely the things of this world. The catharsis that is the result of practising these virtues finds its fulfilment in the 'resemblance with God' : man is already becoming less human and more divine.

Then comes the third stage, still higher, that of the theoretical virtues. Now the soul no longer turns away from but upwards to; it is now ready for 'theoria', for contemplation, the object of which is the Nous. The fruit of contemplation is that the soul can practise the 'paradigmatic' virtues, those of the fourth and highest category - virtues that are proper to the Nous and, therefore, lift one above oneself. We are now fully in the realm of the divine and have left the earth and what is bodily far behind us [400].

The way that is followed is that of a human person that is living 'outside himself' ('ektos anthroopos'). Do not, however, think that the acquisition of true happiness is the result of reasoning. "The quantity of the arguments does not lead to it." What is needed is "a second nature and a life that conforms to these (higher) realities ... We must change our actual life for another life" [401]. In doing this, "we resemble people who, whether voluntary or not, have emigrated to a nation of another race than theirs". There follows a phrase that reveals the dualistic disposition of Porphyry. "Such men have been excluded from the domain that is proper to them" [402]. The domain that was originally proper to them was that of the body.

c. The need of asceticism

In Porphyry it is not the body itself that is bad, but rather a tendency in the soul to stoop and acquiesce to inferior passions and desires [403]. In order to become purified it is absolutely necessay to lead an ascetic life. Porphyry composed a long treatise called 'On abstinence'. The first great element in Porphyrian asceticism is the practice of vegetarianism. "It is in the nature of man to eat meat, but against his nature to consume it raw" [404]. The philosopher distinguishes two categories of beings : the animals who devour their prey raw, and men who also eat animals but only after having cooked, roasted, or baked their meat. He mentions this as a fact but he does not like this fact. There is, however, a third category, namely of those who willingly abstain from meat, the gods, that is.

Consuming meat, not raw but prepared, was seen by the Greeks - as it was by the Jews - 'as a distinctive sign of human nature' [405]. The vegetarian, by eating meat, sets himself apart from all others who enjoy eating meat, especially at festive occasions; the vegetarian of Greek antiquity does so still more by refusing to take part in the public ritual where animals are sacrificed. Speaking of purity, Porphyry says that we do not honour the godhead by eating sacrificial meat [406]. This does not mean that the vegetarian should take the road to the desert, scorning all companionship. Quite the contrary! He wants commensality with the gods who do not need to eat human food, feeding themselves, as they do, on nectar and ambrosia. Of course, the vegetarian cannot imitate the gods since he has to eat. But he expresses his otherness by not eating the most common kind of human food [407]. Porphyry states that our bodies "carry with them the exhalations of the demons of matter [408] ... For this reason an intelligent and temperate man will take care not to partake of sacrifices which risk to him demons of this kind [409] ... In consequence, those who have real knowledge of the gods have every reason to practise abstinence." [410] Porphyry distinguishes here between two worlds, that of the poleis - if they will bring sacrifices, let them! - and that of people with a better understanding of theology.

d. Far from the maddening crowd

What the gods wish to see is a pure mind and an impassive soul [411]. Bad customs (i.e. in religious practice) are neither agreeable to the gods nor useful to humans; the philosopher should avoid them. "He must go following the straight road, without heeding the danger that comes from the crowd ... Well then, should we, from fear of what people will say or because of their unholy ideas, choose to transgress the law of nature and the divine precepts!" [412]. Once again that fundamentally dualistic idea so beloved among Greek thinkers can be detected here, namely that the true lover of wisdom is a being totally different from the common run. Porphyry expresses this graphically by stating that he has 'to die for the others' = to be as dead to them [413].

e. Body and soul

The practice of abstinence, living a sober life, and scorning the things of this world are the necessary conditions for acquiring a true understanding of higher things. Porphyry's metaphysical ideas are not different from those of his master : the gradual descent from the One to Matter, and the ascent of the soul to the One. But he has treated the relation of soul and body, of the spiritual and the corporeal, in his own way. We know that, to Porphyry, the aim of philosophy is to purify the human person so that he or she can begin the ascent to God. The body and what is bodily can form hindrances for this aspiration. Porphyry does not see Matter as an independent principle; it too is an emanation from the One. But in practice it is the opposite of the divine One. "The opposition of what is simple, eternal, and indestructible and of what is composed, transitory, and changing is accentuated by him as sharply as possible" [414]. He does so in many places in his 'Sententiae'.

Porphyry's crucial question is how, in the human person, the spiritual element, the soul, relates to the material element. In his psychology the soul is the intermediate element between God and the body. It may strive upwards and it may fall downwards. If it is looking upwards, it is strong; does it look downwards, it becomes feeble. If it occupies herself with the things outside her, it is treading somewhat out herself and comes into contact with what is not itself. Does it, however, concentrate upon itself, it is thoughtful and remains pure and wholly itself. Porphyry is speaking of the self-determination of the soul rather than of its parts.

In one important respect he entirely agrees with his master, namely, that there is no organic union between soul and body. Porphyry teaches us that the soul, more than it should do, may be interested in what is corporeal and physical. This does not imply that it associates itself with the body to the point that they become a unity. It always keeps itself somewhat apart. But it produces a force of an inferior nature and more material than it itself is, that flows into the body and becomes the link between this and the soul [415]. The presence of the soul in the body is, as Zeller, expressed it, 'dynamic and not substantial' [416]. The term used for this force that goes out from the soul is 'pneuma'. This pneuma is, so to speak, the vehicle that enables the soul to travel through the physical world and, in particular, to dwell in the body. When the human person dies, the soul no longer needs the pneuma and they part ways, leaving the body behind.

3. Iamblichus

a. The man and his work

Another pupil of Plotinus was Iamblichus, a Syrian who was born ca. 245 in the town of Chalcis (now Qinnesrin). After studying philosophy in the West, either in Rome or in Sicily, he returned to his native country where he founded a school of philosophy. He died, about eighty years old, around 325. As with so many other authors, much of his work has been lost or survives only partly in fragments. However, of a compendium of Pythagorean philosophy four volumes are still extant [417].

b. The ineffable

We saw that Plotinus interposed several stages (hypostases) between the One, which is the Good, and the nether world. I suggested that he did this to keep the One as apart as possible from that lower world, as though any contact with it would contaminate it (or him). Iamblichus was not content with this and made the distance even greater by postulating a principle superior to the One, the 'Ineffable' [418]. In this way he situated the Plotinian One one stage lower in the ontological order. This Super-One is the source of all that is.

Why was the One/the Good not sufficient for Iamblichus as the origin of all being? I feel that Wallis is correct when he supposes that, in Iamblichus' thought, "unity has meaning only in contrast to plurality and therefore belongs to the sphere of relative reality" [419]. In other words, the fact that the One is related to the Many, although in contrast, implies that it is contaminated to some degree. What Iamblichus needed was an absolute principle. Plotinus' first principle is preserved but is consigned to the second place. Not the Ineffable but the One/the Good becomes the productive principle [420].

c. The Intelligible

What is brought forth by the One is the 'Intelligible'. Although this Intelligible differs from the One, it nevertheless remains very close to it; it even has its home in it. Just like the One it is simple and eternal; we should not conceive of it as a (Platonic) Idea, not even as the Idea of all Ideas. It is not multiple nor is it composed of parts. It will come somewhat as a surprise after this statement that this non-composite Intelligible is nonetheless a Triad consisting of three elements, the Father, the Force, and the Nous. With the Father reality is meant, with the Force probably a productive power, and with the Nous activity [421]. It seems that each part of this Triad is in its turn composed of three elements, so that there were nine Triads in all, but the bad state in which the fragments of Iamblichus have come down to us prevents us from being more precise on this point [422]. Since nothing at all is known of these nine Triads, we are absolved from speaking about them, which is a blessing, for without this Iamblichus' system is already intricate enough.

d. Two spiritual worlds and the World Soul

The philosopher distinguishes two worlds. The Intelligible is the 'kosmos noêtos', the world of the intelligible; from this comes the 'kosmos noeros', the world of the intellectual beings (these beings are one shade more concrete or one shade less abstract than the intelligible). In the philosopher's terminology these beings are 'gods' or 'fathers'. The first of these is Nous which seems to belong both to the Intelligible and Intellectual worlds and is, for this reason, called 'an intermediary hypostasis' by Copleston [423]. The second is the divine vital force bringing forth all life, and the third the Demiurge, the creative power [424]. The difference between the Intelligible and the Intellectual is that the first is the world of the primal images, the second that of the Ideas themselves. Iamblichus distances himself from Plato for whom the Ideas themselves were primal and primary; in his strong tendency to posit ever more levels between the Ineffable and the actual world - almost an obsession -, he even creates a level above the Ideas.

Plotinus' World Soul did not satisfy Iamblichus. In his system there also is a world soul, the Superterrestrial Soul. From this soul two others are derived [425]. But whereas the Superterrestrial Soul is, as the word says, above the world, the two others are within it. The three souls hang together but are different. The problem is that there is a wide chasm between 'anoo' and 'katoo', between 'above' and 'below', and, in consequence, between the Superterrestrial and Terrestrial Souls. In order to realize the connection he needs yet another Nous, not the first absolute Nous, but a lower one that can intermediate between the upper and lower regions.

e. Terrestrial Souls

Iamblichus was indefatigable in creating ever newer diversions. Speaking of the Terrestrial Souls, we have to distinguish between the souls of gods, angels, demons, and heroes. Being fond of tripartitions, he has three classes of gods : twelve superior gods whose number reminds us of the twelve Olympians; according to his triadic system from these twelve divinities thirty-six other gods are derived, and from these thirty-six three hundred and sixty. Furthermore , there are 'rulers of the world', gods of nature, protective deities without number, altogether an immense and incredibly complicated system.

f. 'Funktionslust'

Having reached this point, the reader will probably feel his or her head reeling. It is not inconceivable that this was precisely Iamblichus' intention. What he was out to do was to make the gap between the Ineffable and the lower orders so unbridgeably, so dualistically wide that it would make one feel so dizzy that one would not dare to raise one's eyes towards the highest summit. The dualistic crunch is that this philosopher, unlike Plotinus, was not content with the One but superposed another entity, utterly incomprehensible and unapproachable. In view of the intricate system Iamblichus built, all those layers - I have not mentioned all of them - between the highest and the lowest, a psychologist would probably speak of 'Funktionslust', the urge to create as many functions as possible. It looks like the effect of a Neoplatonist 'Parkinson's Law', the obsessive drive to create always more intermediate stages which in their turn necessitate the creation of still more stages - all this in order to hold the top and the bottom as far distant from each other as possible.

It reminds one of the Gnosis where we also find some very elaborate systems, for instance, that of Basilides who knows of three hundred and sixty-five heavens [426]. With Iamblichus we overstep, indeed, what many other philosophers would consider the orbit of rational thought. He was an outspoken polytheist and propagated the veneration of the images of the gods; he believed in celestial signs, in auguries and predictions, in miracles, divination, and fortune-telling. The 'mystical' side of Plotinus had reached full growth in him. He was perhaps more of a Neopythagorean than a Neoplatonist. In any case he was a great admirer of Pythagoras and enthused about the Master's theory of numbers.

g. The physical world

But we have run ahead, for we have not yet reached the physical world as yet. Nature originates when superterrestrial forces combine with physical elements. "Nature", says Iamblichus, "is the cause of the cosmos" [427]. Once again he postulates an intermediate stage, this time between the higher immaterial world and the material cosmos. Although higher on in his system a Demiurge figures, we should not think of this entity as of 'him' but of 'it'; it it is not a person, a lower god, for instance, but a creative power. The kind of Demiurge we find in the Gnosis is absent in Iamblichus. In his place 'Nature' ('phusis') is acting as such.

The philosopher attaches an adiective to his word 'cause', namely 'achooristos' which means 'without a definite place being assigned to it'. Since everything material necessarily has a place, Nature is at the same time immaterial and material and can, for this reason, serve as the link between the upper and nether worlds. The manifold phenomena of the physical world finally have only one cause on which they depend and that makes them hang together, in other words, that makes them into a cosmos [428].

But Iamblichus does not explain how matter originates; it seems to have been always there. It has something of a counter-force, for the physical elements are disorderly and chaotic. Like so many other Hellenic philosophers, he has a low idea of matter : it is our fate and no good comes from it. Only the gods can save us from this apparently hopeless situation [429].

h. Iamblichus' psychology

Iamblichus was, according to Zeller, not really interested in physical nature; he was rather a psychologist [430]. Lloyd says that he made 'an important step in the separation of psychology from metaphysics' [431]. We have seen that Plotinus held that there are classes of virtues; these three were not sufficient for Iamblichus, for he added two more. Like Porphyry, he begins with the political virtues : an orderly civic and social life will enable man to raise his thoughts to the realm of Being. The purifying or cathartic virtues free the soul of everything that is not essential (in the last resort the non-essential includes miracles and magic). But then comes a new class, that of the 'theoretical' virtues, which make contemplation of the higher world possible. The next class is, just as in Porphyry, that of the paradigmatic virtues; the soul having now reached the level of the Nous unifies itself with it [432]. Finally, there is a last and highest class, that of the priestly virtues : these enable the soul to proceed beyond the Nous and ascend upwards to the highest beings [433].

j. Conclusion

It is clear : man, or rather his soul, is destined to leave this material world behind and return to the upper world. The body is of no use in this process neither is human knowledge. The way upwards is not easy and not everyone will go along it. The knowledge and the insights one needs have no human origin; they are the result of divine revelation. What we have in ourselves is an innate impulse to return to the One, but not all people will obey this voice. The dualistic separation of the spiritual and the material world is evident. The material world is useless and of no significance; it is only precariously held together. We also see that, in the last resort, even philosophy is no real help. The virtues that bring man's destiny to fulfilment are the 'priestly' ('hieratikai') ones; the priest is thus of far greater significance than the philosopher.

4. Proclus

a. The man and his work

Laurence Rosán says of Proclus that "by the time of his death he surely knew that he was an illustrious link in the 'golden chain' of Platonism [434] - but not that he was practically the final one" [435]. This last great philosopher of Antiquity [436] was born in 412 and died in 485 [437], when the Western Empire had already disappeared [438]. Proclus came from a town in Lycia in Asia Minor, where he attended school; he then went to Alexandria to study. Introduced by his teacher, he was able to frequent the highest circles in town. What he studied there was rhetoric, because he planned to be a lawyer. But on a journey to Constantinople he landed in Athens where he became acquainted with philosophy the study of which he continued when back in the Egyptian capital.

It was a divine inspiration, his biographer thought [439], that brought him back to Athens where he, in time, became the head of the famous philosophical school, the Academy. He stayed there until his death. He never married, in the true philosophical style. He was also a convinced vegetarian. Marinus describes him as being irascible and ambitious but also as kind and solicitous for his friends and pupils, visiting them when they were ill. In all 'a perfectly good man' [440]. But in spite of these endearing qualities, his freely chosen celibacy and his vegetarianism are pointers to it that he did not count himself an ordinary man.

Of Proclus' numerous works only a part has come down to us, mainly commentaries on dialogues of Plato [441]. The name of Plato is also attached to his 'Platonic theology', his most voluminous work, in which many of Proclus' own ideas are to be found. This also applies to the more compressed 'Elements of theology'. Three treatises on moral subjects are only known to us in the medieval Latin of William of Moerbeke. Since the philosopher was a man of a very vast erudition, he also published books on mathematics, physics, astronomy, linguistics, and poetics. Being no friend of the Christians, he wrote a book against them of which fragments remain. Finally, he also wrote poetry which is extant. Ancient philosophy did not therefore wither away 'sang- und klanglos' but instead ended with a great flourish [442].

b. Proclus the mystic

Just like Plotinus and just like Iamblichus, Proclus was not only a philosopher but something more, a mystic, and this probably first and foremost. His fundamental attitude is graphically expressed in his own words : "Our whole life here is a training-school for that life that is divine" [443]. It was the ageing Plutarch [444], called by the twenty-year old young man his 'grandfather' [445], who introduced him to the study of Plato [446]. Soon Plutarch's successor in the Academy, Syrianus, took him into his home [447] and they read Aristotle together. He also led his pupil to what Marinus calls 'Plato's mystagogy', that is, 'to the direct and immediate vision of the really divine mysteries contained in this philosopher'; the first fruit of this was Proclus' 'Commentary on the Timaeus' [448].

On a journey to Lydia, where he stayed a year, he became cognizant of 'the ancient religious institutions which had been there preserved' [449]. After this he began to venerate the Great Mother and celebrate the New Moon 'in great solemnity and with much sanctity'. Since he did not want to be peculiar or fastidious in his religious observance, he also paid much attention to the festivals of other peoples, for, as he used to say, a philosopher "ought to be the common hierophant of the whole world" [450]. He was much given to purifying practices, for instance, to taking ritual baths in the sea, even in winter, and even when he had become an old man [451]. In short, we have here the portrait of a philosopher of a very different kind than, say, A.J. Ayer [452].

c. Eternity and Time

All philosophy thrives on abstraction, and this is not different in Proclus. He distinguishes three 'degrees of abstraction' [453]. The first degree is 'the Individual Thing, or what it means something to be'; the second degree is

'Relationship, or what it means for something to be related to something else'; the third degree is 'Predication, or what it means for something to be not something else'. Apart from these three general principles there are three more that come somewhat lower in the ontological order and are dependent on the already mentioned. The first is the distinction between eternity and time; the second is the doctrine that "all things are in all things", the unifying principle; the third is that everything in the universe is at once an effect and a cause so that each member of the universe is reflected in another member.

Rosán calls the distinction between eternity and time 'the dualistic principle of Proclus' philosophy' [454]. This is so "because it divides the universe into two separate realms standing in eternal opposition to each other and characterized by different attributes". The difference is this that, in the world of eternity, causation means a 'formal relationship' in which "there is neither motion nor change, but everything remains forever frozen into its fixed pattern". The characteristics of the eternal entities are independent of others and immaterial; we may dub them 'self-existent' because they have no physical causes. In the world of time, however, "causation is a constant process which never stops; the chain of causality has had no beginning nor will it ever have and end, but one thing gives rise to another in perpetual motion". Here the causes are of a material nature. In Proclus' view the eternal and immaterial world is reality proper, whereas the temporal and material world is no more than 'the image or appeareance of the former world'. And Rosán concludes : "A dichotomy that splits the universe into two realms that differ as sharply in the degree of their reality as do those of time and eternity, therefore, may be called a dualistic principle" [455].

But there is also that second principle saying that "all things are in all things". This signifies that the dualism described above is not a radical one, because there is a connection between the entities of the higher world and those of the lower world. A general unifying principle operates that holds the two halves of the universe together. As Rosán expresses it, "eternal things exist temporally in temporal things, and temporal things exist eternally in eternal things. Thus the unifying principle interweaves every portion of the universe with every other portion (and) makes one world out of the seemingly conflicting realms of time and eternity" [456]. If the reader will find this somewhat confusing - is there or is there not dualism here? -, he or she must be prepared to find more of such ambiguities in Proclus' philosophy. One of the causes of this lack of clarity in important sections of his doctrine is that he consciously steers apart from the Gnosis. Although he acknowledges two separate and contrasted parts of the universe, he does not want to have them radically opposed to each other; in order to avoid the impression that he is mercilessly contrasting them, he disguises his own dualism.

d. The One and the Many

Proclus' philosophy presents itself as a solidly monistic system since everything is contained in and proceeds from the One. But we shall see that his monism generates its own problems. Stating that the One was fundamental in Proclus' metaphysics also means that the age-old problem of the One and the Many, as old as Greek philosophy itself, was at the centre of his thought [457]. The first section of his most seminal work, the 'Elements of Theology', is devoted to this theme. He starts from the multiple : "Every manifold is posterior to the One" [458]. But the multiple is not multiple tout court; it is also something else, for "every manifold participates unity" [459], so that "all that participates unity is both one and not-one" [460]. However, although the multiple may, to a certain extent or in a certain sense, become unified, it remains, nevertheless, 'other than the One itself' [461]. The conclusion is that the multiple, the Many, to be something more than a chaos, needs the One and is dependent on it. The One benevolently spreads its wings over the multiple or else this multiple would show no coherence at all.

e. Can the One be known?

Proclus says that like is known by like, for instance what is intelligible is known by the intellect. In the same mode that 'what is most one' can be known by the One, and 'what is ineffable by the ineffable'. Does this mean that only the ineffable One can know itself? It seems so. But the philosopher quotes Socrates to the effect that the soul by toning in upon itself and by seeking its own unity and the centre of its life can elevate itself to that higher viewpoint where it can see all that exists. But, it is added, this can only be attained if the soul divests itself 'of the multipliciy and diversity of the infinite powers' [462]. Is this possible?

Proclus' theology is a negative one; it isolates the One from everything else by using negations, by stating what it is not. This 'via negativa' is summarized in the statement that the One is ineffable. But, as he himself admits, the series of negations leads to what he calls an 'adunaton', an impossiblity, an 'aporia'. Since nothing can be postulated of the One, no argument actually applies to it. The One cannot be known by reasoning about it. There can be no definition of the ineffable; everything that is said about destroys itself [463]. The One is beyond all knowledge, beyond all reasoning. As Zeller said, it "has no positive relation to the world" [464]. It is only in a mystical way, using neither intellect nor language, that the soul can communicate with it.

f. Proclus' monism

That there is continuity between the One and the Many would, at first sight, be sufficient to show that Proclus' system is indeed monistic. The fact, however, that he says that the unified manifold remains 'other than the One itself' must make us think twice. Furthermore, since he declares that "everything which participates unity is both one and not-one", it follows that in this not wholly unified multiple something incoherent and chaotic remains; therefore, it stays, at least partly, outside the One. This being one and not-one at the same time cannot be said of the One itself, of course, or else it would not be what it is, the One. "The One itself is not both one and not-one ..., for if identical with the unified manifold, (it) will be the infinitely manifold" [465] which would signify that there is no unity at all.

A contradiction is becoming apparent; it becomes clearly evident when Proclus categorically states that "the One is imparticipable" [466]. Did he forget that he has started with stating that the Many owes the coherence it possesses to its participation in the One? Or that he wrote that "the participant (the Many, that is) was incomplete (= was lacking coherence) before the participation (in the One)" [467]? But now he states that the One, "were it participating, would ... cease to be the cause both of existent things and of the principles prior to existence" [468].

Trouillard, an expert on Proclus, writes that this philosopher "is careful to maintain the most strict continuity between principle (archê) and derivatives; and this notwithstanding he postulates a rupture that guarantees the transcendent and mysterious nature of the cause" [469]. As is often the case in monistic systems, the dualism sets in one stage lower. Here the antagonism is between participation and the ontological impossibility to participate, to communicate itself. In order to make the unification of the manifold possible, Proclus needs a principle, or principles that are participable; these are the 'henads'; "every henad posterior to one One is participable". A henad cannot be one in the same degree as the One itself [470].

g. The essential problem

Still remaining in the multiple world, Proclus now states that "all that exists proceeds from a single first cause" [471]. This 'principium' ('archê') is defined as 'the Good', because the multiple is subjected to unification, and "all unification is a good"; in consequence, "the Good is identical with the One" [472]. But that the One is also the Good does not explain how the multiple proceeds from it, since it cannot communicate itself. The One and the many are dualistically different. True, unity goes forth from the One. But although the unifying force it radiates gives coherence to the manifold, the manifold does not originate from the One. The philosopher seems to say so himself. Like brings forth what is like, he explains; the procession goes by means of similitudes [473]. How then can the One bring forth its opposite, the Many? How does Proclus solve what Beutler calls 'the essential problem of all Platonism' : "how can the finite (the multiple) come from the infinite (the One)?" [474].

h. Being

Perhaps one would think that the One and Being are identical, but in Proclus this is not so. According to his ontology Being is secondary to the One; he is quite explicit on this. Being is 'next to the One', but not identical with the One. It is "the highest participant ... and prior to it there is no further principle save the One ... Being stands immediately next to it". Proclus unequivocally puts the One apart from Being by stating that it is a 'not-Being'. It can only be superior to Being as a not-Being' [475]. This differentiating of Being and not-Being is also something dualistic.

It is in Being, and not in the One, that Proclus combines unity and multiplicity. For "Being is nothing else but a monad of the multiple powers or a pluralistic existence (or substance), and it is for this reason that Being is the one-multiple" [476]. Elsewhere Proclus calls Being 'the unitary manifold' that is a 'composite of limit and infinite' [477]. "All true being is composed of limit and infinite" [478]. However, there is in Being more unity than multiplicity. "The multiplicity finds itself in the primary beings in a hidden and indistinct mode", but the lower we come, the more visibly the multiple manifests itself [479]. Originally, so we learned, it was the One that imparted unity to the multiple world, but now it seems to be Being that is charged with this task.

j. The chain of being

Proclus wants the chain of being to be uninterrupted; no link may be missing. "The processions of the entities ... do not admit of any vacuum; everywhere there exist between the extreme terms intermediates that assure their colligation" [480]. The mechanism with the help of which Proclus makes his chain uninterrupted is the sequel of cause and effect. We might also speak of emanations from which other emanations come, and so on, but the philosopher himself prefers the term 'processions'. The ruling idea is that what is lower has its cause in what is higher, and what is particular in what is more general [481]. In the course of the process the effects multiply : "every cause ... gives rise to a greater number of posterior terms" [482]. In this way the existents constantly proliferate.

Proclus seems to have realized that the coherence in his chain is perhaps not as solid as he wanted it to be. An effect must have a cause, indeed, but something needs not necessarily be a cause by leading to an effect. For "every cause properly so called transcends its result"; the cause is more than and is different from the effect. It cannot be immanent in its effect; it does not need the effect for its existence [483]. What else can this mean but that the emanations are not necessary? This caveat suggests that he postulates his constant processions or productions because he needs them in order to explain why there is a multiple world. In the last resort his ontology does not admit to the existence of it.

Let me quote Beutler who presents the resulting causal chain. We begin at the One that is uncaused. The first effect is Being, the cause of all unity, the uppermost substance and the origin of life. Then follows Nous and next Psychê (soul). At a lower stage come the things that happen, than the things that grow, then the lifeless things, and finally matter. The unifying force becomes ever weaker in the process, so that matter receives very little of it [484]. The consequence is that in Proclus' view all existents hang together, for "all existents proceed from one single first cause" [485].

As conclusive as this may seem, a problem remains. "Cause is not convertible with effect" [486]. The effect is only partially similar to the cause or else it would be identical with the cause. "All that is immediately produced by any principle both remains in the principle (is similar to it) and proceeds ('goes out') from it (is dissimilar from it)" [487]. The consequence is that, the lower we get in the descending line of emanations, the less the effect will resemble the primary cause, the 'archê', so that the resemblance of the ultimate effect to the archê, the One, will be very slight. In the course of the processions the disparity continue to grow.

Proclus jeopardizes the coherence and solidity of his chain of being by making the following curious statement. "Every cause which is separate from its effect exists at once everywhere and nowhere." He then goes on to explain what he means by 'cause' : it is "that which fits all things naturally capable of participating it, which is the cause of all secondary existences (= its effects) and by the fecund outpourings of its irradiations is present in them all." This makes it clear why the chain is a chain : the cause is 'everywhere'. But it is also 'nowhere' which means that it is not linked to anything else. "By its mode of being, which has no admixture of the spatial (i.e. it is immmaterial - F.), and by its transcendent purity it is nowhere"; this applies, of course, in particular to the One. "For if it is separate from its effects, it is enthroned above all alike and resides in no being inferior to itself."

How on earth can anything be simultaneously nowhere and everywhere = linked and not linked to the lower orders, present and not present in them? If a cause were merely everywhere, then "it would not exist separately prior to them all". If it were merely nowhere, then "it would not be omnipresent". But perhaps it is so that one part of the cause is 'nowhere', that is, separate from anything else, and that another part is 'everywhere', that is, present in all its effects. But no! Proclus categorically states that the cause "is entire everywhere and likewise nowhere" [488]. I can explain this in no other way than that the philosopher realizes that his system is dualistic, especially with regard to the One and what emanates from it, but does not want to have it thus [489].

Proclus uses a device that ensures that his chain of being does not desintegrate into its links; this device is the 'triadic development'. This means, in short, that what has descended goes upwards again; what has proceeded from the One will finally return to it. This triadic development [490] has three moments : first the 'monê', say, the element of oneness by which an effect is linked to and remains in its cause, then the 'prohodos', the proceeding, the going forth, that is, the becoming an effect, and finally, the 'epistrophê', the returning to the principle. This triadic process repeats itself at every stage of the emanations [491]. It is succinctly stated by Proclus as follows. "Every effect remains in its cause, proceeds from it, and revers upon it" [492].

Werner Beierwaltes cautions us not to see the triadic movement as something formal or as a manner of classification, but as something that is essential to his system [493]. As Proclus himself put it : "The intelligible and intellectual triads bring all things to perfection and hold them together and lead them to unity" [494]. "The deeper we go in the series of proceedings, the more divided and less perfect being becomes ...; the higher we go, the other way round, in the reversed direction, the more perfect it grows" [495]. Zeller remarks that in this way Proclus designed a world picture that comprised all that is visible and that is invisible. He compared it with the bureaucratic hierarchy of the Eastern Empire (in which all power, even that of the lowest official, came from the Emperor, and in which every official had to refer to the one higher employee, and in the last resort to the Emperor himself); in the same way he compared it to the hierarchy of the Christian Church [496].

k. The One and the Many once again : the role of the henads

Now that we, with Proclus, have once again arrived at the One, we must ask ourselves, or rather him, how the multiple can go forth from it. Since the One can only produce what is one, a number of 'henads' or 'units' come from it. Multiplicity begins here, in fact, but Proclus takes care that the number of henads is only small. "The entire number of henads is finite in number"; multiple, yes, but not too multiple. This restriction is caused by the fact that the henads stand nearest to the One. As direct descendants of the One they have to be as one as possible, although they are manifold. Proclus, by way of speaking, excuses himself for their being multiple; he admits that "the manifold as such is already a departure from the One. But this manifold "is not infinite ...; the infinite is not cognate from the One but alien from it ... It is plain that an infinite manifold is completely bereft of its influence." We have already seen that the henads have influence, since they are, in contrast to the One itself, participable. They are "marked by unit and limit; and this in a higher degree than any other, since of all manifolds it is nearest akin to the One" [497]. The philosopher grapples here with two venerable problems of Greek philosophy, both reaching back to its infant-days, that of the One and the Many and that of peras and apeiron, for these are the Greek terms for finite and infinite. Both figure already in Pythagoras' list of oppositions [498].

The philosopher does his utmost to minimize the nasty manifoldness of the henads. He calls them units in order to stress that they participate in the One in a privileged way and accentuates this by stating that all henads are in each other (= one), "and yet they are distinct" [499]. They are, therefore, one and different at the same time. The henads are 'gods' : "every god is a self-complete henad or unit, and every self-complete henad is a god". And since they share in the divinity of the One, they are also incomprehensible. For "all that is divine is ineffable and unknowable by any secondary being because of its supra-existential unity." However, although the One itself can never be comprehended, the henads can be apprehended, not directly, but indirectly, namely 'from the existents that participate in it" [500].

It remains unclear what these henads exactly are; they are highly abstract beings of whom nothing is predicated [501]. Beutler speaks here of a 'remarkable unclarity' and thinks they are superfluous. What then for did Proclus need them for? To find a nook in his system for the traditional gods? This same scholar thinks that the urge to ramificate and to interpose mediators played a role [502].

It is evident that the function of the henads is to mediate. What the One will not do, they will. They have just enough oneness to stand close to the One and just enough of the multiple for having a relation with the manifold world. "A god is more universal as he is nearer to the One, more specific in proportion to his remoteness from it" [503]. "Every god (= henad) embraces in his substance the function of exercizing providence towards the universe" [504]. The henads extend their influence ever further downwards. "Every god proceeds through all secondary orders ... The procession is from a unity to a manifold [505] ... The sequence of principles which participate the divine henads extends from Being to the bodily nature, since Being is the first and body the last participant [506] ... All the powers of the gods ... descend even to the last existents and the terrestrial regions [507]." In this way the coherence of the universe is ensured. The function of the henads is, in co-operation with the One, to make the existence of the existents possible; every henad is, so to speak, responsible for its own class of existents. "Whatever supra-existential character is proper to a particular divinity (henad) appears existentially in the real-existent which participates it" [508].

1. Syrianus' view of Monas and Duas, Peras and Apeiron

It is necessary to pause on this highest rung of the existential ladder for one moment. We have seen how Proclus coped with the question of the One and the Many, namely by arguing that this henads are one and many at the same time. A cognate question is that of the Finite and the Infinite which are in Pythagoras' list dualistically opposed. The Greeks had as visceral fear of the apeiron, the infinite, which to them was the equivalent of chaos. The cosmos had its peras, its limit, and beyond that lay the apeiron. This image perhaps had its origin in the idea of the polis as a microcosmos, a well-ordered whole; beyond its borders began the terra, if not incognita, then certainly inimica. It was best to stay at home, as did Socrates who rarely left Athens.

The question of the peras and the apeiron was put on the philosophical agenda again by Syrianus, the immediate successor of Plutarch in the Athenian Academy. For this philosopher too the overarching principle is the One. It manifests itself in the existential order as the Monad which, however, is paired with the 'aoristos duas', the limitless duality, right from the start [509]. That Monas and Duas are opposites is shown by the fact that Syrianus, harking back to Empedocles, equates the first with 'philia' = friendship, and the second with 'neikos' = quarrel or discord [510]. They constitute two 'archai', each of them at the head of a cosmos of its own, these being the intelligible and the sensible worlds [511]. Their workings reach down to the lowest layers of the universe, that is, into the 'phusis', into physical nature. Monas and duas are not radical opposites; they relate to each other just as peras and apeiron, as male and female, as paternal and maternal [512]. So we see thus figuring the Pythagorean list of opposites at the beginning and at the very end of Greek philosophy. The universe has a 'unitary cause', indeed [513], but as Seeck wrote, it immediately forks into a dualism [514].

m. Proclus on these problems

The conceptual pair 'peras-apeiron' was something that was debated in the Athenian Academy. It is also to be found in Proclus [515], just as we may expect in the work of a philosopher who is so much dependent on the Pythagorean-Platonist tradition. What this implies is that there is a tendency towards dualism in his work. A.C. Lloyd has argued that Proclus was far from 'the convential Pythagorean-Platonic interpretation', signifying that he was averse from dualism [516]. This scholar says that Proclus makes peras and apeiron collaborate. To prove this, he quotes a passage from the 'Theologia platonica' [517] in which the philosopher attacks certain Platonists whom he accuses of misunderstanding the Master. "If they are crediting intelligible substance (noêtên ousian) with something that has no shape or form or limit (aoriston), then they seem to me to mistake Plato's meaning. The Unlimited (apeiron) is not the matter (hulê) of Limit (peras) but its force (dunamis), and Limit is not the form of the Unlimited but its substance (huparxis)." This is an opaque statement. It is far from clear what is meant by the Unlimited being the force of the Limit. Does this mean that the peras is forced to act upon the apeiron, because it does not want something to be unlimited? Must we conclude on the basis of the above statement that peras and apeiron are 'collaborating'?

Proclus, so much is true, follows Plato by stating that "generation (genesis) is a mixed form of peras and apeiron" [518]. For there to be existents both are needed. "All that is brought forward by nature, with regard to its form resembles the Limit, and with regard to its matter the Unlimited" [519]. We would, however, be wrong to suppose that we are dealing with two sides of the same coin. The point is that there are two 'archai', two principles [520]. This is stated categorically in the following proposition : "Prior to all that is composed of Limit and Infinitude there exist substantially and independently the first Limit and the first Infinity" [521].

These two archai are totally different in quality. The Limit causes the universe to be divinely stable and uniform, whereas with the Unlimited multiplicity begins. Unity, integrality, commonalty of beings, all that is godlike in the universe, depend on the Limit; all division, all going apart, all multiplying, have their origin in the Unlimited. Proclus calls the first 'the better' and the second 'defective', and speaks of an opposition, an 'antithesis'. We are here not far from dualism [522].

It is a curious thing - an unexplainable anomaly in Proclus' system - that, although we heard that the henads come immediately after the One, we now are told that the pair Peras-Apeiron is still prior to them. "Every order of gods (= henads) is derived from the initial principles, Limit and Infinity". And not only that, but the henads are divided into two sets, each headed by a different archê. "Some manifest predominantly the causality of Limit, others that of Infinity" [523]. Wholly in the line of the Pythagorean opposites, Proclus assigns part of his henads to the Limit, declaring them to be paternal, sustaining, creative, and another part to to the Unlimited, saying that this part is 'zoogonic' (= producing living beings) and 'generative' [524]. The difference manifests itself all the way down from the One to Matter [525]. Maybe the philosopher was averse to dualism, but this does not mean that he was no dualist. He wanted to camouflage it in, although he was none too successful in doing so. For say what he may, we can observe a split running through the whole universe with the superior and perfect on one side and the inferior and imperfect on the other.

n. The offspring of the henads

Leaving aside the problem of whether or not the henads form the first emanation, we must see what they produce. From them goes forth the Intelligible (the Nous); true to his predilection for triads, Proclus divides it into three compartments. Just as Iamblichus, he distinguishes the Intelligible proper and the Intellectual, but to make it threefold, he inserts the Intelligible-Intellectual; the Intelligible is Being, the Intelligible-Intellectual Life, and the Intellectual Thought, and the most of these is Being [526]. There is a qualitative difference in this triad, in a descending order. It is here that multiplicity really begins, not yet of factual things, but of intelligibles [527].

Each member of this first triad consists in itself of a triad so that there are nine triads in all. A number of these triads are in their turn subdivided into hebdomads, sevens. The result is a phantastically and confusingly complicated system in which even the most die hard philosopher will lose track. No wonder that, as Beutler remarks, "it had only an ephemeral significance and remained without influence on later periods" [528]. The whole constitutes a very long staircase down which one slowly and haltingly descends from the One to the factual world. Once again we see how a philosopher of Late Antiquity screens his supreme archê from the lower world. It is only when we have reached the last and lowest hebdomad that we can start the descent to the material world. Here we find, in true Platonic fashion, the Ideas. One will, however, search in vain for Evil or for an evil-intended Demiurge.

o. The sphere of the Soul

If the reader might believe that, leaving this immensely intricate system of the Intelligible, he or she can now enter the material world, he or she would be mistaken. For first we have to cross the sphere of the Soul, "which is the intermediary between the supersensible and sensible worlds, mirroring the former as a copy and serving as a pattern for the latter" [529]. Not having lost his gusto for subdivisions, Proclus divides the sphere of the Soul into three sub-spheres, one of divine souls, another of demonic souls (in its turn divined into three), and a third of human souls. All souls, the human ones not excluded, are eternal. Because human souls essentially belong to the sphere of the spiritual, they possess the potency to return to that realm, even if they are housed in physical bodies temporarily.

p. Nature

Have we now reached the material world? Not yet [530]! But we are now indeed at the last and lowest stage of incorporeal entities, that of 'phusis' = Nature. Nature is here not what we understand by it - trees, plants, animals - but an abstract principle. The idea Proclus has of Nature, says Zeller, is not really physical but theological and teleological [531]. Nature carries in herself the 'logoi', the reasons why actual things are as they are. It is very hard to say how the world of the phenomena came into being. It is equally hard to tell how Matter originated. It is by no account something that is independent of the One, for "it takes its origin from the One ... For Matter which is the basis of all things, proceeded from the cause of all things". But the philosopher is not very specific about this; Matter 'is devoid of Form" [532]. It is ethically neutral, neither good nor bad, but entirely 'qualityless'; we should, therefore, not think that it is the home of evil [533].

Matter is receptive, it can take what is good, but the good it takes comes from elsewhere, not from itself. It exists because of what is good, and insofar, Matter is itself good. But this is too simplistic. For it is the very lowest grade of what is; it finds itself at the greatest possible distance from the supremely good, and for this reason it is bad. However, it is 'necessary' [534]. The philosopher hesitates in taking a radically dualistic position, that of opposing Matter as the supremely Evil to the supremely Good. But equally he cannot bring himself to state that Matter is good, although it is the last link in the chain of being that has its starting-point in the supremely Good.

q. Demiurgic functions

Although there is no specific Demiurge operating in Proclus' system, there are demiurgic functions. For in some way or other Matter must have been shaped into the distinct forms of existent beings and things. This was done by those who are grouped under the sign of the Limit, viz. the paternal and demiurgic (creative) ones. The functions of these two sorts of henads are not identical, although both have 'a limitative character'. The paternal henad brings forth 'the processive orders of things existent', or, in short, existence. It enables beings and things to exist. The task of the demiurgic henad is to lend form (eidos) to the existents, that is, to give them shape and make them distinct from each other [535]. But how this process exactly works is not explained, and particularly not how such abstract principles can come to such concrete results.

We should not think of these demiurgic functions as something personal; the creational activity of the Judaeo-Christian God is something personal, but this is not so in the Proclan henads. Demiurgic activity does not result from somebody's free will but from sheer necessity; demiurgic henads simply have to do and to make, because such is their nature that forces them to it, whereas the Judaeo-Christian God creates from his own free volition.

r. The soul's descent

Another question is why the soul agrees to descend into a physical body. Does it do so willingly? Proclus answers this question in this way. As long as the soul is at rest, that is, not in a body, it is absorbed in contemplation. But it also wants to imitate the gods, the henads, who are at once contemplating and provident or generating; therefore, the soul gets moving and descends into a physical shape. Proclus adds that this contributes to the perfection of the world since it enables the 'existents of the last degree', that is, the material things, to participate of reason and intellect. But their complying to the will of the gods does not make the souls really happy, for they become 'filled with trouble and misery'.

The combination with a physical shape is not congenial to them; they do not love "this abrupt passage from the Intelligible to the Sensible, from calm rest to a state of total mobility, as the consequence of disorderly encounters that are naturally inherent to beings composed of such dissimilar elements, the immortal and the mortal, the intelligent and without reason, then invisible, and the discursive". And all of a sudden we are reminded of Gnostic mythology : "Doubtless, the soul ignites a light in the body, but she herself has been plunged into obscurity". The dualism is here already apparent but it is uncompromisingly brought out in what Proclus lets follow. The soul "has given life to the body, but she herself and her intellect have been destroyed ... For the physical connection is the death of immortal life but vivifies the mortal body" [536].

s. The question of Evil

Related to this is the question of Evil. True to his monistic starting-point Proclus cannot classify it as something that is, for then Evil would have its origin in the One, the supreme Good. Consequently, Evil is something that is not. The philosopher consigns it to the lowest layers, to the individual souls and to the bodies. One can only say that God is the cause of Evil 'accidentally', because he is the cause of the invididual souls [537]. The real cause of Evil is that the individual souls are not capable of withstanding the lure of physicality : "The cause of all that is bad is mortality ... We ourselves are the cause" [538]. But there is not only moral but also physical evil; just as moral evil has its seat in individual souls, physical evil is at home in concrete and distinct things.

t. The return of the soul

It is, however, not so that a soul, having served its time in a body, can return to its origin. "Every intra-mundane soul has its proper life-periods and cyclic reinstatements" [539]. With the 'intra-mundane' ('enkosmios') soul an incorporated one is meant; it has to stay here for a fixed time. With the 'cyclic reinstatements' refer to its wanderings from body to body. This is the consequence of its taking part in the general movememt, the 'prohodos' once set in motion, it stays moving until the momentum is spilt, and the 'epistrophê', the return begins. But this return is not automatically guaranteed; it is the result of leading a virtuous life, just as in Plotinus. Here too ethical perfection is reached in stages. It ends, at least for thoroughly virtuous souls, where it began : in the One. It needs no argument that the body is left behind.

u. Conclusion

This last element shows us that Proclus' system is not free of dualistic characteristics. He does not want it to be so; he wants it to be 'holistic', a homogeneous, a monistic system. But through the cracks and fissures in it we find several unbridgeable oppositions. Little else is to be expected from a philosopher who has followed the line of the Pythagorean-Platonic tradition.

NOTES TO CHAPTER I

1. See Vol. VI, Ch. III.4.

2. Pohlenz, Stoa I, 257 : "Die Römer waren ihrem eigentlichen Wesen nach ganz unphilosophisch, ausschließlich den praktischen Aufgaben des realen Lebens zugewandt. Bei ihnen herrschte nicht das Wissen, sondern der Wille".

3. See Lucrezio, Della natura, ed. Armando Fellin 11-14 Diffusione dell' Epicureismo a Roma. P. 11 : "Nello scatenamento degli egoismi, delle ambizioni smisurate, degli odi di ogni parte, il richiamo dell' epicureismo all' interiorità dell' uomo, alla scienza austera, all' amicizia, al distacco della vita politica, fu accollto con trasporto entusiastico". A very detailed review, author by author, with opponents included, of the role Epicureanism played in the Western Roman Empire until its end, is presented by Ferguson, Epicureanism, ANRW, Bd. 36.4, 2257-2327.

4. See Vol. VI, Ch. III.3.

5. Lucr., De rerum natura 2.222.

6. Lucr., De rerum 2.224.

7. Lucr., De rerum natura 2.243-250.

8. Ackerman, Lukrez 212 : "Die natura (ist) Lukrezens Urmythos".

9. Vol. VI, Ch. III.4h and k.

10. Lucr., De rerum natura 1.62. Perelli, Lucrezio, cap. 3 Il timore degli dei, 139 : "Il timore degli dei in Lucrezio è strettamente associato al timore della morte come causa dell' infelicità umana".

11. Lucr., De rerum natura 1.78-79.

12. Lucr., Rerum 1.83.

13. Lucr., 1.101 : "Tantum religio potuit suadere malorum".

14. Lucr., De rerum natura 1.56.

15. Lucr., De rerum natura 5.8-9. Winspear, Lucretius 46 : "The religious reader feels that Lucretius has not fully satisfied himself, that he has not banished his own fears, that his debating opponent is still in a sense himself. They detect some longing for the eternal, some hunger for immortality that Lucretius with his own philosophy has not been able entirely to banish from his own heart".

16. Lucr., De rerum natura 5.52-53.
17. Lucr., De rerum natura 5.1-5. See for this passage Schrijvers, Horror § 19i La religion.
18. Lucr., Rerum 3.18-24.
19. Lucr., De rerum natura 3.1023.
20. Lucr., De rerum natura 1.1.
21. Ackermann, Lukrez 184.
22. Lucr., De rerum natura 1.21.
23. Ackermann, Lukrez 215.
24. Vol. VI, Ch. III, § 3a.
25. Vol. VI, Ch. III, § 3m.
26. Lucrezio, Ed. Fellin 11.
27. Cic., De oratore 3.24.95.
28. Cic., Tusculanae disputationes 5.10.28. For Cicero's polemic against atomism, see Stückelberger, Atomistik 2564-2568. This author concludes that the opposition to atomism of authoritative authors like Aristotle, Cicero, and Augustine, who exercized much influence on medieval thought, were responsible for the fact that for many centuries atomism did not have much of a future (see his § II).
29. Cic., Tusculanae disputationes 4.3.7.
30. Cic., De finibus 2.14.44.
31. Cic., De natura deorum 1.41.115.
32. Lucrezio, ed. Fellin 11.
33. See Vol. VI, Ch. III, § 9b.
34. See Vol. VI, Ch. III, § 9c.
35. A recent exposition of Cicero's significance as a philosopher is presented by Günter Gawlick and Woldemar Görler, Grundriss der Philosophie der Antike, Bd. 4 Die hellenistische Philosophie, 6. Kap. Basel, 1994. It offers useful summaries of Cicero's philosophical works and two extensive bibliographies. The authors conclude (p. 1030) that the contemporaries did not pay much attention to his philosophical works.
36. See Vol. VI, Ch. III, § 2.
37. Copleston, History of Philosophy I, 2, 172/173.
38. Pohlenz, Stoa I, 304.
39. Copleston, History of Philosophy I, 2, 173.

40. Sen., Ep. ad Lucilium 65.1.
41. Sen., Ep. ad Lucilium 65.16.
42. Sen., Ep. ad Lucilium 120.15-16.
43. See Rozelaar, Seneca. 5. Kap., § 6 Dualismus von Leib und Seele, § 7 Absage an den Körper.
44. Sen., Ep. ad Lucilium 65.16.
45. See Vol. VI, Ch. III, § 2b.
46. Seneca, Ep. ad Lucilium 65.2.
47. Sen., Ep. ad Lucilium 65.12.
48. Scarpat, Pensiero religioso 22.
49. Sen., De beneficiis 4.19.2-3.
50. Sen., Naturales quaestiones, Praefatio 1-3.
51. Sen., De beneficiis 4.8.3.
52. Sen., Naturales quaestiones, Praef. 13.
53. Pohlenz, Stoa I, 321. Idem in Scarpat, Pensiero religioso 31 : "Seneca concepisce la divinità alla maniera stoica, cioè strettamente immanentistica e monistica."
54. Pohlenz, Stoa I, 321, believes that in many places Seneca shows "wie nahe ihm die persönliche Auffassung der Gottheit lag". This is glibly stated. True enough, it is possible to quote a text like this one : "God has for good people a fatherly heart and loves them deeply", Sen., De providentia 2.6. But, asks Scarpat, Pensiero religioso 32, does this have the same significance as it would have in a Christian text? Absolutely not, he says. In Stoicism it is the world that is good, the world that is pervaded and guided by the Logos. "God comes to man; what is more, he comes in man", Sen., Ep. ad Lucilium 73.16. The consequence of this is that man, having God in himself, does not have to look up to heaven and pray, Scarpat, Pensiero religioso 39. "The gods are not moved by prayers", Sen., Phaedra 1242.
55. Pohlenz, Stoa I, 305.
56. Sen., Ep. ad Lucilium 82.6.
57. Copleston, Hist. of phil., I, 2, 173.
58. Sen., Ep. ad Lucilium 1.1.
59. Sen., Ep. ad Lucilium. 80.4.
60. Sen., Naturales quaestiones, 2.35.
61. Sen., Ep. ad Lucilium 107.9.
62. Sen., Ep. ad Lucilium 107.12.

101

63. Sen., Naturales quaestiones, 2.38.3.
64. Sen., Ep. ad Lucilium 16.4-5.
65. Copleston, Hist. of phil. I, 2, 179.
66. Bonhöffer, Epiktet 274-281; this author is speaking here of 'supernatural and in consequence dualistic conception of being' in the New Testament; I do not follow him in this.
67. See Bonhöffer, Epiktet. 2. Buch, 3. Teil, 2. Abschnitt A, Stellung zu Gott.
68. Epict., Enchiridion 1.2.
69. Epict., Enchiridion 1.4.
70. 1Cor. 6:19.
71. Epict., Diatribes 4.11.9 sqq.
72. Epict., Diatribes 3.10.14.
73. Epict., Diatribes 3.22.20.
74. Epict., Diatribes 3.22.26.
75. Epict., Diatribes 3.22.41.
76. Epict., Diatribes 4.1.79.
77. Epict., Diatribes 4.1.104.
78. Marc.Aur., Med. 2.17.
79. Marc.Aur., Med. 4.40.
80. Marc.Aur., Med. 4.23.
81. Marc.Aur., Med. 9.3.
82. Marc.Aur., Med. 3.7.
83. Marc.Aur., Med. 4.41; the author presents this as a quotation from Epictetus, but this text is not be found in this philosopher's work.
84. Marc.Aur., Med. 11.19.
85. Marc.Aur., Med. 12.1.
86. Marc.Aur., Med. 12.1.
87. Pohlenz, Stoa I, 343.
88. Marc.Aur., Med. 5.27.
89. Marc.Aur., Med. 12.1.
90. Marc.Aur., Med. 2.13.
91. Marc.Aur., Med. 3.6; see also 5.10.

92. See for instance Vol. IX, Preface § 2.
93. See Vol. III, Ch III, §§ 3, 6, 8, 14a, 20d.
94. Vol. I, Ch. I.
95. Zeller, Phil.d.Gr. III.2.2, 95/96. For the Orphic mysteries see Vol. I, Ch. IV, § 10.
96. Lemma 'Alexander Polyhistor', Der neue Pauly, Bd. 1 (1996).
97. DL 8.24-36.
98. Zeller, Phil.d.Gr. III.2.2, 103.
99. Philostr., Life of Apoll.
100. For a discussion of the Apollonius-tradition see Bowie, Apollonius, ANRW II.16.2 (1978).
101. Philostr., Life 5.37.
102. Dio 78.18.4.
103. Lampridius, Sev.Al. 29.2.
104. Cic., Timaeus 1.1.
105. Scholia in Cic. § 14.
106. Sen., Nat.quaest. 7.32.2.
107. Zeller, Phil.d.Gr. III.2.2, 113/114.
108. Zeller, Phil.d.Gr. III.2.2., 115.
109. Zeller, Phil.d.Gr. III.2.2, 126; Copleston, Hist.Phil. I.2, 190.
110. Sext.Emp., Against the phys. 2.281.
111. Sext.Emp., Againsr the phys. 2.282.
112. Zeller, Phil.d.Gr. III.2.2, 129/130.
113. For instance, Clem.Al., Strom. 1.22; Orig., Contra Cels. 1.67.
114. Frede, Numenius, ANRW II.36.2, 1040, "Numenius ist, seiner Lehre nach, ein Platoniker. Gewöhnlich wird er als Neopythagoreer eingeordnet ... (1046) Es fragt sich ob es nicht irreführend ist, Numenius einen Neopythagoreer zu nennen".
115. Puech, Numenios 454/455, characterizes Apameia, a city of some 170.000 inhabitants, as an important cultural centre and a town where the most diverse influences crossed each other.
116. There are five collections in all, that of Des Places, Numénius, Fragments (see Bibliography), being the most recent.
117. Puech, Numenios 457, answers the question whether Num. was a Jew with "this is at least a possibility".

103

118. Fr. 9 and 10 Des Places knowledge of Moses in Egypt; fr. 13 speaks of God as 'He who is'.

119. Fr. 1a Des Places : "all that has been posited by the Brahmans, the Jews, the Magi, and the Egyptians"; on the influence Num. had on later scholars like Porphyry and Origen, see Frede, Numenius, ANRW II,36.2 (1987), 1034-1037.

120. Frede, Numenius, ANRW II.36.2, 1037 : "(Wir) wissen aber leider immer noch viel zu wenig über Numenius, um uns ein klares Bild von seiner Lehre auch nur in ihren Grundzügen und von ihrer wahren historischen Bedeutung zu machen".

121. Fr. 48, Des Places, from Iamblichus in Stobaeus, Anth. I, 49.40 (Wachsmuth).

122. Fr. 52, Des Places, from Calcidius in Timaeum.

123. This is the view expressed by the philosopher Moderatus, but Numenius rejects it and "returns to the two independent and opposed principles which he finds in the earlier Pythagoreans and Plato", Armstrong, Dualism 36.

124. Karin Alt, Weltflucht (see Bibliography).

125. Alt, Weltflucht 31.

126. Fr. 52, 101-112, Des Places.

127. Fr. 52, 105-108, Des Places.

128. Dillon, Middle Plat. 379.

129. Fr. 3, Des Places.

130. Rudolf Beutler s.v. 'Numenius', PW Suppl. Bd. VII (1940), 669.

131. Fr. 11, Des Places.

132. Fr. 12, Des Places.

133. Fr. 11, Des Places. Most of the time Numenius speaks of two gods, but in Fr. 11.13-14, Des Places, he speaks of a third : "The second and the Third God are one". Probably he made some sort of distinction between the divine Intellect (Nous) and the Demiurge. Frede, Numenius 1057-1090, discusses this question extensively.

134. Fr. 57, Des Places.

135. Fr. 13, Des Places.

136. Fr. 15, Des Places.

137. Fr. 16, Des Places.

138. Fr. 18, Des Places.

139. Fr. 18, Des Places.

140. Fr. 15, Des Places.
141. Fr. 11, Des Places.
142. Dillon, Middle Plat. 369.
143. Fr. 52, 64-66, Des Places.
144. Alt, Weltflucht 33.
145. Deuse, Untersuch. 72/73 thinks "daß die gute Weltseele als Welt-Nous betrachtet werden kann", although he must admit that we "eine gute Weltseele in den Fragmenten und Zeugnissen nicht belegt finden ... Die gute Weltseele ist das schöpferische und ordnende Prinzip des Kosmos, das den Kosmos hervorbringt, <u>indem es sich selbst im Zusammentreffen mit der Materie konstituiert</u>" (emphasis added).
146. Fr. 20, 13, Des Places.
147. Fr. 12, 14-16, Des Places.
148. Fr. 22, Des Places.
149. Fr. 44, Des Places. Porphyry from whom this fragment comes assures us that we should not really think of two or three parts in the soul but of two souls. In the Calcidius-fragment, fr. 52, 70-74, Des Places, it is spoken of two 'parts' of the soul, by Numenius, that is, but Waszink (quoted Deuse, Unters. 71, note 34) thinks that it was Calcidius who added the word 'pars' in order to bring the Numenian text into agreement with his own doctrine, perhaps because he (C.) did not want dualism in the human soul.
150. Alt, Weltflucht 101.
151. Fr. 43, 4-5, Des Places.
152. Fr. 43, Des Places.
153. Fr. 49, Des Places.
154. Deuse, Untersuch. 77.
155. Fr. 46, Des Places.
156. Fr. 46, Des Places.
157. Fr. 52, 73-74, Des Places.
158. See Vol. III, Ch. III. especially §§ 13, 18d, 19c, 20.
159. See Vol. VIII, Ch. I, § 13.
160. Cic., Academica 2.4.11.
161. Cic., Brutus 91.315.
162. Cic., De fin. 5.6.
163. Dillon, Middle Plat. 105.

164. Lueder, Philos.Persönl. 19, "... herrschte schon im Altertum Unklarheit darüber, zu welcher philosophischer Richtung Antiochos auf Grund seiner Lehre gerechnet werden müsse : ob er wirklich das war was er sein wollte, nämlich Akademiker, oder ob er nicht viel mehr Stoiker sei". May we believe her (pp. 71-73), but then Antiochus rejected the Stoa, although according to Luck, Antiochos 45-51, there were Stoic influences in him.

165. We have a collection of fragments, most of them short, in Luck, Antiochos (see Bibliography).

166. Cic., Acad.post. I, 27-29.

167. Dillon, Middle Plat. 83.

168. Cic., Academica 2.132 (Lucullus) : "he was called an Academic, and was in fact, had he made very few modifications, a perfectly genuine Stoic".

169. For Antiochus see also Zeller, Phil.d.Gr. (1963), III.1, 618-630, and, more recently, Dillon, Middle Plat. 52-106.

170. Freudenthal, Albinus (see Bibliography).

171. Whittaker, Plat.phil., ANRW 2.36.1 (1987), 83-102. Only ten years earlier, in 1977, Dillon had seen no reason to mention him in his book on the Middle Platonists.

172. Matthias Balthus s.v. 'Alkinoos', Der neue Pauly (1996) : "Eine Identität des ansonsten unbekannten A. mit Albinos aus Smyrna kann nicht ausgeschlossen werden". Another problem is that we do not know whether the Alkinoos mentioned by Philostratus, Vitae sophistarum, 1.24.23-32, as 'Alkinoos the Stoic' is identical with an Alkinoos mentioned by Hippolytus in a fragment preserved by Photius, Bibliotheca, cod. 48, 11b17-32, see Göransson, Albinus, 132-136. This author (p. 136) believes they are not identical and that (p. 135) "even if the possibility of an identity cannot be totally excluded, it is not probable that the Stoic Alcinous is the same person as the author of the Didaskalikos".

173. The authoritative edition is by Whittaker, Alcinoos (see Bibliography).

174. Both Whittaker, Plat.phil. 109, "Alcinous must have drawn upon a multiplicity of sources", and Göransson, Albinus, Ch. 6 The Didaskalikos : a work of many sources, are convinced that A. was a compiler and that (Göransson 132) he "cannot have been an eminent Platonist philosopher".

175. Alt, Weltflucht 42.

176. Alt, Weltflucht 47.

177. Alc., Didask. 5.156.35-37.

178. Alc., Didask. 16.6-7.

179. Alc., Didask. 17.20-25.

180. Alc., Didask. 17.173.5-15.
181. Alc., Didask. 24.176.43-44.
182. Alc., Didask. 173.17.9.
183. Alc., Didask. 25.177.16-35.
184. Alc., Didask. 16.172.15-19.
185. Alc., Didask. 25.178.38-39.
186. Alt, Weltflucht 151; Deuse, Unters. 86, note 17, is speaking here of 'die Neigung oder die Empfänglichkeit für das was zur eigenen Natur paßt', see also his note 37 on p. 92.
187. Alc., Didask. 178.35.38.
188. Alt, Weltflucht 151.
189. Alc., Didask. 1.152.2-4.
190. Alt, Weltflucht 218.
191. This list is the so-called 'Lamprias catalogue'. It is not complete; a total of eighteen books are not mentioned in it. See for this catalogue Ziegler, Plutarchos 61-66.
192. Jones, Plutarch 24.
193. See Vol. II, Ch. IV, § 4a-h.
194. Vol. II, Ch. IV, § 4h.
195. This section is based on Le Corsu, Plutarch et les femmes. Conclusion. The quotation is from p. 258.
196. Copleston, Hist.phil. I.2, 197.
197. Riès, Plutarque 146.
198. Plut., The E 392 E 19.
199. Plut., The E 392 E 19.
200. Plut., The E 393 A 20.
201. Plut., The E 393 B,C.
202. Plut., De defectu 428 F 35.
203. Bianchi, Plutarch 354 : "Der mythisch-theologische Komplex, wie er sich in der Schrift 'De Iside' darstellt, entspricht ... folgender Typologie von Dualismus : ein radikaler, nicht abgemilderter Dualismus, weil Vollkommmenheit und Unvollkommenheit mit ihren jeweiligen ontologischen 'Prinzipien' seit jeher bestehen, zumindenstens seit Anbeginn der Welt; ein dialektischer und nicht eschatologischer Dualismus, weil die Vollkommenheit niemals die Abgründe der Unvollkommenheit beseitigen kann; und schließlich ein pro-kosmischer

und nicht anti-kosmischer Dualismus, wenn auch mit notwendigen Einschränkungen."

204. Roscher, Lex.d.Mythologie, Bd. 6, 128/129. The story is retold by Plutarch in 'De Iside', 356 A 13 - 358 D 19.

205. See Vol. VI, Preface § 1.

206. Plut., De Iside 382-383 E-F 78.

207. Both Griffiths, Plutarch's De Iside, 17, and Alt, Weltflucht, 21, note 29, believe that De Iside is the later work, but the question is not really important for our theme.

208. Deuse, Untersuch. 38.

209. Alt, Weltflucht 16 : "... das Traktat über Isis und Osiris, in welchem Plutarch dem iranischen Dualismus geradezu Modellcharacter zumißt".

210. Plut., De Iside 369 E 46.

211. Plut., De Iside 369 B 45.

212. To my astonishment Valgiglio, Divinità 32/33, does not speak of these two principles. To Plut., according to this scholar, man himself is the cause of his own evil, which seems to an unwarranted conclusion.

213. Plut., De Iside 369 C-D 45.

214. Dillon, Middle Plat. 203.

215. Plut., De Iside 370 D-F 48.

216. Plut., De procreat. 1014 F.

217. Plut., De procr. 1015 A.

218. Plut., De procr. 1015 C.

219. Plut., De procr. 1015 E.

220. Plut., De procr. 1015 A.

221. Alt, Weltflucht 17.

222. Alt, Weltflucht 18.

223. Plut., Quaest.plat. 1001 B-C.

224. Plut. De procr. 1014 E.

225. Plut., De procr. 1014 B.

226. Plut., De procr. 1014 C.

227. Copleston, Hist.phil. I.2, 198. In his introduction to his Loeb Classical translation of 'De procreatione animae', 140-149, Cherniss showed that, although Plut. constantly appeals to Plato, he did not follow him at all faithfully; he manipulated Plato for his own philosophical ends.

Alt, Weltflucht 29, concludes : "Man wird Plutarch den ontologischen Dualismus zwischen Geist and Welt und die Anerkennung des Transzendenten nicht absprechen können ... Die Frage nach dem Bösen innerhalb des Kosmos sucht er von verschiedenen Seiten her zu lösen, in engerem Anschluß an den Timaios oder aber in einem für einen Platoniker kühneren dualistischen Konzept".

228. Plut., De sera 563 B 22 - 568 33.
229. Vol. I, Ch. I, § 7, Ch. III, §§ 9 and 15, pp. 158-159, and especially Ch. IV, § 11, pp. 243-247.
230. Plut., De facie 943 A 28.
231. Plut., De facie 943 B-C 28.
232. Alt, Weltflucht 96.
233. Plut., De facie 945 A 30.
234. Plut., De facie 945 D 30.
235. Plut., De facie 945 A 30.
236. Plut., De facie 945 A 30.
237. Plut., De facie 945 C 30.
238. Plut., De facie 945 A 30, F 30.
239. Plut., De genio 591 D-E.
240. Plut., De genio 591 E.
241. Plut., De genio 591 E.
242. Plut., De genio 592 C.
243. Plut., De genio 592 C.
244. Plut., De genio 592 A-B.
245. Alt, Weltflucht 100/101.
246. Dillon, Middle Plat. 211. Deuse, Unters. 45, speaks of 'eine klare Trennung von nous and psuchê' and of a 'dichotomische Deutung der Menschennatur'.
247. Att., Fr. 1.2.1.
248. Att., fr. 35. See also Deuse, Unters. 52.
249. Att., fr. 23.
250. Att., fr. 24.
251. Att., fr. 22.
252. Att., fr. 23.

253. Att., fr. 26.
254. Att., fr. 19.
255. Att., fr. 38b' this text is found in the Byzantine author Ioannes Philoponus, De aeternitate mundi 13-15.
256. Moreschini, Attico 486 : That the world is created does not mean that it is not eternal. "Il mondo è eterno ..., non in quanto è increato, ma è eterno in quanto lo conserva tale il volere e la provvidenza di dio" (fr. 4 Des Places).
257. Att., frs. 19 and 20.
258. Att., fr. 13.
259. Dillon, Middle Plat. 253 : "Here he is much more the dogmatic theologian than the philosopher".
260. Proclus, In Tim. comm. 394.17-22.
261. Att., fr. 11, from Iamblichus in Stobaeus.
262. Deuse, Unters. 55, note 31. See for this section also Baltes, Weltentstehung 45-62.
263. The classical source for his life is Porphyrius, Vita Plotini (see Bibliography).
264. See Vol. XI, Ch. III, § 61.
265. The reader will find a list of Plotinus' titles in Gerson, Plotinus X/XI. The chronological ordering is indicated in brackets; it corresponds by no means with Porphyry's ordering of the essays. Gerson's book also contains a very extensive Bibliography, the most recent as far as I am aware.
266. I am following here Zeller, Phil.d.Gr. III.2.2, 527/528 (1963).
267. Armstrong, Dualism 379.
268. Copleston, Hist. of Phil. I.2, 216.
269. Copleston, Hist. of Phil. I.2, 215.
270. Gerson, Plotinus XVI : "The fruit of his philosophy is obscure and only harvested with difficulty".
271. Porph., Vita 17-18.
272. Arnou, Désir de Dieu 33.
273. Porph., Vita 8.
274. Porph., Vita 13.
275. Porph., Vita 8.
276. Porph., Vita 9.

277. Porph., Vita 9.
278. Porph., Vita 1.
279. Arnoud, Désir de Dieu 23.
280. Arnou, Désir de Dieu 24/25.
281. Plot., Enn. 6.7.26.
282. Plot., Enn. 6.7.27.
283. Plot., Enn. 3.5.9.
284. Plot., Enn. 6.5.1.
285. All the quotations from Plot., Enn. 5.5.12.
286. Quotations from Plot., Enn. 6.7.26.
287. From Plot., Enn. 6.7.21.
288. From Plot., Enn. 6.9.9.
289. From Plot., Enn. 5.4.1.
290. Plot., Enn. 3.8.9.
291. About, Plotin et la conquête de l'un 7, says that after Plotinus every metaphysician will have to choose "sans compromis possible', between 'se définir comme philosophie de l'être et comme philosophie de l'un'. Halfwassen, Der Austieg 9, characterizes all Neoplatonism as a 'metaphysics of the one'. He speaks extensively of Plotinus' metaphysics of the Absolute in his Erster Teil, pp. 34-182.
292. Plot., Enn. 3.8.8.
293. Varessis, Andersheit 64 : "Das Eine/Gute ist das ontologische Prinzip der Wirklichkeit".
294. This does not mean that absolutely nothing can be said of him : the philosopher himself says that his God is simple, self-sufficient, perfect, eternal, infinite, omnipresent, and supremely good. See Gerson, Plotinus 16-20.
295. Varessis, Andersheit 70 : "Die Unaussagbarkeit des ersten Prinzips ist durch seine absolute Transzendenz bedingt; daher kann das Eine/Gute nicht durch Affirmation bestimmt werden und bleibt in gewissem Maße dem menschlichen Denken unzugänglich".
296. Plot., Enn. 6.9.6.
297. Plotinus seems to have felt that he was manoeuvring himself into a dead end in this way. Would non-awareness not mean that the One is simply non-existent, a void? For in the same passage he added that absence of self-knowledge does not comport ignorance. "Ignorance is something outside - a knower ignorant of the knowable - but in the solitary there is neither knowing nor anything unknown." The One has

'no need of self-intellection'. The ordinary reader will feel that he or she is led around in a circle here. Obviously Plotinus felt he was causing insolvable problems, for he said that "the mind reels before something thus alien to all we know", Enn. 6.9.7.

298. From Plot., Enn. 6.8.9.
299. Plot., Enn. 1.2.3.
300. Arnou, Désir 127.
301. "When the dead rise, there is no marrying nor giving in marriage", Mc. 12:25.
302. From Plot., Enn. 3.5.2.
303. Copleston, Hist.Phil. 2.1, 210.
304. Philip Merlan s.v. 'Emanationism'. Enc. of Phil. 1/2, 473 (1972).
305. Zeller, Phil.d.Gr. III.2.2, 560/561.
306. Arnou, Désir 158.
307. Plot., Enn 1.7.1.
308. Plot., Enn. 6.4.3.
309. Plot., Enn. 1.7.1.
310. Dodds, Preface XXV of Plot., The Enneads (see Bibliography).
311. In secondary literature it is often spoken of Plotinus' three 'hypostases'. However, he himself does not use this term exclusively for his three entities. He prefers to speak, in the true Hellenic tradition, of 'archai' or principles, see Gerson, Plot. 3.
312. Dodds, Preface XXVI to Plot., Enn.
313. Dodds, Preface XXVI/XXVII to Plot., Enn.
314. Plot., Enn. 5.1.6.
315. Plot., Enn. 6.9.5.
316. Baladi, Pensée de Plotin 92. Trouillard, Procession 4/5 : "Chez Plotin, l'altérité accentue son caractère d'opposition et d'inversion. Chaque ordre écarte de soi son origine en même temps qu'il la recherche; il la trahit en l'exprimant ... Et c'est sur cette puissance de négation que s'appuie l'âme qui déchoit. Elle se fixe et se captive dans l'antithèse ... Elle s'exalte et se nourrit d'opposition ... C'est dans par une prolifération de la négation, que nous passons de l'intelligible au sensible".
317. Plot., Enn. 5.1.7.
318. From Plot., Enn. 5.1.6.

319. As Gerson, Plot. 45 expresses it : "The One is necessarily productive, (but) what it produces is necessarily other than it".
320. Once again a problem remains unsolved.
321. Plot., Enn. 5.1.7.
322. Nous is 'closest to the One', Plot., Enn. 5.4.2. "Therefore, the closer something is to Intellect, the closer it is to the One, and the farther away from Intellect, the farther away from the One", Gerson, Plot. 46.
323. Plot., Enn. 5.9.6.
324. From Plot., Enn. 5.3.15.
325. Dodds, Preface XXVII to Plot., Enn.
326. Plot., Enn. 6.2.2.
327. From Plot., Enn. 5.9.9.
328. Dodds, Preface XXVII to Plot., Enn.
329. Plot., Enn. 4.1.1.
330. From Plot., Enn. 4.2.2.
331. From Plot., Enn. 4.3.4.
332. Plot., Enn. 2.9.
333. From Plot., Enn. 4.2.3.
334. Alt, Weltflucht 113.
335. From Plot., Enn. 4.8.8.
336. Plot., Enn. 3.4.3.
337. Plot., Enn. 1.1.10, 2.3.9; elsewhere he says that we are 'polla' = manifold, 1.1.9.
338. From Plot., Enn. 1.1.10.
339. From Plot., Enn. 2.1.5.
340. From Plot., Enn. 6.4.14.
341. Alt, Weltflucht 119/120.
342. From Plot., Enn. 6.4.15.
343. On Plotinus' soul-body dualism see Emillson, Plotinus, in Companions 2 (1991).
344. Porph., Vita 1.1.
345. Porph., Vita 8.
346. Plot., Enn. 2.4.

113

347. Plot., Enn. 2.4.2.
348. Copleston, Hist.Phil. I.2, 213.
349. It is a moot point whether Matter really is an emanation, albeit the last and lowest one. To quote, O'Brien, one of the scholars expressing himself with regard to this point [Plotinus on the origin of matter], shows himself firmly convinced that in Plotinus Matter is an emanation, see his Chapter I. He is combated on this point by two scholars, H.-J. Schwyzer and Kevin Corrigan. The first one holds that Matter cannot be generated, since Plotinus says it is 'indestructible'. I agree with O'Brien that indestructible does not necessarily mean ungenerated. In Christian theology the soul is generated but also indestructible (O'Brien's Chs. II & III). Corrigan assumes that there are in Plotinus levels or kinds of Matter, so that there are also several generations of Matter (O'Brien's Chs. IV-VII). I think, along with O'Brien, that there is very little in the Enneads to corroborate this point of view.
Varessis too, Die Andersheit 6, characterizes Plotinus' view as a 'system of emanations' in which physical reality is gradually derived from an absolute principle, with multiplicity gradually increasing in the same way. Pp. 12/13 she says that this principle of multiplicity is deduced from an all over-arching super-One in the context of a monistic emanation. She concludes (p. 13) that the question of the origin of Matter must exclusively be understood in the context of Plotinus' emanation concept. Matter (p. 16), as the lowest level of reality, cannot be considered without referring to his framework of emanations. She adds, however, that Matter is incorporeal, indestructible, and timeless, which is so because it exists as 'a product of eternal overflowing'.
350. Plot., Enn. 2.4.3.
351. Varessis, Andersheit 308 : "Als Andersheit schlechthin ist das Nicht-Seiende der Gegenpol zum Guten".
352. From Plot., Enn. 2.4.6.
353. From Plot., Enn. 2.4.8.
354. From Plot., 3.6.7.
355. From Plot., Enn. 2.4.14.
356. Terms from Plot., Enn. 2.4.14.
357. From Plot., Enn. 2.4.10.
358. Armstrong, Dualism 37.
359. Armstrong, Dualism 37.
360. Plot., Ennn. 1.5.

361. Trouillard, Purification 205, situates Plotinus on a very long line that began long before Plato : "Pourque le Plotinisme naquît, il fallait que des préoccupations religieuses venues principalement de l'Orient rejoignissent les exigences rationelles de la culture hellénique et platonicienne, déjà empreinte d'ailleurs de traditions religieuses. Il fallait que le très ancien dualisme du monde impur en du monde pur rencontrât la distinction platonicienne du sensible et de l'intelligible et fût transposé dans le registre noétique". It is known that Plotinus combated the Gnosis, but we may well ask how great the distance was between the Gnosis and himself, when we read in Trouillard, Purification 5, that "toute la doctrine des Ennéades peut être regardée comme une tentative de faire la **genèse de la connaissance humaine**. ou bien comme l'élaboration d'un **processus de l'affranchissement** pour l'esprit qui est dans chacun de nous" (Trouillard's emphasis).

362. From Plot., Enn. 1.8.5.

363. From., Plot. Enn. 1.8.3.

364. From Plot., Enn. 1.8.5.

365. From Plot., Enn. 1.8.3.

366. From., Plot., Enn. 1.8.8.

367. From Plot., Enn. 1.8.14.

368. From Plot. Enn. 1.8.3.

369. Plot., Enn. 1.8.4.

370. Plot., Enn. 4.7.13.

371. Plot., Enn. 1.8.14.

372. Armstrong, Dualism 37.

373. Plot., Enn. 2.9.9.

374. Plot., Enn. 4.4.22.

375. Plot., Enn. 4.3.12.

376. Plot., Enn. 4.3.12.

377. Plot., Enn. 3.2.1.

378. Plot., Enn. 3.2.2.

379. Plot., Enn. 1.8.15.

380. Plot., Enn. 3.2.2.

381. Plot., Enn. 2.9.9.

382. Plot., Enn. 4.3.15.

383. Plot., Enn. 4.3.24.

384. Plot., Enn. 4.8.1.
385. 2Cor.12:1-4.
386. Plot., Enn. 1.2.1.
387. Plot. Enn. 6.7.9.
388. Plot., Enn. 1.3.4.
389. Plot., Enn. 1.3.7.
390. Plot., Enn. 6.9.10.
391. Plot., Enn. 6.9.9.
392. Plot., Enn. 6.9.11.
393. Plot., Enn. 6.9.11.
394. Copleston, Hist.Phil. I.2, 216.
395. Gerson, Plotinus 138 says that "Plotinus is not interested in a crude soul-body dualism". It is not his primary concern, maybe, but this kind of dualism certainly is there. This scholar speaks here of 'a refined dualism'. P. 136 he writes that Plotinus' "distinctive form of dualism ... is something of a non-hylophormic composite and an additional principle, the true self. The composite is a part of nature, the product of the universal soul. The self is an independent principle in a human being, with a separate lineage in Intellect". I do not really understand this, but Gerson seems not to understand it either since he adds that "even if we grant the need to postulate a separate actuality to account for intellection, it remains deeply obscure how this is to be related to the actual composite". Perhaps it cannot be related at all, since the relation is dualistic.
396. Gerson, Plotinus 127 : "Plotinus can be described as a post-Aristotelian Platonic dualist".
397. Plot., Enn. 6.9.11.
398. Nonetheless, Wallis, Neoplatonism 97, calls him "a constructive metaphysician'. A good introduction to Porphyry is the article of Rudolf Beutler s.v. 'Porphyrios', PW XXII (1954).
399. Socr., HE 3.23.
400. Porph., Sententiae 32.
401. Porph., De abst. 1.29.
402. Porph., De abst. 1.30.
403. Porph., Ad Marc. 29.
404. Porph., De abst. 1.13.2.
405. Bouffartique et Patillon, Introduction (to Porph., De l'abstinence) LXII.

406. Porph., De abst. 1.57.
407. See also Vol. I, Ch. IV, § 11 (pp.248-250) and Vol. IX, Ch. IV, § 23a,b.
408. Porph., De abst. 2.46.2.
409. Porph., De abst. 2.43.2.
410. Porph., De abst. 2.47.1.
411. Porph., De abst. 2.61.1.
412. Porph., De abst. 2.61.6-7.
413. Porph., De abst. 2.61.8.
414. Zeller, Phil.d.Gr. III.2.2, 703.
415. Porph., Sent. 4.
416. Zeller, Phil.d.Gr. III.2.2, 708.
417. The classical source for Iamblichus' life is Eunapius, Lives of the philosophers 457-461. The fragments are edited by Dillon (see Bibliography) "from which", the editor writes p. 3, "solid information can be extracted only with difficulty and in small amounts". He concludes that "we know virtually nothing about the subject".
418. Damascius, Traité 1.86.3.
419. Wallis, Neoplatonism 118.
420. Damascius, Dubitationes 43.
421. Damascius, Dubitationes 54.
422. Zeller, Phil.d.Gr. III.2.2, 748.
423. Copleston, Hist.Phi. I.2, 219.
424. Proc., In Tim. 94C-D.
425. Procl., In Tim. 214A.
426. See Vol. VIII, Ch. VII, § 4b.
427. Stobaeus, Eclogae I.186.
428. Stobaeus, Eclogae I.184.
429. Stobaeus, Eclogae I.80; Iambl., De myst. 8.7.
430. Zeller, Phil.d.Gr. III.2.2, 765.
431. A.C. Lloyd s.v. 'Iamblichus', Enc. of Phil. 3/4 (1972).
432. Olymp., In Phaedr. Plat. nr. 142 = p. 114, 16-21.
433. Olymp., In Phaedr. Plat. nr. 143 = p. 114, 22-25.

117

434. Marinus, Life 26 (see Bibliography). Rosán presents his own translation of Marinus' Life in his 'Philosophy of Proclus', pp. 13-35.

435. Laurence J. Rosán s.v. 'Proclus', Enc.of Phil. 5/6 (1972).

436. Beierwaltes, Proklos 1 : "in Proklos ... hat die griechische Philosophie ihre Vollendung gefunden". Rosán, in the subtitle of his book on 'The Philosophy of Proclus' (see Bibliography), spoke of 'The Final Phase of Ancient Thought'.

437. We happen to know - it is really a rarity! - the exact dates of his life : 8.II.412-17.IV.485. This is possible because Marinus, Life 35, presents the horoscope of his birth and relates the date of death to a total solar eclipse (37).

438. The classical source of his life is the biography by his pupil Marinus, Life of Proclus (see Bibliography). For a modern decsription of his life and writings see the work of Bastid, Proclus, Chap. I La vie, le caractère et l'oeuvre de Proclus (see Bibliography).

439. Marinus, Life 10.

440. Marinus, Life 17.

441. For this subject see Bastid, Proclus, Ch. III Proclus commentateur de Platon.

442. The reader will find a list of his writings in Rudolf Beutler s.v. 'Proklos', PW XXIII.1 (1957), 191-208. Rosán, Philosophy of Proclus, has a long chapter (Chapter Three) on 'The Works of Proclus'.

443. Procl., Comm. in Plat. Parm. 1015.

444. This is Plutarch of Athens, not to be confused with the far better known Plutarch of Chaeronea.

445. Marinus, Life 29.

446. Marinus, Life 12.

447. Marinus, Life 12.

448. Marinus, Life 13.

449. Marinus, Life 15.

450. Marinus, Life 19.

451. Marinus, Life 18.

452. For the 'mystagogy' of Proclus see Trouillard, Mystagogie, Chap. II Le merveilleux dans la vie et la pensée de Proclus.

453. I am following Rosán, Philosophy of Proclus, here, Chap., Four Ontology.

454. Rosán, Philosophy of Proclus 94-95.

455. Rosán, Philosophy of Proclus 95.
456. Rosán, Philosophy of Proclus 96-97.
457. Bastid, Proclus 213.
458. Proclus, El.Theol., Prop. 5.
459. Proclus, El.Theol., Prop. 1. The somewhat singular use of 'participate' is explained by Dodds in Note 1.
460. Proclus, El.Theol., Prop. 2.
461. Proclus, El.Theol., Prop. 4.
462. Procl., Theol.plat. I.3.7.
463. Procl., Theol.plat. II.10.109.
464. Zeller, Phil.d.Gr. III.2.2, 854.
465. Proclus, El.Theol., Prop. 4.
466. Proclus, El.Theol., Prop. 116.
467. Proclus, El.Theol. Prop. 24.
468. Proclus, El.Theol., Prop. 116.
469. Trouillard, Mystagogie 71.
470. Proclus, Elem.Theol. Prop. 116.
471. Procl., Elem.theol., Prop. 11.
472. Procl., Elem.theol., Prop. 13.
473. Procl., Theol.plat. III.2.118.
474. Rudolf Beutler s.v. 'Proclus', PW XXIII.1 (1957), 210.
475. Procl., Elem.theol., Prop. 138.
476. Proclus, Theol.plat. III.9.39.18-19.
477. Proclus, Elem.theol., Prop. 138.
478. Procl., Elem.theol., Prop. 89.
479. Procl., Theol.plat. III.9.39.20-23.
480. Procl., De prov. 4.20.
481. Procl., Elem.theol., Prop. 56.
482. Procl., Elem.theol., Prop. 57.
483. Procl., Elem.theol., Prop. 75.
484. Rudolf Beutler s.v. 'Proklos', PW XXIII.1 (1957), 211.
485. Procl., Elem.theol., Prop. 11.

486. Procl., Elem.theol., Prop. 11.
487. Procl., Elem.theol., Prop. 30.
488. Procl., Elem.theol., Prop. 98, from which proposition also the foregoing quotations are taken.
489. Bastid, Proclus 209 : "La complication de ses doctrines a beaucoup nui à son prestige. Il témoigne d'un goût assez fâcheux pour les explications aussi contournées que minutieuses. Il cherche partout ses tirades, des oppositions, des analogies trop souvent artificielles, et d'où les contradictions de détail ne sont pas absentes. Il en résulte une prolifération extravagante d'entités inutiles".
490. See for a discussion of this subject Gersh, Kinêsis, Ch. III.
491. See Procl., Elem.theol., Prop. 30, 31, 33.
492. Procl., Elem.theol., Prop. 35.
493. Beierwaltes, Proklos 24.
494. Procl., Theol.plat. 4.16.209.
495. Zeller, Phil.d.Gr. III.2.2, 849.
496. Zeller, Phil.d.Gr. III.2.2, 851.
497. Procl., Elem.theol. 149.
498. See Vol. I, Ch. I, §§ 11 and 12.
499. Procl., Comm. in Parm. 6.1049.
500. Procl., Elem.theol., Prop. 123.
501. Zeller, Phil.d.Gr. III.2.2, 854.
502. Rudolf Beutler s.v. 'Proklos', PW XXIII.1 (1957), 218.
503. Procl., Elem.theol., Prop. 126.
504. Procl., Elem.theol., Prop. 120.
505. Procl., Elem.theol., Prop. 125.
506. Procl., Elem.theol. 139.
507. Procl., Elem.theol. 140.
508. Procl., Elem.theol., Prop. 139.
509. Syrianus, Met.comm. 144.4/5.
510. Syrianus, Met.comm. 11.28-32.
511. Syrianus, Met.Comm. 129.4, 165.34, 184.9,12.
512. Syrianus, Met.comm. 166.1, 167.9.
513. Syrianus, Met.comm. 11.21, 43,21.

514. O. Seeck (whom I am following in this passage) s.v. 'Syrianos', PW IVA (1932), 1757.
515. See for this subject Beierwaltes, Proklos 50-60.
516. Lloyd, Anatomy 109/110.
517. Procl., Theol.plat. 3.9, p. 137.
518. Procl., Theol.plat. 3.10, p. 138.
519. Procl., Theol.plat. 3.8, p. 134.
520. Procl., Theol.plat. 3.8, p. 134.
521. Procl., Elem.theol. 90.
522. Procl., Theol.plat. 3.8, p. 134.
523. Procl., Elem.theol., Prop. 159.
524. Procl., Comm. in Tim. 31A, 441.
525. Rudolf Beutler s.v. 'Proklos;, PW XXIII.1 (1957), 223.
526. Procl., Elem,Theol, Prop. 101.
527. Procl., Theol.plat. 3.14, p. 143.
528. Rudolf Beutler s.v. 'Proklos', PW XXIII.1 (1957), 228.
529. Copleston, Hist.phil. I.2, 223.
530. Bastid, Proclus 383 : "A travers toute l'oeuvre de Proclus il est beaucoup moins question du monde des phénomènes que de l'univers supersensible qui constitue pour lui la réalité véritable et qui semble suffire à expliquer toutes les apparences concrètes".
531. Zeller, Phil.d.Gr. III.2.2, 870.
532. Procl., Elem.theol., Prop. 72.
533. Procl., De mal.subs. 208.30.
534. Procl., De mal.subst. 220.37.
535. Procl., Elem.theol., Prop. 157.
536. Procl., Comm. in Tim. 43A (324-325).
537. Procl., Comm. in Tim. 30A (380).
538. Procl., Comm. in Tim. 42E (313).
539. Procl., Elem.theol., Prop. 199.

CHAPTER II

DUALISM IN THE NEW RELIGIONS
OF LATE ANTIQUITY

INTRODUCTORY

In the Graeco-Roman world, not excluding ancient Israel, religion was everywhere a public affair. Closely intertwined as it was with the state, it formed part of the public domain. The strict separation of Church and State that is characteristic of many modern democracies - one could think here of the Netherlands, France, and the United States, for instance - was completely alien to the world of Antiquity. On the other hand, there is Great Britain, where the Queen is the official head of the Church of England; we have also the Islamic countries (with the exception of Turkey) and Japan where this separation of Church and state does not exist. In the Graeco-Roman world public officials were, as a part of their function, the performers of the religious rites.

The citizens participated in them, thus fulfilling their civic and religious obligations (they would not have understood the distinction) simultaneously. Nobody thought of shirking these duties, with perhaps the exception of some eccentric philosopher. Doing so would have put down one as a bad citizen. Being unchurched or non-denominational did not exist for them. People might be irreligious, irreverant, or indifferent, but this would not prevent them from taking part in the public cult. There was no overt atheism either [1], no pertinent denial of there being a supernatural world. 'Impiety' existed; what was understood by it was the denial of the existence of the

Olympian gods. Socrates, for instance, was not accused of being an atheist but of introducing 'other gods'. But those who turned their backs on the Olympians, mainly philosophers, had divinities of their own, like Plato with 'the Good' or Plotinus with 'the One'.

It has been debated whether the ancients, the Greeks for example, recognized personal piety. There were prayers, and offerings were brought; people had their own favourite deities, often minor ones. Certainly. But on the whole the official cult as it was left little room for the personal and affective. In Volume I I wrote that "in Hellas the public domain was so extensive that it threatened to swallow up the religious life of the individual ... The veritably religious mind of the Greeks of whatever class or rank suffered painfully from the dominating official status of the Olympian system" [2]. Add to this that they did not feel wholly comfortable with their gods. They found them untrustworthy, capricious, and arbitrary; criticisms were directed against their moral behaviour. Furthermore, state theology showed considerable defects. The gods were neither eternal nor all-powerful; they were subjected to fate. Their blatant anthropomorphism was not compatible with authentic religion. The system did not contain an explanation of the origin of evil nor did it tell people how the cosmos and mankind had come about [3].

All this applies equally to official Roman theology and to the Roman public cult. No wonder, then, that ways out were sought and found. The escape routes were, of course, superstition and magic, which we find all over the ancient world. These enabled people to penetrate into the unknown and to gain some control over it by manipulating the gods, the unseen powers, and the forces of nature.

Some of the institutional escapes have already been discussed. Judaism and Christianity both presented a coherent world view. They spoke of the godhead as a person who could be approached as such, in a 'cor ad cor loquitur'. Since their God was a Creator, they could explain how the world and the human race had come into being. And, very importantly, they knew of the origin of evil. Both advocated a life of high moral quality - in contrast to the depravity of so many circles of the Roman society of Late Antiquity.

The Gnosis did not present such a coherent world view, because 'the' Gnosis did not exist. There were countless Gnostic sects with almost as many ideologies [4]. The attraction the Gnosis had for many people consisted in this that it concentrated on the origin of evil. Christianity and the Gnosis both won many adherents because they were religions of redemption; they taught people how to escape from a life that was sinful and morally imperfect. In the end Christianity won the day, the Gnosis being too fragmentated and too pessimistic, and Judaism being seen as fundamentally ethnic, in contrast to the universal appeal of the Christian creed.

However, long before the Gnosis and Christianity had begun to make their presence felt in the Roman Empire, and long before Judaism began to mean an alternative to some pagans, there had already been some deviant groups. In the sixth century B.C. and for some time later Pythagoreanism surely did not move within the orbit of the official Hellenic religion [5]. The clearest expression of its being non-conformist was the existence of the Pythagorean fraternities with their own peculiar life-style. Pythagoreans were vegetarians, for instance, an evident sign that they repudiated what was considered normal.

In Hellas proper we find several manifestation of the desire for an alternative. Let me first of all mention the popularity of the mysteries of Eleusis [6]. What attracted people to them was the promise of immortality, for the Olympian religion had very little to offer with regard to an afterlife. It is true that the mysteries stood under the protection of the city of Athens and were part of the official Athenian state-religion. They did not constitute a danger to official theology but rather added something to it, namely an eschatology. But when all is said and done, they were 'extra-territorial'. The mysteries took place, not in Athens where all events of importance occurred, but at some fifteen miles distance from the town in a 'temenos', a sacred domain. This means that the mysteries were fundamentally different from the polis religion and for all that Athens stood for as the capital of Hellenic culture, and of religious culture also.

Next there was Orphism [7], a vague subject admittedly. Anyhow, there existed Orphic poems. A religion based on scripture was something unheard of in the Hellenic world. In these poems incestuous and syncretistic elements are not uncommon. In the fragments a cosmogony and a cosmology can be detected that try to improve on Hesiod's Theogony. Then there is an anthropology or rather an anthroposophy that speculates on the nature and destiny of man. Finally, there is a strong tendency towards pantheism. It is a moot question whether Orphic sects existed, but there were people who called themselves Orphics and who possessed books upon which rites and mysteries were based. In any event we are dealing with tendencies and with people who stood more or less apart from the official polis religion.

PART I '... KOMMT DER NEUE GOTT GEGANGEN' : DIONYSUS-BACCHUS

1. Dionysus and the Greek religious establishment

a. A wild and elusive god

In Orphic theogony the last descendant in the line of the progeny of Chronos is Dionysus to whom we now turn [8]. His cult, or that of Bacchus, as he was also called, became very important [9]. Its origin was partly Greek (Mycenaean-Minoan), partly non-Greek (Thracian, Phrygian). In its Asian homeland the cult doubtless had a wild, emotional, even ecstatic character. That Dionysus did not form part of the original historical establishment of Hellas becomes apparent from the fact that Homer was negative about him : this god was 'mainomenos' = mad, frenzied, driving to madness [10], a term not used in praise.

Dionysus was a wild god. However, once he had arrived in Greece, his cult was tamed and made more fashionable. He became a member of the Olympian pantheon and changed from a vegetation god into a generic god of nature. And he made his way into Delphi where his star continued to rise, although he never succeeded in dislodging Apollo from his place of honour there. This god had a 'civilizing' influence on the newcomer. The two gods belong together and together they reign at Delphi, but they are different. Apollo's statue stood in front of the great temple, that of Dionysus at the back, at the dayside and at the nightside of existence. Apollo was associated with the sun, with light, with life and wisdom, Dionysus with death and revival, with frenzy and ecstasy [11]. There are marked elements of 'otherness', of dualism, in Dionysus and his cult. Louis Gernet says that he makes us think of the 'Other' : "he is an elusive god ... He is at the antipode of the world of the the Ideas". He is the embodiment of the antithesis, that is, he is fundamentally different from and opposed to the regular politico-religious establishment [12]. And Marcel Detienne writes that Dionysus is an "epidemic god which sets him apart from the other gods with their regular epiphanies that are programmed and embedded in the cultic order of the official feasts, everyone in its own time ... One meets him everywhere and he is nowhere at home" [13].

Nietzsche found this distinction so telling that he built his famous book 'The Birth of Tragedy' on it, with the opposition between the 'Apollinian' and the 'Dionysian' as its Leitmotiv [14]. And how is this today? Is there not a sharp opposition between, on the one hand, the logics of science, technology, bureaucracy, and on the other, the frenzy that, for instance, football evokes? Do many people not try to escape from the drabness and the boring regularity of ordinary life and their jobs (or from not having one) by using, preferably in company, hallucinogenic, psychedelic drugs that are considered to be 'mind-expanding'? And is not one of these drugs, one of the most powerful, called XTC = ecstasy?

In spite of all their efforts, the official authorities never succeeded in getting the Dionysus-cult fully under control. They tried to absorb it into the regular polis festivals but there always remained a residue of licentiousness and wildness in it, demonstrated by the fact that an enormous phallus, symbol of fertility and procreation, was carried around in processions. That the poleis were unable to regulate the cult wholly as they wished to do and felt uneasy with the situation [15], is shown by Euripides' 'Bacchae'. Pentheus, king of Thebes, is a fervent opponent of the cult. Disguised as a Bacchant, he goes out into the hills in order to see what the women, venerators of Dionysus, are doing there. But they discover and kill him [16].

The most disquieting and disturbing element of the cult were the 'orgies', outbursts of wildness. Mainly women, the inferior members of Greek society, took part in them. In winter-time they left city and home and hearth behind them and departed for the mountains. Clad in animal skins, they danced and shrieked ecstatically; they tore the sacrificial animals to pieces, devouring their meat raw. All that is connected with the Dionysiac cult stands diametrically opposed to the law and order the polis represented. It manifested a deep 'Unbehagen in der Kultur', in that very culture that we consider authentically 'Greek', a dissatisfaction with its religious aspects in particular.

b. The Dionysiac cult in the hellenistic Orient

It is to be expected that that cult of Dionysus, as a manifestation of religious discontent, would not be easily repressed nor that it would remain restricted to Hellas proper. We find it in the whole hellenistic Orient, in fact, and later in the romanized West. The conquest of the East by Alexander the Great opened the way for its spread.

The traditional polis religion had always been at home in Hellenic towns that were mostly small and homogeneously Greek. The hellenistic cities that were founded on the trail of Alexander's conquest, were usually much bigger. They also had mixed, cosmopolitan populations; one could think here of Alexandria, a real metropolis, with its large Jewish element. In these cities the ethnic Greeks often constituted only a minority. All kinds of divinities were venerated there. Many of these had their own 'thiasos'; the term denotes a religious guild or confraternity [17]. Such 'thiasoi' brought together the venerators of a specific godhead and took care of its cult, its festivals and sacrifices. Those of Dionysus-Bacchus were the most conspicuous and important among them, so much so that 'thiasos' could come to mean 'Bacchic revel or rout'. The inhabitants of hellenistic cities in the East could witness tumultuous processions, accompanied by frenetic dancing.

c. 'The religious crisis of the end of the fourth century'

Jeanmaire, whom I am following here [18], asks our attention for an important factor in what he calls 'the religious crisis of the end of the fourth century'. Socrates and Plato had given the impulse to a new development in Greek theology. Among the cultivated classes of Hellenic society the old polis religion had lost its appeal. It was considered too phantastic, too mythological, too close to superstition, and too much based on fear. The new philosophical concept preached an ideal of divine beauty, order, and goodness that was universalist and cosmic; it embraced the cosmos and mankind. Later philosophical developments, like Epicureanism and Stoicism, went into the same direction. The adherents of these new ideologies no longer wanted to have anything to do with the caprices and the vindictiveness of the gods. To be 'cool' was the new ideal, to have no fear, to remain impassive, even impassible, in short, to be what we call 'stoical'.

This new attitude, very much in vogue among the hellenized élites, met the Dionysian cult on its way. True enough, the members of its thiasoi concurred with the Epicureans and Stoics in this that they were not interested in the ancient social, political, and religious preconditions of polis life. But they were not 'cool', quite the contrary! The philosophical contempt for all that was physical was not theirs neither did they put a high price on reason. The venerators of Dionysus could find no satisfaction in the polis cult but also not in the new philosophical concepts. The Dionysian thiasoi recruited their members not from ranks of the intellectuals but among the common folk, among the city dwellers of different races, especially among women.

The populist character of the Dionysian sects is the reason why we possess only very few written testimonies about them. In a letter to his wife, Plutarch, in the second century A.D., states the difference between the philosophical creed and the Dionysian cult very clearly. He opposed the opinion that there exists no evil, no affliction (he is aiming at Epicureanism); instead, he praises the mysticism of the cult of Dionysus of which "we, as initiated, share the knowledge among us" [19].

Dionysiac celebrations were very popular in the cities of the hellenistic East. It is not diffucult to guess why. Dionysus/Bacchus was the god of the wine so that great quantities of this elixir were consumed in honour of the god. There was joyous, exuberant revelry with dancing and music in which male and female, old and young, and people of high and low social status took part. And all this was not just a fair or a colourful pageant; it was a religious occasion, even a sacrament. The theatre in particular stood under the protection of Dionysus.

2. Dionysus comes to Rome

We find Dionysiac celebrations and associations at a very early date in Sicily and southern Italy. This is no wonder, because these lands were thoroughly colonized by the Greeks. Much later, after Alexander, the cult found also a welcome home in Egypt. Some of the Ptolemaean Pharaohs acted as its official protectors.

As was to be expected, the cult travelled from southern Italy northward, to find a home in Rome. There were Bacchics in Rome and in Middle Italy around 200 B.C. The fate that befell them is related by Livius who found abhorrent what he had to tell; he was obviously stricken by fear. At first, he does not mention the name of the cult but soon it becomes apparent that he is speaking of that of Bacchus. The one who introduced it into Rome he says, was a nameless Greek, 'a dabbler in sacrifices and a fortune-teller' [20]. It is as if he asks the reader : can anything good come from such a man? The Greek operated in broad daylight but was 'a priest of secret rites performed by night' [21]. Livius says that the cult spread from Etruria to Rome like wildfire [22]. When the affair came to a head in 186 B.C. [23], one of the consuls publicly stated that the Bacchanalia "have long been celebrated all over Italy and now even within the City in many places"; he added that "there are many thousands of them (i.e. Bacchants)" [24].

3. The affair of 186 B.C.

a. The authorities investigating

At first, what happened in Rome remained concealed, but soon enough a consul was alerted and began to gather information [25]. He heard witnesses, and when he found he had been fully informed, he briefed the Senate. The horrified Patres entrusted the two consuls with the further conduct of the afffair.

Yet what were the Patres told? Everything we know about the occurrences of 186 B.C. stems from the pen of Livius, who wrote his report one and a half century later. Being more or less the official historiographer of Rome, he was wholly on the side of the authorities, of the public religion, and of the old and well-tested Roman customs. The horror of these already far-off days still echoes in Livius' words; to him nothing could be more alien to what he viewed as Roman than the Bacchanalia. So it was too with the authorities of 186 B.C. who acted against the Bacchics with the utmost severity, in a truly dualistic manner. No compromise was possible, not an inch given.

Livius did not attach much weight to the religious element, although he does mention it. It was, he thought, 'the delights of wine and feasts' that attracted so many people. We hear the same kind of accusations that were in later times directed against the Christians : the meetings soon degenerated into sexual orgies and promiscuous matings of free men and women. Worse still, there were also poisonings and secret murders. Livius did not ask himself for what reason Bacchics would kill one another. And how was it possible that such a horror remained unknown for so long? Well, "not even the bodies were found for burial ... Amid the howlings and the crash of drums and cymbals no cry of the sufferers could be heard as the debauchery and the murders proceeded" [26]. It was enough to send a shiver down the spine of a virtuous Roman.

One of the witnesses, a woman, knew more gruesome details still. At first, she declared, the rites were only for women; matrons acted as priestesses. The rites, originally confined to three days per year, were held with increasing frequency, finally taking place during five days every month. Men were now admitted too. "No form of crime, no sort of wrongdoing was left untried"; it was suggested that much homosexuality was practised. Even men and women of high rank participated. The behaviour of the Bacchics is described as frantic. Men sprang around, uttering prophecies, 'with fanatical tossing of their bodies'; women, dressed as Bacchantes, ran about with dishevelled hair and blazing torches [27]. When the consuls had informed of all the evidence, they informed the people from the Rostra [28].

b. Why Livius wrote as he did

Having perused this whole long report, the reader will be struck by the fact that the names of Dionysus-Bacchus are not so much as mentioned. What the nature of this cult exactly was is not divulged. Livius concentrates wholly on the sensational and unsavoury aspects of it : debauchery, promiscuity, frenzy. It is not inconceivable that, even at this distance of time, Livius did not want to be too specific about the Dionysiaca due to a residual fear that such things might recur. Instead, he tried to instil a healthy fear into his readers of what would come from it. However, it cannot be wholly fantasy what he had to tell. There can be no doubt that Bacchic thiasoi existed in Italy, even in Rome, and that this cult had an orgiastic character.

c. Action against the Bacchics

The authorities reacted with great vehemence, obviously intending to stamp out the cult root and branch. The citizenship was asked to offer the names of Bacchics to the authorities. Many of them were caught when trying to flee; the leaders of the cult could be arrested. It was said that more than seven thousand men and women were involved. The whole neighbourhood of Rome was scoured for culprits who had succeeded in escaping from the city. Many were thrown into prison, but many more were killed, probably summarily. It may suprise the reader that the Bacchanalia were not completely forbidden, perhaps from fear of offending the god. But the praetor urbanus was to be informed of meetings with more than a hundred persons present; sacrifices might be offered but by no more than five persons [29].

d. What the authorities feared

Yet what made the authoirities clamp down on this cult, causing so many fatal victims, many of whom will have been innocent of the atrocities they were accused of? What made them suggest to the people that, if this horror was allowed to grow, it would 'crush the state'? "It is already to great to be a purely private matter; its objective is the control of the state" [30], no less. Was the cause of their terror their opinion that the Bacchic cult was 'a false religion' [31], and that its rites were 'vile and alien' [32]? This certainly was an important motive for the repression. The authorities who were the guardians of the public cult were highly distrustful of rites that were imported from elsewhere, especially from the East. But the fear of contagion also played a role. "I am not free of anxiety", said the consul on the Rostra, "lest even some of you, citizens, might go astray through error" [33].

There is yet another element in this affair that may easily be overlooked. The speaker on the Rostra sketched it as something that was typically feminine. "A great part of them are women, and they are the source of this mischief." And the men? The men who partake are effeminate, 'very like the women' [34]. Obviously the authorities detected in the Bacchanalia a threat to the macho society that Rome was and to its fundamentally masculine character. Another thing to which they objected was the foreign origin of the cult; it was felt as un-Roman, even as anti-Roman, thriving as it did on ecstasy and frenzy. And then there was its secrecy, its preference for the veil of darkness. Authorities nowhere and never feel at ease with movements and societies that operate in obscurity. All this was felt as a threat to the fabric of Roman existence.

e. Dualistic oppositions

There were quite a number of dualistic oppositions in the affair of 186 B.C. : day versus night, openness versus secrecy, public religion versus private piety, reason versus frenzy, the austere versus the emotional, male versus female, masculine versus feminine, the authentically Roman versus foreign trash. My definition of dualism says that the unbridgeable opposition can grow so strong that the inferior pole must be destroyed. The Romans found the Bacchic cult to be deeply inferior indeed. The campaign of destruction led to an almost complete result, for afterwards very little was heard of it in Rome and Middle Italy.

4. The survival of Dionysus-Bacchus

In the much smaller proportions that were permitted by the senatusconsultum the Bacchic cult subsisted, probably mainly in the higher circles of Roman society. There is hardly evidence of this in writing but somewhat more in iconography [35]. Pictures that have been preserved show that Dionysus was venerated and celebrated long after 186 B.C. But Jeanmaire feels that it is impossible to decide whether in these pictures we are dealing with simple acts of devotion or with a full-blown initiation into the Bacchic mysteries such as still occurred in the hellenistic East [36]. From a later time, around the beginning of our era, we have those magnificent frescoes on the walls of a villa in Pompeii, baptized the 'Villa of the Mysteries', and those discovered in a villa in the Farnesina gardens in Rome. There cannot be the slightest doubt that they represent an initiation [37].

This shows already that not all members of Roman high society were impervious to the lure of the Bacchic cult. We can also point to Mark Antony who, during his stay in Asia Minor and Egypt, posed as the 'new Dionysus', while his paramour Cleopatra was the 'new Isis' [38]. Their success in the hellenized East was great, but Roman officialdom was not pleased with what they considered an unworthy masquerade. That other contender for Caesar's heritage, Octavianus-Augustus, won the struggle for power by posing as the guarantee of Roman religion and austerity. But the idea was not wholly dead, for later Emperors like Traian and Antoninus Pius thought also fit to dub themselves 'neos Dionysos', the new Dionysus, that is to say, only in the East. This shows that the Dionysian cult continued to flourish until it was finally superseded by the Christian religion.

PART II ISIS

1. The lure of the Orient

In spite of often grim opposition by the authorities, oriental religions always had a great fascination for the public at large, especially when they were connected with 'mysteries', cultic rites with a mysterious and secret character. These appealed to large sections of the pagan world, not only in the East, in the West too; they seemed to fill a gap, to supply something that people missed in the rather arid official theology. The state cult was too public to many people, not private, not personal enough. In Vol. XI I related how Judaism, although this was not really a mystery religion, had the sympathy of many educated Romans, especially women, and that the authorities did not approve of this [39]. However, Judaizers, proselytes, and sympathizers were not persecuted as the Christians were.

Christianity, that was far more a mystery religion than Judaism, had much against it in the eyes of the pagan Romans : it was accused of secrecy and of holding nightly conventicles in obscure places; it was of foreign, oriental origin, never a recommendation in official circles; its adherents did not take part in the official cult and were, in consequence, bad citizens. But the real crux was that, whereas the Roman Empire was a universal one, the Christian Church had its own claim to universality. All this has been sufficiently related in the long Chapter I of Volume XII. But in these first centuries Christianity had to compete with other mystery religions. One of the most successful of these was the Isis cult.

2. The home of the Isis cult

With the goddess Isis we find ourselves in ancient Egypt, but not in the time of the pyramids and the Old Kingdom, when she is hardly mentioned, nor in the Middle Kingdom, when she is known but not yet venerated. Her cult begins in the New Kingdom, particularly in the Delta and further south in the region of the Fayûm [40]. From then on she went from strength to strength, rapidly becoming the most imposing Egyptian goddess, the Mistress of the House of Life, who absorbed many other divinities so that she came to be called 'the one with the innumerable names' [41]. Equated with many godheads as she is, she also had many functions, mostly connected with matters of life and death. She protects the dead and brings about rebirth; it is she who causes the Nile to flood and makes nature start all over again at the New Year; she provides the harvest, and she is also a magician.

3. The myth of Isis and Osiris

a. The original version of the myth

As everyone knows who has only once heard Sarastro's great, solemn bass aria in Mozart's 'The Magic Flute', the names of Isis and Osiris are quoted in one breath. In the oldest Egyptian version [42] - but the myth was constantly rearranged - Isis was the wife of King Osiris who was at the same time her brother. But Seth, the evil god of darkness, kills Osiris out of jealousy, because he is a good king, such as Seth never can be. Osiris is buried in some unknown place, but Isis, helped in this by her sister Nephthys, finds the grave over which the sisters sit in mourning. Isis stretches herself over the corpse in which, however, still so much vital force is left that she becomes pregnant. Osiris is revived and now becomes the king of the dead in the underworld. Isis retires to the marshes of the Delta where she gives birth to her son Horus. Later we see him as the heir and successor to his father Osiris. This is the basic form of the Isis-myth [43]. Later versions adorned it with many colourful details, but the upshot is that Isis became the great goddess of nature and, more in particular, the mistress of its mysterious forces, including magic. No wonder then that she had such a wide appeal.

b. Plutarch's version

The best-known version of the myth, beloved in the Hellenistic world, is that presented by Plutarch in his 'De Iside et Osiride'. I related this story in the Preface to Vol. VI (§ 1). The reader who knows that volume must forgive me for repeating what I wrote there. Plutarch's story is of the utmost importance to our overall theme, for in that Preface I called him a precursor of me as an historian of dualism. Had he known the term already, he would have used it. Plutarch, who had travelled in Egypt, was fascinated by the antagonistic elements in Egyptian religion and mythology. In his version Seth is called Typhon and is a mythological monster. Rather fantastically, the author explains the name 'Isis' by deriving it from the Greek verb 'oida' = to know. In this way he turns the goddess of nature into one of knowledge for which he uses the word 'gnoosis'. Of course, divine knowledge is meant. The mortal enemy of that wisdom is Typhon who kills Osiris. Later Isis restores her brother to life.

Plutarch interprets this myth, as he says himself, 'philosophically'. He distances himself from the crude details it contains and wants to present a loftier version, instead. Although it appeals to him to turn the old mythological lore into a geographical allegory in which Osiris is the Nile, Isis the earth, and Typhon the sea, this does not really satisfy him as an explanation. The divine trio is also identified with fundamental and opposed natural forces, such as generation and decay. Plutarch speaks here of 'two opposed principles and two antagonistic forces' in nature and the universe. In his dualistic cosmological theory the universe has its origin in two opposed principles or 'archai'.

Plutarch did not present his theory as something shockingly new. Quite to the contrary, he was entirely in tune with the ideas that were current in his days. Most philosophers and most educated people thought along dualistic lines. What he did was to provide this dualism with some sort of theory and with a history. It is important to note that he gave the popular Isis-myth a strongly dualistic colour, for, to quote his concluding words, "the creation of this world is complex, resulting, as it does, from two opposing influences". Let me quote what Solmsen has to say on this subject. "The myth as Plutarch presents it does not point to monotheism but to a dualistic scheme, two opposing principles, one benevolent, the other destructive. They are engaged in a perennial struggle for domination" [44]. In this dualistic version the myth made its way through the Roman world.

4. Isis' entry into Rome

Egyptian deities were venerated in Sicily and in South Italy already in the second century B.C. [45]. There was a statue of Isis in Pompeii [46]. Apuleius says that an Isis-society existed in the days of Sulla, but he does not state where. Perhaps in Rome? In any case, he is not speaking of the cult in Magna Graecia [47]. It was a secret and private cult at first but soon enough it came into the open. Isis appeared even in such a hallowed place as the Roman Capitol, for altars of this foreign divinity stood there; in 59 B.C. the Senate ordered them to be destroyed, but this action had to be repeated in later years [48]. Venerators of Isis were bold enough to brave the Senate obviously; they were numerous and influential enough to force the Patres to give in. In 43 B.C., one year after Caesar's death, it was officially decided to build a temple for Serapis and Isis in Rome [49] which of course implied a recognition of their cult by the state. There is, however, no evidence that this temple was actually erected [50].

But it was not the Senate that took this decision; it was the triumviri (Octavian, Mark Antony, Lepidus) who were responsible for it. They probably hoped to win the favour of the populares among whom sympathy for Isis was strong and who were just as much pro-Caesar as the Senate was anti. According to the Belgian scholar Lambrechts, "in this period Isiacism in Rome reprensented a force to be reckoned with" [51]. In that same year a Roman official, M. Volusius, was in danger of losing his head, because he sympathized with the murderers of Caesar. He clad himself in the vestments of an Isis devotee; the robe was lent to him by a priest of the goddess. In this disguise he made good his escape from Rome to the camp of Caesar's enemies, quite alone and along the public road. In order not be recognized, he wore an Anubis mask. Could anything be more 'Egyptian' [52]?

5. The offensive against Isis

This spring was soon over. Octavianus, the later Augustus, was contested by Mark Antony in his bid for power. The fact that his rival and his Queen Cleopatra had paraded themselves as Dionysus and Isis made him very averse to Egyptian deities. Once back in Rome, now completely triumphant, Augustus no longer hid his utter contempt for all those new oriental religions that were invading Rome [53]. "He did not allow the Egyptian rites to be celebrated inside the pomerium (= the sacred domain of the inner city)" [54]. This was in 28 B.C., but seven years later it was established that "the Egyptian rites were again invading the city". The prohibited area was then enlarged to one mile from the town [55]. It is, however, remarkable that the cult itself was not forbidden; obviously, its eradication was considered impossible and imprudent.

The irritation the Roman authorities felt against the Isis cult was brought to a head in the days of Tiberius. Flavius Josephus has an odd story to tell about an event that took place in A.D. 19. Fulvia Paulina, a married high society lady, was known for her exemplary behaviour. A Roman knight, Decius Mundus, being madly in love with her, did all he could to seduce her, even to the point of offering her an exorbitant sum to spend one night with him. All his efforts proving hopeless, he decided to commit suicide. But when he was about to kill himself, Ida, a freedwoman of his house, informed him that she would need no more than a quarter of the sum he had offered to Paulina, in order to bring her to his bed.

Ida knew that the lady in question was very much devoted to Isis. Accordingly, she went to the priests of her cult and promised them the sum Mundus had given her, if they were ready to help her. Having heard of Mundus' infatuation and being not averse to the money, they visited Paulina and told her that the god Anubis had fallen in love with her and desired not only to have dinner with her but also to sleep with her. She went to the temple and in the dark Mundus - yes, who else? - came to her and had intercourse with her. The next day the stupid woman bragged left, right and centre about her having been visited by a god. Two days later she met Mundus who revealed to her that this Anubis had really been him; he had the affrontery to add that this trickery had saved him a lot of money.

Paulina was beside herself when she heard this; she informed her husband who told Tiberius. The Emperor took the most drastic action. The guilty Isis priests and Ida were crucified; the temple was razed to the ground [56], and the statue of the goddess was thrown into the Tiber. Mundus himself got off with being exiled, for Tiberius found that the deed he had committed was what the French would today call a 'crime passionel' [57].

A few elements deserve our attention. The Isis cult was supposed to be popular especially with women; it had a reputation of lasciviousness. It is evident that it had found its way into Rome again, although in all probability not into the pomerium. The Roman authorities would have nothing of it. Tiberius hated foreign cults, this Egyptian one too, "compelling all who were addicted to such superstitions to burn their religious vestments and all their paraphernalia" [58]. The telling word here is 'superstition' : the Isis cult was profoundly different from its official Roman counterpart.

6. The triumph of Isis

The triumphant march of the Isis cult proved unstopppable; there was no fighting against its popularity. It was Caligula who, around A.D. 40, accorded it the status of a recognized Roman religion. A temple for Isis and Serapis was built in Rome around A.D. 70, but outside the pomerium, on the Campus Martius so that it got the name of the Temple of Isis Campensis = Isis in the fields. Apuleius says that she was 'the object of pious devotion' there [59]. There was a three-days Isis festival during which Osiris' death, Isis' complaint, and the god's resurrection were reenacted and celebrated. That the cult had a public character appears also from the fact that the rites began with prayers for the sovereign, the Senate, and the entire Roman people [60]. Still higher rose the star of Isis when Caracalla allowed her around A.D. 200 to enter the pomerium; both she and Osiris were then afforded magnificent temples on the Quirinal and the Caelius.

It is evident that, in the course of time, Isis had acquired an outstanding position in Roman life. She even became, as Witt expresses it, 'the goddess darling of the Roman Emperors' [61]. Processions marched through the streets of the city in which priests in white vestments and with shorn heads walked, dancing to the music of exotic instruments. How far Rome had drifted from her religious moorings is shown by the fact that the spectators could see the priests wearing the dog's head of Anubis [62].

Two groups of people will have viewed this spectacle with disgust : pagans who remained true to their forefathers' religion, and Christians. Indeed, Wissowa was right when he stated that all those oriental mystery religions were destroying the Roman state cult. This scholar is convinced that they would have triumphed if the Christian religion had not finally won the day [63].

7. The interior life of the Isis cult

What made the Isis cult so attractive to the Roman public, especially, so it seems, to the less privileged [64]? Sharon Heyob writes that "many of the foreign cults that made their way to Rome at the beginning of the second century B.C. were well suited for the gathering of subversives from the lower classes of Roman society. Such religions appealed greatly to the masses to whom the Roman religion was dry and meaningless. The pomp of their festivities and the awesomeness of their mysticism were a welcome substitute for the perfunctory contractual tone of the state religion" [65]. The Isis cult appealed strongly especially to women, because she was a woman herself and was acquainted with birth, marriage, and death [66].

An important feature of the cult is that it was well organized; it was really a 'Church'. It had its temples and chapels, its liturgy and festivals. There was also a priesthood, so conspicuously different from that of the

Roman state religion. Isis priests were numerous, while there were also female ones. This gave women the idea that they were fully acknowledged. Perhaps there resided a kind of high priest in Rome.

As is usual in esoteric communities with their predilection for the sacred number 'three', the Isis cult knew three degrees of initiation. The last and highest degree was that of the 'pastophoroi'; these formed the college of those who possessed the right to carry around in the processions the little shrines with the sacred statues. Apuleius relates that he enjoyed the privilege of becoming a member. He had to shave his head and proudly showed his bald pate to everyone, without in the least feeling embarassed by it, as balding Romans usually were. Earlier, in preparation to his acceptance into the first degree, he had decided to abstain henceforward from animal food; vegetarianism is quite common in esoteric societies [67].

This same author left us a description of an initiation (into the first degree). On the day before the initiate was bathed and purified; fasting all day and abstaining from wine formed part of the preparations. When the sun declined, the priests clad him or her in a white robe and led the candidate into the temple to spend the night there. In the early morning the initiate was placed on a wooden platform, right in front of the statue of Isis, with a long precious cope on the shoulders, a garland of flowers on the head, and a lighted torch in the hand. When the initiation was over, there were banquets, with a ceremonial dinner on the third day [68].

The Isis liturgy was really impressive. Every morning, when the temple was opened, the white curtains that hid the statue of the goddess, were drawn back. The priests in their white linen vestments appeared and prepared the altars; they brought fire and water for the libation. This ceremony was called the 'opening' of the godhead; the fire and the water were thought to have a (spiritually) therapeutic function. The matins were sung, to announce the beginning of the day [69].

But however attractive this daily liturgy might be, the really grand thing for a novice was the initiation into the sacred mysteries. We know nothing of their contents ; the strictest secrecy was imposed upon the devotees. Apuleius mysteriously speaks of books kept in a secret place in the temple, "books written with unknown characters, partly printed with figures of beasts declaring briefly every sentence, partly with letters whose tops and tails turned round in fashion of a wheel, joined together above like the tendrils of a vine, whereby they were wholly strange and impossible to read of the profane people". Priests interpreted these signs for him [70]. We here detect the dualistic distinction of the initiated and the common run, of the sacred and the profane. You, studious reader, says Apuleius, would love to know what I saw and heard, but alas, my tongue is tied; I may not disclose anything. But then he lifts a tip of the veil by telling us that "he approached near hell, even to the gates of Proserpina, and after I was ravished throughout the elements, I returned to my proper place. About midnight I saw the sun brightly shine; I saw likewise the gods celestial and the gods infernal, before whom I presented myself and worshipped them" [71].

8. The great prize

What would the Isis devotee win by dedicating him- or herself to the goddess? The prize was very great, indeed, but would be gained only on the condition that the devotee would always remain bound and subjected to her; he must stay in her service forever. But when this basic condition was fulfilled, "you shall", so speaks the goddess herself, "live glorious by my guide and protection, and when after your allotted space of life you descend to the underworld, you shall see me there in that subterranean firmament, shining ... in the darkness of Acheron and reigning in the deep profundity of Styx, and you shall worship me as one who has been favourable to you. And if I perceive that you are obedient to my commandment and addicted to my religion, meriting by your constant chastity my divine grace, know then I alone may prolong your days above the time the fates have appointed and ordained" [72]. Now we see what the great prize was : a long life followed by immortality.

9. How to not be an ass

We should not lose sight of the fact that the story of 'the golden ass', as Apuleius' 'Metamorphoses' are often called, is an allegory [73]. It is about a certain Lucius (the author's name was Lucius Apuleius) who relates it in the I-form. Travelling through Greece, this Lucius comes to Thessaly where he encounters a wealthy lady called Byrrhaena in whose house he stayed for some time. Here he becomes enamoured by a slave girl called Fotis; he was not yet addicted to chastity then.

This slave girl was the servant of a famous enchantress whose name was Pamphile. One day, spying on the sorceress, he saw how she rubbed herself with a certain ointment and in doing so changed herself into an owl. Having seen this scene, Lucius vehemently desired to become an owl himself, for this bird that can see in the dark is the image of wisdom, the favourite emblem of the goddess Athena. He implores Fotis to bring him this ointment - "O, Fotis, my honey, I pray you by your sweet breasts!" -, but cautiously makes her promise that he will return to his human shape after the experiment. But the girl inadvertently brings him the wrong ointment which changes him into an ass. Worse still, Fotis has no idea how to transform him back into a man. So he has willy nilly to live in an asine shape. Thus far the meaning of the allegory is clear. Lucius is living in such a stupid way that it can hardly be called human. He fritters away his time and hopes to find wisdom in the wrong way and the wrong place. He really makes an ass of himself.

As an ass he has to serve many masters but finally he manages to escape. Having arrived on the sea shore near Corinth he decides to implore the help of Isis. Seven times he plunges himself imto the sea "which number of seven is convenable and agreeable to holy and divine things, as the worthy and sage philosopher Pythagoras has declared" [74]. Once again, it is evident what is happening. The 'ass' frees himself of his savage and inhuman masters (= the passions) and is now turning into the direction into which real wisdom is to be found. While praying to Isis, he has a vision of her, rising out of the sea and coming to him. She reveals herself to him as "the natural mother of all things, mistress and governess of all the elements, the initial progeny of worlds, chief of the powers divine, queen of all that are in the underworld, the principal of them who dwell in heaven, manifested alone and under one form of all the gods and goddesses" [75].

Isis orders him to go to the town where a solemn procession in her honour will take place. She does not say which town she means, Corinth, or Rome perhaps? Anyhow, Lucius, still in the shape of an ass, does as he is told and sees the great procession walking through the streets. At the end the great priest strides whom, in a vision, Isis has ordered to give a garland of roses to an ass. As soon as Lucius has devoured this garland, he feels himself changing from an ass into a man. The priest tells some attendant to give him a linen robe and says that he has suffered enough now for turning to servile pleasures and enjoying the folly of his youthfulness. It had all been poor Fotis's fault who had entangled him in this maze of miserable wanderings [76]. What now happens to him is that he is 'renatus', reborn [77], 'a man raised from death to life' [78]. This is the gist of the whole story. It bears out the dualistic opposition of the sensuous, really subhuman life of ordinary people and the high-minded, truly human life of the Isis devotee.

PART III MITHRAS

1. The home of Mithras

Mithras (or Mithra or Mitra) is one of the oldest names in the Indo-European pantheon. He is an Iranian divinity, or even more ancient than that, dating from the time that the Aryan tribes had not yet split into Iranians and Indians [79]. His name contains the root 'mei' = to bind [80]; if this is correct, his name may be rendered as 'compact'; he is the protective deity of contract and agreements, but also of cattle-herding and the light of dawn [81].

Our knowledge of this god comes from two main sources, Vedic literature and the Avesta [82], and here in particular from the tenth Yasht [83], and from the incredibly numerous archaeological remains, a great many of them within the frontiers of the Roman Empire. Beck mentions over four hundred find-spots; further there are some thousand dedicatory inscriptions and about eleven hundred and fifty pieces of sculpture. But, as this scholar somewhat ruefully adds, "literary references to Mithras are as scarce as the material remains abound" [84].

2. Mithras as an Iranian godhead

Mithras began his career as an Iranian godhead. 'As part of the dual divinity 'Mithra-Varuna', he was an important figure in Vedic theology [85]. But when Zoroaster and his theology gained the upper hand in Iran, Mithra suffered a serious setback. The great prophet had no use for other divinities than Ahura Mazda and his eternal opponent Ahriman. Mithras does not belong to the divine beings that surround Ahura Mazda, the Amesha-Spenta. In orthodox Zoroastrian theology Mithras is no more than a subordinate spirit without much significance [86].

We know, however, that Zoroastrianism did not long exist in its pure original form. Discarded divinities reclaimed and regained their places. Mithras celebrated a come-back for which he had to pay a price : he had to adapt himself to the dualistic Zoroastrian system. Thus he became an ally of Ahura Mazda and helped him combat the Evil Spirit; in consequence, he had the function of a war-god [87]. "The entire world is divided into two : those who claim to be the true worshippers of Mithra and those who are branded as not". And woe to those who provoked his anger! "Usually he smashes an entire nation to punish a few miscreants who seem to be readily available to provide the pretext for the carnage" [88]. Mithra was given his great festival, the Mihragan, which lasts six days, between 2nd and 8th October [89].

3. Mithraic legends

Mithras was at the centre of a great many legends. He is said to have been born from a rock. Since it was often thought that the firmament was made of bluestone, this may explain why he was a light god. On images we see the little boy covered with a Phrygian cap and armed with a knife. Once grown up,

Mithras encounters the Sun with whom he has a conflict. He remains triumphant and enters into an alliance with his defeated enemy. The god is often identified with the sun, the Sol Invictus, the sun who is invincible [90]. A very important element of the legend is the struggle with the bull. Mithras acts like a toreador. He seizes the animal by the nostrils with his left hand, hurls it to the ground, and with his right hand plunges his knife into its flank. Presentations of this bull-killing were found in a great many Mithras sanctuaries; they played an important part in the mysteries.

4. The functions of Mithras

a. Mithras as a protective deity

Mithras was not the supreme godhead of the Iranian religion - this was Ahura-Mazda -, but he mediates between the highest god and mankind. By the same token he stands midway between Ahura-Mazda and Ahriman [91]. As the protector of the human race we see him constantly fighting malevolent elements and providing the earth with good things. He prevents the sun from scorching the earth (as Ahriman wanted it to do) by subjecting it to his will. He pierces a rock with an arrow so that water gushes forth from it. And what about that bull that is slain? In all probability we should see in this bull-killing a sacrifice, the 'sacrificium mithraicum'. The gore of the animal fructifies the earth, while from his seed other animals originate. But the spirit of evil does not sleep! A scorpion, an animal that typically belongs to Ahriman, appears and makes away with the bull's testicles.

b. The cosmological Mithras

Mithras is not only the protective deity of mankind, he is even the origin or creator of all that is on earth. He is the firm opponent of all that is bad and impure. There was no room for orgiastic rites in his cult. All that he wanted was purity and chastity. Whoever lived up to his lofty precepts would be guaranteed a place in the hereafter.

The cosmological nature of the Mithras religion appears from its predilection for the number seven. This is a sacred number, because there are seven main celestial bodies, the five planets visible with the naked eye plus the sun and the moon. In consequence, Mithraists venerate seven divinities and have a week of seven days. There were also, as we shall see, seven degrees of initiation [92]; each one of these degrees was placed under the protection of one of the celestial seven [93].

5. The westward journey of the Mithras cult

The Mithras cult slowly found its way westward from the Iranian highland. The god became popular in Babylon; his cult spread north along the two streams into Armenia and Bactria, and along the southern shores of the Black Sea to Pontus. The fact that this country had six kings with the name 'Mithradates' ('Mithridates') is sufficient proof of his popularity there. His cult was also found in other parts of Asia Minor, especially in Cilicia, the home of the pirates whom Pompey fought [94]; Plutarch relates that they instituted the rites of Mithras there [95]. The Cilicia of the pirates was an important turntable on Mithras' road from Iran to the West. According to Robert-Alain Turcan, in this robbers' nest the god had become "already sufficiently differentiated from the eastern Mithra to contain the seeds of Graeco-Roman Mithraism" [96].

For a long time Mithras came no farther than the eastern half of Asia Minor. Cumont stated that he remained unknown to the Hellenic and hellenistic world [97]. "Ancient Greek authors speak of him as a foreign godhead [98] ... That he remained so far distant from the great centres of ancient civilization explains why Mithras came so late to the Romans" [99]. It was only when Rome had conquered the whole of eastern Asia Minor, together with Armenia, that the Mithras cult began to spread westward again [100]. His triumphant entry into the Roman Empire occurred not earlier than the first half of the second century A.D. It is typical, for instance, that not one reference to the eastern god is found in Pompeii, that fell in A.D. 79.

The earliest mention of Mithras in Rome is an inscription saying that a certain Alcimus made the gift he had promised to the god [101]. This Alcimus was in all probability a slave of the prefect of Traian's Praetorian Guard; if this is correct, the date of the inscription must be A.D. 102. Vermaseren remarks that this points to the fact that it was through the slave population that the new cult penetrated into Roman high society [102].

6. Devotees of Mithras

Slaves formed only one of the groups that introduced the cult into the Empire; there were many orientals among them who found masters even in distant parts of the western Empire. A second group were the legionaries among whom were also many easterners; military reallocations brought them to the farthest corners of the Empire [103]. Soon enough the Mithras cult was discernible along the Rhine [104]. A third group were the merchants who maintained the commercial contact between East and West, but they imported not only material goods. The Mithras cult spread over the whole breadth and length of the Empire, 'from Britain to the Black Sea, from the Rhine to the Nile, and this over a period of almost three centuries' [105].

Manfred Clauss cautions us, however, against the idea that the population of the Empire adhered to the cult to the last man; it were, he writes, only a few chosen who were initiated into the mysteries. Nevertheless, the devotees were at home everywhere : in 462 locations in all traces of the cult have been unearthed [106]. Even in the imperial capital Mithras was conspicuously present; he had a great number of sanctuaries there, fifteen of which could be localized [107]. The devotees were found among all classes of society. The names of eleven senators and thirty-seven knights are known, together with those of eighteen members of city councils. Then there were the military, privates as well as officers; Clauss estimates that somewhat more than ten percent of all adherents were legionaries, in Britain, however, seventy-five percent. Finally, the free Roman citizens who were Mithras devotees should not be forgotten [108].

7. A male cult

And now a very curious and telling thing : no women were ever initiated into the Mithraic mysteries. "A cult of men was wholly adequate to a society that was destined for men" [109]. It is not known why women were not permitted. R.L. Gordon wrote that "women constituted part of the 'world' which one had to escape from" [110], but Clauss combats this, saying that this is seen too much from the restricted vision of the soldiers [111]. I feel, however, that Gordon may not be too far off the mark. The Roman state was first and foremost a machinery for conducting war; its society was wholly geared to war [112]. But war is a typically masculine occupation. Roman women, who wholeheartedly sustained Rome's fundamental option for war, by doing so put themselves on the male side [113]. But this did not make them the equals of men. Just as women do not figure on whichever level of political and military management, we do not find them in the cult of Mithras. For we should not lose sight of the fact that Mithras was a war god, a god for men, that is. There is an evidently dualistic element in this exclusion of the women.

8. Was the Roman Mithras the Mithra of Iran?

The great question now confronting us is whether the god Mithras whom so many Romans revered was identical to the ancient Iranian deity. Or did he undergo important modifications during centuries long journey that led him from the Iranian plateau to York in Britain? The great founder of Mithraic studies was Franz Cumont, 'a giant of a scholar' [114] who published his 'Textes et monuments figurés relatifs aux mystères de Mithra' in the years 1896-1899. Since then, for decades to come, what Cumont said of Mithraism was the law.

The reason that his opinions remained so long unscathed is that Mithraism is an exceedingly difficult study object. To be really competent an expert needs to have knowledge of quite a number of languages, of the history of all the lands from the West to India, of anthropology, of sociology, and of whatever else. It is, therefore, not surprising that the First International

Congress of Mithraic Studies was held as late as in 1971, in Manchester. There was a second congress in Teheran in 1975. In later years Cumont's conclusions came increasingly under fire. Some of these are now viewed as quite unwarranted [115].

One of the organizers of the Manchester congress, John R. Hinnells, states that "perhaps the basic problem for Mithraic studies is the question of the continuity or discontinuity between the Eastern (particularly the Iranian) and the Roman worship of the god". Cumont and almost all other scholars after him assumed that there existed a linear continuity so that, "to understand Roman Mithraism one had first to understand Zoroastrianism (specifically, Middle Persian Zoroastrianism) and to a more limited extent Vedic thought". Hinnells's conclusion is that Roman Mithraism may perhaps best be studied in its own right; if it is to be compared, then it must be "studied in comparison to the other cults prevailing in the Empire and to the Gnosis" [116]. And yet another conclusion of importance is that of Gordon, namely that "the origins of the belief system are of no help whatever in assessing the function and significance of the Mithraic mysteries in the Roman Empire". Nevertheless, it should not be forgotten that the devotees themselves did not see it like this; they "believed their cult to come from Persia ... It is this claim which is important, not the reality, which ... is not recoverable" [117].

9. The foreign god

Correctly or not, the adherents of the Mithraic cult saw it as something Iranian. Mithras was a foreign god, coming from beyond the eastern frontier of the Empire. Foreign gods were not popular with the politico-religious authorities. What is more remarkable still is that Mithras was a divinity of the Persian arch-enemy. Since the fifth century B.C. the West had been in almost perpetual combat with Iran. In its later centuries the Empire was locked in a deadly struggle with its Persian neighbour in the East, first with the Parthian Empire, later with that of the Sasanians. In Vol. XI I have characterized this struggle as dualistic [118]. One of them both had to be destroyed; there was no room for two great Empires in the East.

Must we not see then the sympathies Mithras evoked as conflicting with what was essentially Roman? As a perfidious assault on the 'romanitas'? But there have even been Emperors who showed themselves well deposed to the Mithras cult [119]. What to think of Diocletian, not exactly a lover of foreign gods, who around 300 dedicated a votive stone to Mithras in the castra of Carnutum (now Petronell in Lower Austria)? Did he do this only to please his soldiers? But he described the god on this stone as the 'fautor imperii', the protector of the Empire [120]. What about Juppiter Capitolinus then? But the imperial god is not far away, indeed, for on the same dedicatory slab or stone the Emperor describes himself as 'Iovius', as 'one of Juppiter'. Could it be that Diocletian attempted to steal the thunder of the Sasanians by annexing the Persian god, equating him somehow with the Roman imperial divinity, and thus rendering him harmless?

But if this is correct, as I feel it is in the last resort, the trick worked against the Roman religious system. This assimilation of entirely foreign gods, who were worlds apart from what was authentically Roman in religion and cult, watered it down, made it lose something of its virility and resilience. And since Roman religion was considered the true fundament of the state, this acceptance of what was foreign to it weakened the political fabric also. A man like Diocletian, who made a dedication to a Persian god, acted from well-pondered considerations, says Bianchi. It is for this reason that he called the sympathy certain Emperors showed for the Mithras cult 'enigmatic' [121].

10. Initiation

As is appropriate in a mystery religion with an esoteric character, a newcomer had to be initiated. The lowest grade was that of 'corax' or 'raven' [122]. A raven might act as a server during the liturgy. His protective deity was Mercury. The second grade was that of 'nymphus'. This is a curious term, for the Greek word 'numphê' means 'bride', while a bridegroom is a 'numphios', not a 'numphos'. How must we then interpret the term 'nymphus'?

Vermaseren thinks that a 'nymphus' is a male bride (remember that Mithraism did not admit women). If this is correct, the nymphus was 'married' to the godhead, that is, brought into an intimate and personal relation to him. This is also expressed by the fact that he is covered with a long yellow veil, and that his protective deity is Venus [123]. The third stage is that of 'miles', soldier or warrior, whose protective deity is of course Mars. The milites began their service by taking an oath, the 'sacramentum'.

Then came the 'leo', the lion, placed under the protection of Juppiter which signifies how important this function was. With the leo we reach the inner core of the initiated. Two still higher stages are that of 'Persicus', protected by Luna, the moon, and of 'Heliodromus', the 'sun-walker', under the protection of the sun. The seventh and highest degree is that of 'Pater', the father, the superior, who is the head of the Mithras community. Mithras himself is his god. He is the great expert on the mysteries.

11. Mithraic ritual

Restricting ourselves to the Mithras mysteries of the second, third, and fourth centuries A.D., as they existed in the Roman Empire, we must state first and for all what the aim of these mysteries was. This was the unification of the devotee with his god Mithras, spiritually as well as physically, to such a degree that the god became 'internalized' by the devotee. [124] To achieve this a ritual was needed. Here a problem presents itself, for although the basic elements of the ritual were everywhere the same, the details could differ considerably according to place and circumstances. Colpe sums up elements of ritual behaviour that were, as he expresses it, 'magically charged' to make the internalization possible, 'eating, drinking, viewing, coition, disguising, enduring pain and hunger, touching, ecstasies, turning inward'. [125]

The Mithras cult contained several elements that were wholly alien to ordinary Roman religion. It all began with a baptism [126]. Then there was the sacramental oath of the milites. It seems that they wore a special sign. The candidate was committed to secrecy : he promised not to divulge what he knew of the doctrine and the rites [127]. The transition from grade to grade was accompanied with, or rather effectuated by, certain rites and ceremonies of which we know very little. The Church Fathers told horror stories about them. Lucianus jestingly wrote that the gates of Hades were opened 'taking down in safety anyone they (the Magi) would and guiding him back again". He ridiculed the rites in his usual vein, making a caricature of them [128].

More seriously, Gregory of Nazianze stated that there were 'eight degrees of chastisement accompanied by a descent and an ascent' [129]. Porphyry is quite outspoken about the initiation rites. "The Persian mystagogues initiate their candidate by explaining to him the downward journey of the souls and their subsequent return, and they call the place where this occurs a 'cave'" [130]. It will be clear what this means : the initiate had to die and to be revived ritually; in this way he broke radically with his former life.

There were also purifications, ablutions, and anointments. A kind of eucharist was celebrated. Blessings were spoken over bread and water which were then given to the faithful. Wine was also drunk, for its charismatic effect.

12. The sanctuaries

Porphyry wrote of a 'cave'. He added that "the custom of performing the mysteries in caves and grottoes, whether natural or artificial, caught on among others as well" [131]. Actually, the Mithraic religion did not build temples as we know them in the ancient world [132]. The original adherents preferred natural caves in the rocks, but where there were no rocks, as in the cities, they built semi-subterranean sanctuaries in the form of a cave. These were not very big and could contain only a limited number of faithful, no more than a hundred. The best preserved 'Mithraea' have been unearthed in Ostia, Rome's harbour-town, where no fewer than fourteen sanctuaries have been excavated [133]. This predilection for such simple sanctuaries shows once more how much Mithraism differed from the official Roman cult with its splendid edifices.

Descending into the cave the initiated left the ordinary world on the surface of which the unknowing mortals trod, and entered a world of their own. The main aim of the Roman cult was to honour and pacify the gods and, by doing so punctually, to secure the stability of the state. Mithraic religion, however, was a religion of redemption. It aimed at freeing people from the shackles of this imperfect existence with its ignorance and immorality.

13. Mithraic dualism

There are strong dualistic elements in Mithraism. I began with mentioning the radical exclusion of women. There was then the esoteric, the mysterious character of this cult. By descending into the Mithraeum the faithful almost literally turned their backs upon the world from whence they came. It was like a 'metempsychosis', a 'transmigration of the soul'. There is social dualism in this and also 'psychological dualism'. "Man finds himself caught in an evil world, and he seeks for a way out of this existential impasse, by ascent, by means of magical formulas, toward immortality, or by going through a ritual of rebirth." This psychological dualism is accompanied with an 'ethical dualism', for the initiated wanted to live an ascetic life of purity and chastity, radically different from what was deemed permissible in pagan Roman society [134].

The descent into the cave had a definitely archaic side to it. It symbolized a return to the earth, into the earth. The Mitraic faithful tried to regain the natural security which urban life had robbed them of. But here a problem arose [135]. No real 'retour à la nature' was possible for Roman city-dwellers of Late Antiquity. "Natural religion turned into mystery religion when the dualistic attack upon the natural experience of man forced him desperately to search for his roots. And therefore, what was originally natural re-enactment became artificially recreated re-enactment ... In the Mithraea man experienced something which the 'world' could not give him and which he did not find in Roman paganism. The symbolization transplants the myth" [136].

Without any doubt, Mithraism presented a dire threat to Roman paganism. We have already seen how some Emperors attempted to stave off the danger by assimilating the new cult to the official one, therewith damaging, however, its fundamental ideology. Did Mithraism also present a threat to Christianity? One would almost think so when we see how vehemently the Church Fathers fulminated against it. In their view Mithraic liturgy was a devilish imitation of the Christian cult. Mithraism too had a baptism, a eucharist, a sort of confirmation, to say nothing of its high morality. And it was also a religion of redemption. Once the era of the Christian Emperors had begun, Mithraism steadily lost ground. Sometimes Mithraea were destroyed. Cumont thinks that even the private cult of the god was no longer celebrated after 400 [137].

PART IV 'ENEMIES OF THE ROMAN ORDER'

1. Roman order

Behind the use of the term 'Enemies of the Roman order' - it is the title of a book by Ramsay MacMullen [138] - is the supposition that there was such a thing as 'the Roman order'. And of course there was! How could this enormous political complex, called the 'Imperium romanum', ever have subsisted without a very high degree of order? This order rested on the devotion to the imperial cause, the loyal collaboration and the faultless efficiency of countless authorities, functionaries, employees, and institutions. Who does not think here of the Emperor himself, of the Senate, of the provincial governors? Then there was the Roman army, the main guardian of the Roman order. There was also the imperial city of Rome itself, the centre of all political activity. Relations and transactions were regulated by the detailed stipulations of Roman Law. And underlying all this and crowning it and giving it sense was the Roman public cult with its two great divinities, Juppiter Capitolinus, the imperial god, and Mars, under whose guidance the wars were fought.

2. Imperfections of the Roman order

But no system in the world is perfectly watertight. There are always some anomalies and badly fitting parts; not uncommonly there are loopholes in it. The tax systems of modern democracies are wonders of perfection so that the state is able to fleece its citizens at its convenience. But every now and then a clever money-earner discovers a backdoor which makes him save a lot of money. Normally well-organized system are elastic enough to cope with attempts to escape from them. The Roman order also had its imperfections, of course. But the question is how elastic it actually was.

The problem of the Roman Empire, which was the political expression of the Roman order, was that it had been brought together by means of war and violence. There is hardly an instance of a nation or a tribe that joined the Roman political system voluntarily - if there is any at all. The subjected nations and regions were kept within the Roman order by means of suppression. The Romans preached, sung, and vaunted the 'Pax romana', the peaceful and harmonious cohabitation of countless nations under the aegis of Rome [139]. In Vol. XI, Ch. IV, Part I Subjected nations, the reader will find the story of the endlessly recurring revolts and their brutal repression. In many parts of the Empire rebellion was simply endemic. Rome may be characterized as the enemy of her own order.

It should also be mentioned in this context that Roman society was a slave society; the economy was to a very large extent dependent on slave labour. Slavery meant that a considerable part of the population was considered inferior, not fully human, virtually as non-beings. Roman society was horizontally split along a line with above the free and below the slaves. This situation was not conducive to order, since the free were viscerally afraid of their discontented slaves. There were several slave uprisings indeed some of which were very extensive. I have related this in Vol. XI, Ch. IV, Part IV The slaves.

3. The philosophers as disturbers of the Roman order

In his afore mentioned book MacMullen devotes a chapter of nearly fifty pages to the philosophers. At first sight this may seem astonishing. Philosophy is ordinarily considered an innocuous pastime, something entirely unpractical, pure theory. But we should keep in mind two thinkers, one in the early days of philosophy, and one of a much later time, Socrates who was condemned because his thought was viewed as an attempt on the Athenian religious order, and Karl Marx who found that philosophy was worthless if it remained without practical consequences.

The Romans were not a philosophical people; they were a nation of 'Macher', of managers and rulers, and above all, of warriors. They were not given to deep thought or to meditation, and they were impatient of speculation. The study of philosophy was not viewed as something that befitted a young Roman who wanted to make a career. An able man could demonstrate his wisdom in the arts of governing and warfare. Keeping this in mind, one might say that philosophizing would unfavourably affect the Roman order. This does not mean that the Romans were totally disinterested in philosophy, but the systems they favoured had to suit their social, political, and economic interests. They adapted them to their own practical interests and, by doing so, made them harmless.

Since philosophy was not congenial to the Roman mind, what they had of it was Greek import. Many systems were known among the Romans, but they were used in a eclectic as well a syncretistic way; a pot-pourri was often made out of them. But the idea that was common to Greek philosophers, namely, that the truly wise should live in private and abstain from action, did not appeal to young and ambitious Romans.

To the question "why philosophy and subversion went together (as they undeniably did)", MacMullen supplies the answer that philosophical thinking and "Stoicism in particular sharpened the impulse and courage to say what one felt, without any specific political program [140] ... It was actually made a sort of crime to 'philosophize' or to 'Stoicize', partly because a censorious bearing seemed to rebuke the government" [141]. Hence, Vespasian banished the philosophers in A.D. 71, an order that had to be repeated more than once. And before that, Seneca had already lost his life at the command of Nero.

4. The new religions

a. Judaism

MacMullen does not speak of the new religions that reached Rome from the East, the cults of Dionysus-Bacchus, Isis, and Mithras, although he devotes some attention to Judaism and Christianity. The Roman government treated Judaism as a 'religio licita' which means that it tolerated it. Nonetheless, the Romans felt uncomfortable with the Jewish religion; the presence of Jews in their midst often irritated them. Jews did not acknowledge the imperial god, Juppiter Capitolinus. They worshipped their own God, Jahve, exclusively; venerating any other god was in their view idolatry.

In Vol. XI, Ch. V, Part IV Greek and Roman authors on Jews and Judaism, I showed that these pagan authors and the intelligentsia of the Roman Empire had a very low idea of Jews and their religion. The main reason why the government tolerated Judaism was that it did not regard it a real threat to the Roman order. Judaism was an ethnic religion, a religion of one specific nation only. Although there was some proselytizing, and although some Romans, even high-placed persons, showed sympathy for Judaism, on the whole the Jews kept very much to themselves. The Diaspora Jews loved to live together in their own streets and quarters. They were different from the rest of the population and easily distinguishable by their clothing, their habits, their liturgy, and their own sacred language. This 'apartheid' made it easier for the authorities to keep them under control.

b. Christianity

The Christians presented a totally different case. Their religion was not an ethnic one. It slowly spread from east to west, winning adherents among all nations of the Empire and in all classes of the population. The faithful were not recognizable by their clothing; they did not have a sacred language of their own (it was either Greek or Latin) nor did they live together in Christian districts. This was already sufficient to make the authorities feel uneasy about them. But there was more. Just like the Jews, the Christians refused to acknowledge the imperial god and the divinity of the Emperor. And they could not be overlooked, because they were omnipresent, ever growing in numbers. The authorities could not allow themselves to ignore this refusal to pay homage to Juppiter and the Emperor. The Christian 'gran rifiuto' was viewed as an outright attack on the Roman order.

What made it absolutely impossible for the authorities to view the Christian religion as a 'religio licita' and for the Christians to accept wholeheartedly the pagan Empire was its claim to universality. The Empire viewed itself as the god-given instrument to rule the world, not only politically, but also spiritually. But the Christian religion also saw itself as universal, as the one and only religion for the people of all times. The pagan Empire felt, and from its own point of view with reason, that Christianity presented a deadly threat to its order.

c. The mystery religions

The attitude of the authorities towards the oriental mystery religions, those of Dionysus-Bacchus, Isis, and Mithras, was different. Taken at their face-value these religions presented an evident threat to the Roman order, to its religious and cultic identity in particular. They stood at right angles to what old-fashioned Romans viewed as religion, what with their mystical, very personal, and ecstatic characteristics, and with their tendency to secrecy and esoterism. They were fundamentally different from the state cult.

No wonder then that the authorities were at first averse to these strange oriental cults. However, slowly but certainly their attitude changed and they became more friendly and positive. The last centuries of Antiquity bore witness to a strong tendency towards religious syncretism. All kinds of foreign gods came to be viewed as equivalent to or even identical with Roman ones, the supreme one not excluded. Juppiter-Zeus had many names and many manifestations. As a consequence, the authorities saw no objection in allowing the new gods a place in their pantheon. But when all is said and done, even this syncretistic solution constituted an attack on the Roman order, all the more vicious because it was indirect. The insertion of the new gods into the Roman fabric adulterated it. With its emotionalism, with its cult of personal devotion, its love of being enraptured and transported, it weakened the basis of the old religion which was public, austere, and impersonal, and as such more suited to the Roman character. However, it is not improbable that this character underwent changes under the influence of these new religions.

NOTES TO CHAPTER II

1. See for this subject, Vol. I. Ch. IV, § 4 Atheism as an alternative?
2. Vol. I, Ch. IV, § 6.
3. Vol. I, Ch. IV, § 3 The defects of the Olympian system.
4. I refer the reader to Volumes VII, VIII, and IX.
5. See Vol. I, Ch I Pythagorica.
6. See Vol. I, Ch. IV, § 8 The mystery of Eleusis.
7. See Vol. I. Ch. IV, § 10 'About the Orphic poem'.
8. See Vol. I, p. 234.
9. See Vol. I, Ch. IV, § 10.
10. Il. 6,132.
11. See Vol. I, Ch. IV, § 7. Versnel, Inconsistencies 132/133, remarks that Dionysus' "personality is marked by ambiguities ... The very Greek Dionysos was neither autochthonous nor a genuine Olympian; he displays both human and animal traits ... Dionysus has both masculine and feminine traits. Embodying the vitality of life, he has also marked connections with death and afterlife." And on p. 134 it is said that he shows "two contrasting aspects ..., the threatening side of the ecstatic, potentially asocial, dangerous and disorientating experiences, on the one hand, and the comforting aspects of happiness and euphoria, on the other."
12. Gernet, Anthropologie de la Grèce antique, Ch. II Dionysos et la religion dionysiaque 114.

13. Detienne, Dionysos 55. Dabbad Trabulsi, Dionysisme, Ch. XIV Les mythes de résistance 191 : "Dans son rapport à la cité, le dionysisme est défini (ou se définit) par une série d'oppositions ou de distantiations, telles que ville/montagne, grec/barbare, homme/femme, sophrosunè/mania, pouvoir du dieu/pouvoir politique".

14. In his booklet 'Apollon und Dionysos. Dualistische Streifzüge' (Stuttgart, 1904) the German author Wilhelm Michel took up this Nietzschean Leitmotiv. He begins the first of the four essays in this book with a programmatic statement : "Sobald wir denken, spalten wir die Welt in eine feindliche Zweiheit entgegengesetzter Prinzipien". The reader who is somewhat conversant with my opinions, will know that I do not agree with this.

15. De Cazanove, Quelques théories 89, speaks of the Dionysiac thiasos as "oscillant sans cesse d'un pôle à l'autre, de l'orthodoxie à l'hérésie, du centre de la cité à ses marges, de l'ouverture au monde au repli sur soi, du peuple aux élites, telle paraît bien être l'image qu'ont mise en valeur les diverses enquêtes menées ces dernières années, dans le domaine grec que comme dans le domaine romain".

16. See Vol. I, pp. 217/218.

17. De Cazanove, Quelques théories 1, cautions us that the term 'thiasos', with a history of a thousand years, can denote different things at different times.

18. Jeanmaire, Dionysos. Ch. IX Dionysos dans le milieu hellénistique à l'époque gréco-romaine.

19. Plutarch, Consolation 10.

20. Liv. 39.8.3.

21. Liv. 39.8.4.

22. Liv. 39.9.1.

23. The events of 186 B.C. form the subject of a bulky volume by Pailler, Bacchanalia (see Bibliography).

24. Liv. 39.15.6 and 8.

25. Liv. 39.9.1.

26. Liv. 39.8.8.

27. Liv. 39.13.9-14.

28. Liv. 39.15-16.

29. Liv. 39.17-18. The relative senatusconsultum De Bacchanalibus, printed in CIL I.2, 581, 30, was found in Tiriolo in Calabria (now in the Kunsthistorisches Museum in Vienna).

30. Liv., 39.16.3-4.
31. Liv. 39.16.7.
32. Liv. 39.15.3.
33. Liv. 39.16.6.
34. Liv. 39.15.9.
35. The reader will find a fascinating picture history of Dionysus/Bacchus (144 pictures, the first dated 540 B.C. and the last 1983) in Hamdorf, Dionysos (see Bibliography).
36. Nilsson, Dionysiac mysteries 20 : "The energetic and merciless action of the Senate did at last repress the Bacchanalia and in the following years nothing is heard of them. A small remnant, however, was left, and the public cult continued. It can surely be assumed that the Bacchic movement lived on underground".
37. Jeanmaire, Dionysos 459-463. See also Nilsson, Dionysiac Mysteries, Ch. VI The Bacchic Mysteries in Italy.
38. See Vol. X, Ch. V, § 5e.
39. See Vol. XI, Ch. V, Part V, § 1.
40. All information regarding the spread of the Isis cult in the oriental basin of the Mediterranean is to be found in the monumental work by Françoise Durand, Le culte d'Isis (see Bibliography). There also exists an excellent and extensive bibliography of this cult : Leclant, Inventaire bibliographique (see Bibliography).
41. Plut., De Is. et Os. 372E. See for this subject Witt, Isis, Ch. IX The one whose names cannot be numbered.
42. Le Corsu, Isis, Ch. I, § 2 Le mythe d'Isis et Osiris : la version égyptienne, la version de Plutarque.
43. Cumont s.v. 'Isis', Roscher, Bd. II.1; Richard L. Gordon s.v. 'Isis'. Oxf.Class.Dict. (1996).
44. Solmsen, Isis 65.
45. Heyob, Cult of Isis 12.
46. Wissowa, Religion 351. Heyob, Isis 14 : "The rich finds in Pompeii reveal that Isis and Sarapis flourished there at the time of the eruption of Vesuvius". See for the coming of Isis to Italy Witt, Isis, Ch. VI To the shores of Italy.
47. Apuleius, Metamorph. 11.30.
48. Tert., Apologia 6 and Ad nationes 1.10. See Wissowa, Religion, 351, note 6 : in 53, 50, and 48 B.C.
49. Dio 47.15.5.

50. Wissowa, Religion 352.
51. Lambrechts, Augustus 12.
52. Val.Max., Memorabilia 7.3.8; Appian, Rom.hist., Civil wars 4.47.
53. Suet., Augustus 93.
54. Dio 53.2.4.
55. Dio 54.6.6.
56. Wissowa, Religion 352, believes that under the first Emperors there were not yet temples of Isis but only chapels.
57. Jos., Ant. 18.65-80.
58. Suet., Tiberius 26.
59. Apuleius, Metamorph. 11.26.
60. Apuleius, Metamorph. 11.17.
61. Witt, Isis, Ch. XVII.
62. Apuleius, Metamorph. 11.8-12, presents a picturesque description of such a procession.
63. Wissowa, Religion 95.
64. The spread of the Isis cult all over the western half of the Empire is treated in detail by Takacs, Isis and Sarapis (see Bibliography).
65. Heyob, Cult of Isis 14/15.
66. Heyob, Cult of Isis 128.
67. Apuleius, Metamorph. 11.30.
68. Apuleius, Metamorph. 11.23-24.
69. Apuleius, Metamorph. 11.28; Porph., De abst. 4.9.
70. Apuleius, Metamorph. 11.22.
71. Apuleius, Metamorph. 11.23.
72. Apuleius, Metamorph. 11.6.
73. For this subject see Le Corsu, Isis, Ch. III, §§ 3,4,5.
74. Apuleius, Metamorph. 11.1.
75. Apuleius, Metamorph. 11.4.
76. Apuleius, Metamorph. 11.20.
77. Apuleius, Metamorph. 11.13-16.
78. Apuleius, Metamorph. 11.18.

79. Franz Cumont s.v. 'Mithras', Roscher II.1, 3028/3029; Cumont, Mystères XV, categorically stated that "Mithra est un dieu indo-iranien".

80. Ernst Wüst s.v. 'Mithras (Name)', PW XV (1932), 2132.

81. Roger L. Beck s.v. 'Mithras', Oxf.Class,Dict. (1996³), 991. I refer the linguistically interested reader to an essay by P. Thieme, Concept of Mithra (see Bibliography), according to whom (p. 23) the 'most generally accepted' meaning of 'Mithra' is 'contract'. The conclusion of Turcan, Mithra 6/7, is that "Mithra serait donc initialement le garant de la fides, de l'accord qui consacre l'ordre du monde et de la société ... Cette fonction fondamentale élucide à la fois les représentations védiques et avestiques, voire l'identification ultérieure du dieu avec le soleil et la lumière". Still more information in G. Bonfante, The Name of Mithra (see Bibliography), and in Manfred Mayrhofer, Etymologien (idem).

82. For Vedism see Vol. V, Ch. II, § 2a, and for the Avesta Vol. IV, Ch. IV, § 7.

83. He is mentioned one hundred and seventy times in the Avesta of which one hundred and twenty-six times in the tenth Yasht alone; one hundred and eleven times he is given the title of 'master of the grasslands', see Jarafey, Mithra 55.

84. Roger L. Beck s.v. 'Mithras', Oxf.Class.Dict. (1996³), 991. For the iconography, see Merckelbach, Mithras, Bildteil, with its 169 plates.

85. John R. Hinnells, Editor's Introduction. Mithraic Studies I, XI. Turcan, Mithra 7 : "Mitra et Varuna Védiques sont couramment accouplés ... comme les deux faces antithétiques et complémentaires de la souverainité. Mitra incarne l'aspect juridico-sacerdotal, bienveillant, conciliant, lumineux, proche de la terre et des hommes; Varuna, l'aspect magique, violent, terrible, ténébreux, invisible et lointain". It was especially the positive side of the couple that became important in later times. "Le Mitra védique annonce à certains égards le Mithra hellénique et occidental".

86. F. Cumont s.v. 'Mithras', Roscher II.2, 3029. Autran, Mithra 42 : "Dans les Gâthâs, hymnes formant la partie la plus ancienne de l'Avesta, *il n'est plus question de lui*" (italics of Autran).

87. Kristensen, Het mysterie 25/26; F. Cumont s.v. 'Mithras', Roscher II.2, 3029/3030. Turcan, Mithra 9/10 : "Ahura Mazdah prévalait comme dieu suprême et Mithra, tout en lui demeurant lié plus ou moins étroitement, prend un caractère guerrier qui le rapproche de la deuxième fonction", i.e. that of the violent god Varuna, without, however, becoming entirely negative. "Cette annexion du domaine militaire est dans la logique des attributions en tant que dieu garant de l'ordre et proche de l'homme, donc défenseur de l'homme ... Gardien secourable des créatures, omniscient et victorieux, il a déjà la vocation

du dieu sauveur et solaire que deviendra le *deus invictus* du Mithraicisme gréco-romain".

88. Jarafey, Mithra 58.

89. Jarafey, Mithra 59. This Mihragan festival is still celebrated in modern Iran, see Boyce, Mihragan 106-118.

90. Bianchi, Tipologia 2123 : "il complesso rapporto tra i due personaggi, che va fino all'identificazione".

91. Plut, De Iside 46, 369E : "Midway between the two is Mithras; for this reason the Persians give to Mithras the name of 'mediator'".

92. Bianchi, Topologia 2118.

93. Beck, Planetary gods, Ch. I The planets and the grades : the problem of unique order.

94. See Vol. X, Ch. IV, § 18.

95. Plut., Pomp. 24.6.

96. Turcan, Mithra 23. Beskow, Routes 12/13 : "There is no evidence at all for the common idea that the Cilician pirates, mentioned by Plutarch, should have carried the mysteries to Rome", i.e. after they had been resettled in South Italy by Pompey.

97. Cumont, Mystères 31 : "On peut dire d'une façon générique que Mithra resta toujours exclu du monde hellénique".

98. Merckelbach, Mithras 43, note 1 : "Für die Griechen blieb Mithras immer der Gott jener Persen, die einst versucht hatten ihr Land zu erobern".

99. Cumont, Mystères 33.

100. F. Cumont s.v. 'Mithras', Roscher II.2, 3022.

101. CIL VI, Pars IV, fasc. II, 3018.

102. Vermaseren, Mithrasdienst 25.

103. Cumont, Mystères 39 : "Le principal agent de sa diffusion est certainement l'armée. La religion mithriaque est avant tout celle des soldats". Will, Origine 535 : "On s'aperçoit qu'il (le mithriacisme) est volontiers accueilli dans de petits groupements, groupements, pourrait-on dire, de déracinés, d'hommes éloignés de leur patrie, coupés de leurs familles plus vastes, par leurs occupations professionelles. Le fait est évident pour les militaires". Cumont, Mystères 74 : "Dans toutes les provinces, les modestes employés des services impériaux eurent une part considérable dans la diffusion des cultes étranges ... Ainsi l'administration transféra de gouvernement à gouvernement avec les scribes et les comptables la connaissance des mystères".

104. Daniels, Roman army 273, concludes that "the role of the army, and particularly of the legionaries, seems reasonably certain, both in the introduction and in the later spread of mithraism ... In the way of general conclusions, we see a very uneven distribution of mithraism throughout the Western provinces ... Generally, and with the exception of Greece, the cult was stronger in Central and Eastern Europe than in the West (excluding Italy)".

105. Clauss, Cultores 8.

106. Clauss, Cultores 9. A map at the back of Cumont, Mystères, shows that they were found all over the Empire.

107. Clauss, Cutores 17. Vermaseren, Mithrasdienst, Ch. III De verbreiding te Rome.

108. See for this Clauss, Cultores, Anhängerschichten.

109. Clauss, Cultores 264.

110. R.L. Gordon, Mithraism in the Roman Empire, 115. Cambridge, 1972, quoted by Clauss, Cultores 264. I was unable to consult this essay since it exists in typewritten form only.

111. Clauss, Cultores 264.

112. See Vol. X, Ch. I, § 5.

113. See Vol. XI, Ch. IV, Part III § 5.

114. Hinnells, Editor's Introduction, Mithraic Studies I, XII.

115. For a detailed discussion see R.L. Gordon, Cumont and the doctrine of Mithraism (see Bibliography). Of a somewhat later date is an essay by the Canadian scholar Roger Beck, Mithraism since Franz Cumont, ANRW 2.17.4.

116. Hinnells, Editor's Note. Mithraic Studies I, XII/XIII.

117. Gordon, Cumont 247. The conclusion of Speidel, Mithras-Orion 46, is still more categorical : "The conclusion is inescapable that Mithraism is a Greek and Roman, not an oriental religion". Beskow, Routes 17 : "Some kind of Iranian background is generally supposed. On the other hand, there is increasing agreement that the Mithras of the mysteries and the Mithra of Iranian religion are very different".

118. Vol. XI, Ch. III, § 6a.

119. For the interest Roman Emperors took in the Mithras cult, see Turcan, Mithra, Ch. III, § V Mithra et les Empereurs, and Cumont, Mystères, Ch. III, Mithra et le pouvoir impérial.

120. CIL III.1, 4413.

121. Bianchi, Tipologia storica, 2218.

122. For an extensive discussion of the seven grades, see Merckelbach, Mithras. Die römischen Mithrasmysterien. III Die einzelnen Weihegrade.
123. Vermaseren, Mithrasdienst 126.
124. Colpe, Mithra-Verehrung 386.
125. Colpe, Mithra-Verehrung 387.
126. Tert., De bapt. 5.
127. Cumont, Mystères 166. It is possible that the sign was 'une marque gravée au fer ardent' (ib.).
128. Lucianus, Menippus 6.
129. Greg.Naz., Oratio contra Iul. 6.
130. Porph., Cave of the nymphs 6 (60).
131. Porph., Cave of the nymphs 6 (60).
132. For this subject see Turcan, Mithra, Ch. V, § I Typologie du Mithraeum.
133. Groh, Ostian Mithraeum (see Bibliography).
134. Laeuchli, Mithraic dualism 61/62. This author makes the apt remark that "the dualistic problem has been confused by two rigid assertions. The first limits dualism to an extreme of an Iranian type of two gods, one good and one evil. The second limits dualism to only the metaphysical, religious, or philosophical aspects of such duality. This narrow definition of dualism prevents the observer from grasping the dualistic problem in the ancient world".
135. Laeuchli, Mithraic dualism 61.
136. Laeuchli, Mithraic dualism 63.
137. F. Cumont s.v. 'Mithras', Roscher II.2, 3068. For this subject see Turcan, Mithra, Ch. VII La fin du Mithraicisme. Merckelbach, Mithras. Die römischen Mithrasmysterien. X Das vierte Jahrhundert. Die Mithrasmysterien verlieren die Unterstützung des Kaisers.
138. MacMullen, Enemies (see Bibliography).
139. See Vol. X, Ch. I, § 4a.
140. MacMullen, Enemies 53.
141. MacMullen, Enemies 57.

CHAPTER III

ATTITUDES TO THE BODY AND SEXUALITY IN THE GRAECO-ROMAN WORLD

PART I ON NATURALNESS

1. How natural is the human body?

How natural are human beings? Are we just as natural as dogs or pikes? Most people find that we are somewhat more than animals - which, irrevocably, means that we are less natural than they are. A new-born calf can stand, walk, and find the udders of the mother-cow without help. A new-born baby can breathe, drink (but has to be laid at its mother's breast), cry, sleep, defaecate, and urinate. Not more, that is all. Eating, speaking, walking, potty training, even laughing, it has all to be learned, which is tantamount to saying that it is not natural. Let us not even speak of the simplest intellectual skills, like reading, writing, doing sums. Basically, we are natural beings, indeed, with that most of the time faithfully functioning machine our body is. But then there is that enormous 'superstructure' of thinking and acting, of planning and preparing, of attitudes and estimates, that, as the product of learning and experience is not natural at all.

Is our body something natural? This seems a pointless question to which the answer seems obvious. We did not choose to be male or female, tall or short, blond or dark, black or white. But there are not many older people whose bodies have not undergone medical treatment, operations, for instance, ranging from tonsillectomy to open-heart surgery, not to mention having teeth extracted. Many people have some implement built into their bodies; there is a wide variety of them (I do not even mention spectacles), dental protheses, pace makers, or even artificial limbs. And what to think of the countless people who are not satisfied with their physique? Coloured people who want to have their hair bleached or to wear it less frizzy, women who want to have smaller or bigger breasts, or who lie on the sunbed in order to get artificially tanned? The catalogue is endless.

The consequence is that our attitude to the body is complicated. Partly, of course, we allow our physique to be as natural as it wants to be; over many of its functions we hardly have any control at all. But it also causes us many problems and anxieties. The body has to be looked after, taken care of, petted even; many people spend much time and money on bodily care. But ascetics find that Brother Ass should be kept in check and tamed; it does not deserve so much attention. Attitudes to the body can vary greatly, not only between people, but also between ages and civilizations.

2. Dressing and undressing

But, one will object, what about the nudist' beach? Are not people perfectly natural there, and happy with it too? Does the Bible-word not fit them perfectly : "They were naked but not ashamed of one another" [1], even if they would not win a beauty contest? But look more closely! You will see people sitting and lying on their towels, shunning direct contact with Mother Earth; you will see them using creams and sun-glasses to protect them against the sun; you will see them wearing wrist-watches, rings, and bracelets. They are not quite so naked as they like to think they are; in other words, they are less natural, even there, than they imagine themselves to be.

Visitors leaving the nudists' beach put on their clothing again. Back to normalcy! For we almost constantly wear some garment, even in bed. Why do we wear clothes? To protect us against the inclemency of the weather? Partly true, of course. In my country, the Netherlands, the nudists' beaches remain deserted most of the time, even in summmer. But there are few countries where people can do without clothing almost always. Nevertheless, clothes are also worn there, often many layers of them.

It is not because of the weather that we dress ourselves. The first reason is that we wish to hide our physical deformities and deficiencies. The clothes we wear may make us seem taller or slimmer or with straighter shoulders and less paunch, that is, less natural once again. Secondly, dress expresses something about ourselves, whether we are children or adults, male or female; it can reflect what we are doing, whether we are working or relaxing, sleeping or playing. It indicates our profession : soldier, policeman, professor, clergyman, farmer, trucker, nurse. The more we adorn ourselves - grand gala - the more we want to accentuate our position - King Charles X of France in ceremonial attire -, the farther we distance ourselves from our natural state.

3. Is sexuality natural?

Is sexuality something natural? It seems so, for sexual activity is made possible by glandular secretions. But even the staunchest materialist knows that there is something more to it. We give this surplus the name of 'love'. If sexuality were no more than something purely physical or biochemical, then what would there be against general promiscuity, against everyone mating with everyone, regardless of age and sex? But not even the greatest defender of sexual freedom would plead for this. There are always prohibitions. Not everyone can become everyone's sexual partner.In this field too there are conventions, rules, and even laws, which restrict possibilities and prevent opportunities. Even sexuality, the great pet of modernity, is less natural than it looks. The codes which regulate sexual behaviour may differ from culture to culture, but they are always there.

Just as the human relationship to the body may be difficult and painful, which is to say, unnatural, sexual intercourse is never free from ambiguity. Sex can be a great source of joy, as the expression of true love between human beings. But I should not know what has caused ordinary people the worst problems : money or sex. Or money and sex combined. Horrible crimes are committed in the name of sex; all is permitted in war and love, as the saying goes. But most people will deem much that is done in order to get sexual gratification highly unnatural. Each civilization and each society tries to cope with sexuality, lawless as it is, in its own way. Pagans, Jews, and Christians do not differ in this, although their attitudes do.

It is here that the man-woman relationship comes into play. It is not so, of course, that this relationship, of whichever kind it may be, is always of a sexual nature. Almost all women are sexually entirely uninteresting to men; the reverse is also true (perhaps even more so). But all human relations, from man to woman, for woman to man, from man to man, from woman to woman, have something of Eros in them. The people we encounter or with whom we have to do always make a certain impression on us, whether pleasant or unpleasant, attractive or repulsive, and anything in between. However vague this impression may be, there never is complete indifference.

The erotic impression may become sexual attraction. The more intimate and personal the relation, the stronger the urge to sexual fulfilment becomes. The man-woman relationship is always and everywhere the most obvious (and regular) means for gratifying this urge, with the marriage-bed having pride of place. Whichever form sexual behaviour may asssume, I know of no society in which marriage would not be its principal expression.

4. The man-woman relationship as the test-case

We have a complex with three elements now : the body, sexuality, and the man-woman relationship. The attitude towards all three of these can become dualistic. All that is corporeal and physical may be spurned and scorned, with exclusive attention for what is 'spiritual'. Sexuality may be rejected as dirty and not worthy of human beings. In the man-woman relationship each of the two partners, but usually the woman, can be utterly degraded as an inferior being.

In this tripartite complex the man-woman relationship is the true test-case. If this is disharmonious - which in practice almost always means that the woman is considered far below the man -, then we may safely guess that there is something basically wrong with the attitude to body and sex. I am not speaking of individual cases, of course, but of attitudes prevailing in society. We shall now have to see, first, which attitudes were dominant in the Graeco-Roman world.

PART II PAGAN ATTITUDES

1. A macho society

In Volume X I characterized the Roman state as a machinery geared to war [2]. During the twelve centuries of this state's existence, warfare was its principal occupation; endless wars were waged for conquest, countless others to suppress rebellions. This never ending state of war had its consequences. First of all, it turned Roman society into a macho one; this irrevocably meant that the men were more than the women. The men marched out to do the fighting, to enlarge the realm of the state, to protect it, while the women stayed at home. Secondly, it signified that soldierly prowess and bravery in battle stood in high repute; Romans wanted to be known as valiant soldiers above all. When fighting, they relied on the abilities of their bodies, when marching in heat and cold, to their endurance. But at the same time the men realized that they should not estimate their physical integrity too highly. All too often men returned home mutilated, even as complete invalids. If they returned at all ... For in the course of the centuries hundreds and again hundreds of thousands of men lost their lives on the battle-fields or to the epidemics that frequently ravaged the armies.

2. Not a secularized state

The Roman Empire was a god-given, a divine instrument for governing the world. In this respect it was totally different from a modern secularized state. Politics and religion were closely intertwined; state officials were also the functionaries of the public cult. Roman politics were the fulfilment of the will of the gods. The centre of the Empire, or rather of the whole world, was not the Senate House on the Roman Forum, but the Temple of Juppiter

Capitolinus, the imperial godhead, on the Capitol Hill. To him, the personification of Rome's claim to rule the world, all citizens owed allegiance. The really telling token of subjection to the Roman dominance was offering to the statues of Juppiter and of the divinized Emperor; this subjection was, therefore, primarily something spiritual or mental. The Emperor claimed the whole person, in contrast to modern democracies that leave what is most essential to the citizens themselves.

This conception of the Empire as something divinely ordered had important consequences. All that was necessary for its functioning was carefully looked after. The Empire was a well-organized complex, what with its government, its officials, its armies, its laws, its management of the provinces, its infrastructure of roads and harbours. All this was the practical elaboration of the basically divine order.

3. 'Horror materiae'

The individual needs of the citizens, however, were less well cared for. They had to obey, to march and fight, to pay their taxes, and to behave in an orderly manner. The Roman state knew no social-welfare system, no state-provided education, no hospitals, no public health organization. Individual citizens simply had to fend for themselves in all these respects. The only thing the authorities did for them, at least for the population of Rome and some other big centres, was providing them with sufficient grain, not because they wanted their citizens to lead the good life, but for fear they might rebel if they became hungry.

The upshot of these considerations is that the Roman state was not interested in material matters, in the way modern democracies are. There was in the whole Roman world a distancing from all that is material, of matter. In almost all philosophers of Late Antiquity and also in not a few Christian theologians we find this as contempt and even as a wholesale rejection of Matter, with a capital M, since in these philosophies it is an ontological entity. It is always very hard to gauge how far the influence of philosophers reaches. Not very far in the direct sense, we may assume. The vast majority never open their, not rarely unreadable, volumes. But some of it trickles down, a little distorted perhaps, via popularizations, courses, and lectures, sayings and catchwords, and thus they become part of the mainstream. On the other hand, thinkers do not operate in a vacuum, even if they keep themselves apart from the unthinking behind the walls of their academies and philosophical institutes. They too swim with the mainstream and are impregnated by it. Their negative attitude to Matter surely has something to do with the fundamental anti-materialism that forms part of the Roman mental substructure.

4. Highs and lows

Considering this, we must not expect that the general attitude of the Roman world towards the three elements of our complex would be positive, a model of harmony. On the contrary! But there were highs and lows in this respect, unevenly distributed over the centuries and over the population groups. An absolute low was reached with the Gnostics. Nowhere within the frontiers of the Roman Empire do we find such a radical rejection of Matter as the ultimate evil. This is made concrete in the abhorrence of all that is physical and bodily, the abomination of sexuality, and the vilification of womanhood. The high was doubtless ancient Israel, with Egypt as a good second. Men and women were considered fairly equal in both societies, although with different functions. Sexuality was not denigrated, matter and body were not spoken of in any negative sense. Israel appreciated large families, which were viewed as a divine blessing, and such families do not originate without frequent intercourse [3]. However, Israel as well as Egypt stood somewhat outside the mainstream of Graeco-Roman civilization, Egypt as an ancient, immensely proud culture, and Israel as an entity that was just as god-given as the Roman Empire.

5. The austerity of the Roman Republic

The idea that is prevalent in these days of sexual liberation and the breaking of taboos is that, whereas Christianity is and has always been inimical to sex, the ancient pagan world was far more liberal in this respect and knew how to enjoy it. Actually, ancient republican Rome was very austere and strict in sexual matters. We find nothing here of the tolerant attitude the Greeks had with regard to paedophilia, the sexual relation of an adult man with an adolescent boy. Homosexuality in whichever form was despised as effeminate and unworthy of a true man. Marriage was strictly regulated and not left to the impulses of the spouses. Unmarried daughters (who had to marry as soon as possible) and married women were strictly guarded; illicit sexual behaviour was severely punished.

It was the family who controlled this behaviour, not the state. Adultery, either by the husband or by the wife, very often led to divorce. Adulterers, whether male or female, could be maltreated or even killed by the offended family. The men were somewhat freer, of course, since they were so long and so often away from home on military expeditions. But there was no double standard. Although the men were less controllable, they held no brief for licentious behaviour. The Republic viewed sexuality at the same time as something positive - for the state needed 'Nachwuchs', especially soldiers -, and as something dangerous that, as a potentially destabilizing force, had to be kept under strict control and led into narrow channels. There is no indication that sex was viewed as a liberating power or celebrated as something joyful. There is no text comparable to the biblical Song of Songs in which the pleasures of erotic love are sung in hardly veiled terms. This basic Roman attitude did not change much in the course of the centuries.

6. Mutations in the basic attitude

Towards the end of the Republic there were occurences which made it doubtful that the opinions of the learned men, as described in the foregoing paragraph, were wholeheartedly adhered to by the population as a whole. It is even conceivable that the learned had their reasons to be extra-severe. The last century B.C. was a period of constant turmoil. One civil war after another had been fought; there had also been a war with the slaves and an other with the allies. The number of victims was astronomical, destruction was widespread, and the most heinous crimes and cruelties were committed. The inevitable result was the demoralization and destabilization of Roman society. Individual persons and social groups were swept of their moorings and went adrift. Much seemed permitted and even praiseworthy that had been deemed utterly reprehensible in more stable times. It goes without saying that the old sexual mores had not gone unscathed. Sexuality is a field in which people in troubled times seek compensation for what they suffer, taking the chances that normally are denied to them.

With the return of Octavian-Augustus to Rome political order was restored and built again on stable foundations. But it is not be expected that the confusion in the moral field would disappear immediately. The imperial family itself was not exactly a paragon of strict sexual behaviour [4]. Laws do not change much in human behaviour, nowhere and never, and certainly not the legislation of sexual morality. Laws to this effect were indeed issued by Augustus and his successors, but it proved impossible to force back the citizens, by means of measures in the public sphere, to the rigidity that had prevailed in the days of the Republic. The result was a curious mixture of severity and laxness.

7. 'Benevolent dualism'

Peter Brown speaks of 'benevolent dualism' here, meaning with this the unbridgeable opposition of soul and body. "The soul met the body as the inferior 'other' to the self. The body was as different from the soul, and as intractable, as were women, slaves, and the opaque and restless populace of the cities" [5]. This meant that a little leeway had to be given to that intractable body. Keeping it under too strict a control would have averse effects; Plutarch spoke of "that exact and strictly ordered way of living we are trying to avoid" [6]. Officially the government advocated regular sexual behaviour, that is, sexual intercourse only in marriage with the aim of procreation. Couples should have children, preferably many, since many died at a very tender age.

The Republic had needed children, boys because it wanted to provided with soldiers, and girls who would, in their turn, bear future soldiers. But the Empire was in dire need of children, because the very real danger of depopulation had to be staved off. Premiums were put on having large families. Nevertheless, it proved impossible to tie the men to the marriage bond. Marital chastity was not a thing to brag about; there were too many husbands who offended against it. "In your sex-life preserve purity, as far as you can, before marriage, and if you indulge, take only those privileges which are lawful. However, do not make yourself offensive, or censorious, to those who do indulge" [7]. 'Live and let live!' was the motto. There was no room for moralism.

A young man's adventures were looked upon with tolerance, for there is no fighting against nature. If young men do not cause damage to other people's lives, or subvert respectable houses by their behaviour, let them! They will end as grave and sober men [8]. Even homosexual relations did no longer meet with strong disapproval. It was somewhat different with girls, for they were expected to enter marriage as virgins. Not that this was hard to achieve : girls were often married when they were only fourteen; it happened that a girl became a bride before she had had her first period. But in case she had previously lost her virginity, this was not viewed as though 'the temple of the Holy Ghost' had been violated, but rather as a bad sign that, once married, she would not behave well [9].

8. Sexual norms

A very interesting source for ideas on human sexuality is the 'Onirocritica', the Dreambook, by Artemidorus, a Greek from Ephesus, who flourished in the second half of the second century A.D. This book, that remained very influential, was meant as a 'key to dreams', a help for people to interpret their often disturbing dreams. Many dreams have a sexual nature or present sexual images. What do they signify? Artemidorus' book is not a handbook of sexual morality, but we find in it precious indications of what was found acceptable and what not. Foucault thinks that the morality on which the text is based was traditional [10].

Artemidorus distinguishes three categories in the sexual acts that occur in dreams : those 'kata nomon' = socially acceptable, those 'para nomon' = socially inacceptable, and those 'para phusin' = contrary to nature [11]. Having sexual relations with women is quite normal, with your wife, with a mistress, with slave girls, with a prostitute. This does not mean that the author finds all these relations commendable. Visiting prostitutes he views as somewhat degrading. The background of this is that the male seed is spilled in this case; a prostitute will have no children by her client [12]. Although adultery act is quite normal sexually, the author does not approve of it : a married woman belongs to her husband. In consequence, although intercourse with a mistress is something 'normal', it is against the law [13].

What is really 'para nomon' is incest. This is understood as sexual relations between parents and children. It is typical for Roman mentality that brother-sister incest comes into the same category as that between father and daughter : a brother should be as a father to his sister [14]. If incestuous acts are not unnatural, although absolutely blameworthy, what then is 'para phusin'?, the astonished reader will ask. But he or she will be still more astonished to hear that Artemidorus recognizes only one posture as legitimate : the so-called 'missionary position'. All other postures are wrong, intemperate, excessive [15]. This disapproval is very probably caused by the fact that mammals copulate 'a tergo' [16]. Other sexual acts that are deemed unnatural are oral sex, sex with animals, and lesbian relations [17]. The author thought very lightly of masturbation, which seems illogical, since by this act too seed is spilled. But he saw it probably as an hygienic measure in which only one person is involved.

9. Superiority and inferiority

The general idea Artemidorus had of sexuality seems typical of the pagan mentality to me. Foucault states that it is primarily situated in the context of a 'scénographie sociale'. With this Artemidorus means that the sexual act is not perceived as the intimate, essentially personal encounter of loving partners. There is always superiority and inferiority in it, domination and subjection, victory and defeat [18]. It is doubtless for this reason that Artemidorus so strongly recommends the missionary position. For if the man stretches himself over the woman, he takes possession of her whole body; his partner has to do nothing but obey and consent [19]. It will be evident that there is dualism in this.

Allow me to quote a somewhat longer passage by Foucault, who looked deeply into this matter. "The landscape evoked by the chapters of Artemidorus that are devoted to sexual dreams is a landscape that was familiar to Antiquity. It is easy to find in them elements of morals and customs that could be attested by a great many other testimonies, anterior as well as contemporaneous. We are in a world that is very strongly marked by the central position of the male person and by the importance attached to the virile role in sexual relations. We are in a world where marriage is sufficiently estimated as the best possible context for sexual pleasure. In this world, the married man may also have a mistress, dispose of his servants, boys as well as girls, and frequent prostitutes." It will be clear that the Roman man did not rack their brains about what was acceptable and what not. Foucualt even adds that the line between what was natural and 'contrary to nature' was not sharply drawn. The domineering man allowed himself considerable latitude [20].

Pagan Romans had no high idea of sexuality. Given the fact that they considered women inferior beings, they cannot have attached that much meaning to it. For women it meant having too many children at too early an age, even to a premature death in childbed. The men, who might sow their oats left, right, and centre, will not have had a higher opinion. Their sex was too casual and impersonal.

10. What the learned thought of it

The old republican austerity not having been re-established, the learned men began to feel uncomfortable with the lasciviousness and the sexual licence they detected in pagan society. But their attitude remained somewhat ambiguous. They did not, as Christian authors did, advocate total renunciation in the form of male and female celibacy. But they did not hesitate to fulminate and to warn against what they saw as excesses. Sexual relations were only acceptable when their aim was to procreate - an opinion that is often thought to be typically Christian, but that we meet here in a pagan context [21].

This minimalist attitude had certainly something to do with that 'horror materiae' that was so widespread in Late Antiquity. "Contempt for the human condition and hatred of the body was a disease endemic in the entire culture of the period." In Dodds's opinion it was "an endogenous neurosis, an index of intense and widespread guilt feelings" [22]. It is also worthwile to quote Derrick Bailey who expresses his opinion with regard to this point very accurately. "Against this laxity in moral standards and depravity in sexual behaviour the philosophies of the age proclaimed an ascetical ideal which, though contemplative and mystical rather than disciplinary, had always inclined towards mortification of the flesh. Though chiefly the product of a pessimism which abandoned the realm of the material and the phenomenal as the irreclaimable domain of evil, this asceticism, in its sexual aspect, was partly due also to the low contemporary view of woman and marriage" [23].

With regard to medical opinion in the first period of the rule of the Emperors, Foucault mentions "distrust of pleasures, insistence on the effects of their abuse on body and soul, high valuation of marriage, unbelief respecting the spiritual significance that were attributed to the love of boys : there is in the thought of the philosophers and the doctors of the first two centuries (A.D.) nothing but severity." [24]

True, Aretaeus, a Greek doctor writing in the second half of the second century A.D., found that sex, and he is speaking specifically of male sex, contributes to health, to the vigour of body and soul, and to procreation.

"However", he adds cautiously, "this function should be used only sparely" [25]. But sex can also be dangerous. Several doctors compare it to illnesses, to epilectic fits, for instance. Or it may lead to physical exhaustion, caused by a state of continuous excitement. This is what Aretaeus calls 'satyriasis', never having enough, 'an insatiable desire of sexual intercourse', which causes 'convulsion of the nerves, and slackening of the muscles, the groin, and the perineum' [26]. There is hardly an ailment that cannot be attributed to the abuse of sex : digestive troubles, loss of sight and hearing, loss of memory, general enfeeblement of the senses, convulsive trembling, painful joints, toothache, inflammation of the throat, spitting of blood, illnesses of the bladder [27].

Galenus, another Greek, who had a medical practice in the second half of the first century A.D., says in a somewhat more balanced way that the effect depends on a person's general condition; healthy persons will experience no bad consequences, but it will bring down those who are already in a weakened state [28]. He thought, nevertheless, that "sexual relations are fatiguing for the breast, the lungs, the head, and the nerves". And with an audible sigh, he admits that it is not possible to prohibit people from having sexual relations [29]. Peter Brown quotes this same author to the effect that he admitted that it was strange that the gods should have decided to maintain the humans species by means of a pleasure so sharp and anti-social, for "a very great pleasure is coupled with the exercise of the generative parts, and a raging desire precedes the use" [30].

The corollary is, it goes without saying, that abstinence is better than sexual activity. But since in the pagan world only a few eccentrics remained unmarried and almost all persons had sexual relations of one kind or another, the doctors tried to diminish the risk by prescribing many precautions : body and soul should be in a healthy state, periods of voluntary abstinence were necessary, food should be good but frugal, and not too much wine must be drunk. The right moment must be chosen in order to have good offspring : perhaps winter and spring are better than the hot season, or the day of the full moon.

Taking an overall view, it is evident that well-meaning authors found sex a tricky affair, They never advocated total abstinence in the form of celibacy for whatever reason, but they hedged in sexual activity with so many precautions and pointed out so many dangers that we can only conclude that they were afraid of it. The spectre of dualism is looming in the background, but it moves squarely into the foreground with the following categorical statements by Soranus, a Greek medical doctor (A.D. 98-138) who practiced in Rome. "Every emission of seed is harmful to health" and "sexual relations are injurious in themselves" [31].

11. A dualistic attitude

It should, however, be noted that there nowhere a wholesale condemnation of sex, in whichever form, as a moral evil, is to be found. Rufus of Ephesus, for instance, is against homosexuality but only because it is more fatiguing, more 'violent', than heterosexual intercourse. As Aline Rousselle writes, the great problem of the aristocratic clientele of the famous society doctors, was not desire but fatigue [32], the constant fear that sexual activity would harm one's health. And this, in spite of occasional utterances to the contrary, signifies that sex was viewed as something that not really belonged to a complete person, something even that made that person less complete.

The attitude of the pagan inhabitants of the Graeco-Roman world was characterized by reticence and fearfulness, so much so that it may be called dualistic. It must be admitted that we are speaking of those who were articulate; we do not know really much of the attitudes of the general population. The males tried to overcome this by playing the domineering macho who could lord it over the women and their bodies. This of course did not make the relationship more harmonious.

PART III CHRISTIAN ATTITUDES

1. The Jewish heritage

The main Christian Church could draw upon the Jewish tradition. This tradition was neither averse of sex nor inimical to women. How could this be if the Jews saw in large families the blessing of the Lord? Earlier in this chapter I restated my argument that the situation of the women in Israel was far better than that in the rest of the ancient world, with the exception of Egypt. We find no condemnation of sex in the Old Testament; its is not viewed as evil or as bad for one's health. The biblical authors do not appear to be greatly interested in the subject. The same is true for the New Testament.

2. The New Testament

a. In the Gospels

Jesus's attitude towards women is relaxed. He does not show signs of being erotically interested in them. When Mary Magdalen tries to embrace him after the Resurrection, he wards this off, saying "don't keep me", the famous 'noli me tangere' [33]. There is not a word about sex as such in the Gospels, neither pro nor contra. Marriage is mentioned only rarely, first in the passage where Jesus declares the marriage bond indissoluble, with a reference to Gen. 2:24, and also in another passage where he says that marriage is a temporary institution, because in heaven there will be no marriage [34]. He praises those who remain single because of the Kingdom of heaven [35]. This may be seen as an announcement of Christian celibacy, but at that particular moment nobody understood what Jesus meant.

Finally, there is a 'hard saying' of Jesus about adultery. "I say to you that everyone who looks at a woman lustfully has already committed adultery with her in his heart" [36]. What Jesus wants to convey is that not only the acts count in moral matters, but also what happens in foro interno, in 'the heart'. "For from within, out of the heart of man, come evil thoughts" [37]. He rejects the notion that the secret thoughts and desires one has are not immoral because they hurt no one.

There has been much speculation on the question why the Gospels remain virtually silent on the subject of sex. Some people complain about this; they had expected guidance in this field but they receive barely any help. Jesus becomes somewhat less than human in their eyes by this neglect.

Could it be that his own view of sex was so unfavourable that he did not even wish to mention it? It is true that he did not advocate it but he did not fulminate against it either. Although he himself was not married, he found marriage was to be a perfectly acceptable institution. In Jesus's teaching the origins of an anti-sex tradition in the Christian Church cannot be found.

Joseph Blenkinsopp quotes an opinion brought forward by Tom F. Driver [38]. Driver wrote that Jesus appears in the Gospels as 'the great neutralizer of the meaning of sex'. "Hence the silence is positive and full of meaning. For Jesus sex was neither a mystical force emanating from the divine world nor a demonic force emanating from Satan. It is simply a fact of life, an area of experience in which it is possible to sin as it is in others. Jesus is not isolated from sexuality, but he refuses to confer on it a religious status and meaning." We see Jesus taking a position between the heathen world with its unmasked hedonism and the Gnosis with its whole condemnation of body, sex, and marriage. We should also not forget that he, while remaining almost entirely silent on the subject, assumed that his hearers knew perfectly well how things stood in this field, since they had 'the law and the prophets'.

I feel that Jesus found sex less important and interesting and more matter-of-fact than modern people. Nowadays sex is so highly glorified, we are so constantly bombarded with sexual imagery, that is seems that sex is the supremely important thing in life. Only a few days ago I read an interview with a well-known Dutch stage-manager [39] in which he categorically stated that sex is the only thing that counts. Jesus's 'neutral' attitude may seem surprising, even shocking, to people like him. This causes speculations about Jesus's 'hidden sex-life', for instance, that he was taken off the cross only apparently dead, recovered, married (yes, with Mary Magdalen, with whom else?), had children by his wife, and died peacefully in Rome around A.D. 60. We may see this as a desperate attempt to 'to save Jesus for sex'.

b. In the Letters of Paul

It should be realized that Christianity began its career in a world that was very much given to erotic hedonism. It was also a world in which people relaxed and enjoyed themselves by viewing how gladiators fought another to death, how they combated wild animals and were killed and maimed by them, and how Christians were torn to pieces by lions and panthers. These were favourite pastimes to which Emperors and wealthy Romans treated the populace. Can we expect that people who relished such cruel, degrading spectacles, would be very tender and caring in their erotic relations? The Emperors and the members of high society provided a bad example, adultery and divorce were endemic in these circles [40], and the populace followed suit.

A city like Corinth had a proverbial reputation in this respect : 'korinthiazesthai' came to mean 'to fornicate', and a 'korinthiastês' a 'whore-hopper' [41]. In consequence, Paul knew that he had to be very strict with his Corinthian Christians who lived in a town that thrived on profligacy as well as on commerce. Only a few of them will have had a Jewish background, but the great majority came straight from paganism. It is not probable that they had left the old Adam submerged in the baptismal font. And indeed, says Paul reproachingly, "there is fornication among you", perhaps worse than that among the heathen [42]. He sternly admonishes them that husband and wife should be content with one another. It seems to have a negative sound when he writes : "It is good for a man not to touch a woman", thus extolling religious celibacy. But he knows quite well that this is too high an ideal for his Corinthians, for they lack self-restraint. And because they have no self-restraint, let them marry! It is important to note that he tells husbands and wives that they have mutual obligations in respect of sexuality. If the husband may have the disposal of the body of his wife, she may equally have the disposal of his body. The term 'have the disposal of a body' may sound somewhat crude, but the Greek word used here is 'exousiazoo' which means 'to have authority over'. The meaning will be clear. Paul rejects the pagan notion that the man is the sole 'disposer'; he proclaims the equality of man and woman, even in the nuptial bed [43].

Paul may sometimes sound woman-unfriendly. This is especially so when he is quoted out of context, for instance when he writes that "the man is not out of the woman, but the woman out of the man; the man is not created because of the woman, but the woman because of the man". This is the literal interpretation of Gen. 2:21-23. Does not the apostle know that every male is 'from woman born'? He does. "For just as the woman is out of the man, so is the man out of the woman; and all is out of God. Therefore, in the Lord, the woman is nothing without the man, and the man nothing without the woman" [44].

The apostle is often vehemently criticized for his injunction that wives should be 'submissive' to their husbands [45]. If ever, then the context should be consulted here, in Greek of course. Read Eph. 5:22 carefully, looking for the injunction that wives should be 'submissive' to their husbands. Then one will see that this incriminated word 'submissive' does **not** occur in verse 22; it has been borrowed by the translator from the foregoing sentence, verse 21, which says that people should be 'submissive' to one another. The Greek word used here is 'hupotassemenoi', from the verb 'hupotassoo'. According to the LSJ Lexicon, this verb means, in the passive mood, 'to be obedient', rather than to be 'submissive'. What Paul seeks to convey is that all Christians should be 'obedient' to one another, be helpful and attentive. Nobody should lord it over another person. If Paul repeats this injunction especially to the married women, he does, in my opinion, not want to say more than that wives should not lord it over their husbands - which, as everybody knows, sometimes happens. He does certainly not mean that a wife should be the slave or the servant of her husband or that she is inferior to him.

To Paul the man-woman relation is more than a juridical contract, as it was with the pagans. According to them, a girl passed from the hands of her father or brother into that of her husband; she was transferred from one family to another. In the eyes of the apostle the marriage-bond is something quite different. He goes on to say - once again the context is decisive - that wives should be obedient to their husbands, just as the ecclesia is obedient to Christ. It is altogether out of the question, of course, that Christ would be lording it over his Church, or that the ecclesia would stand in a relation of servility to him. In a Christian marriage the man-woman-relation is a 'mystery', says Paul, meaning with this that it is something sacred, something not merely natural. He has also to say something to the men. They should love their wives as themselves, just as much as their own bodies, and in the same way as Christ loves his ecclesia and gave himself up for her [46].

I do not think it can be argued, as is often done, that Paul had a dualistic attitude to women, marriage, and sex. But he recognizes a hierarchy of values. Religious virginity is something that is higher than marriage which does not mean that marriage is inferior or even evil. And in marriage the supernatural, the sacramental side, is higher that the natural side, with its juridical implications and its sexuality. If he admonishes the women not to be bossy, he warns the men not to be rude to their wives [47], and the fathers not to embitter their children [48]. For if he knew the women, he knew the men too [49].

3. The practice of the early Church

a. The danger of 'over-spiritualising'

The Church of the Graeco-Roman world was engaged in an uphill fight with regard to sexual morality. It had to steer a course between the looseness of pagan morals and what Frank Bottomley calls 'over-spritualising' on the Christian side [50]. Although ecclesiastical authorities and Christian authors were wholly averse of moral laxity and permissivenes, the converts were not immune to it. But on the other hand, it was always so that the need for asceticism, for the self-restraint being necessary for a truly spiritual life, could degenerate into that 'over-spiritualising', with the rabid rejection of marriage, sexuality, and procreation as its corrolary, such as we find it in Tatian, the prophet of Encratism [51]. "In Tatian, the principle of sexual abstinence was almost the prime ingredient in his notion of Christian life" [52]. But Clement of Alexandria, himself a celibate and an ascetic, would have nothing of this. True enough, he rated virginity higher than marriage. But one should not embrace the celibate state out of contempt for marriage or sex. It should be chosen for a higher motive, namely, out of love for God [53].

b. The status of widows

When it came to spreading and sustaining the creed, the earliest Church did not make any distinction between men and women. At the end of his letters Paul always has a word of praise for women who had been particularly helpful. A special role was assigned to the widows. These did not form a religious order with vows and rules, but they nonetheless enjoyed a specific status. But who was a widow? Clearly not every woman who had lost her husband. The First Letter to Timothy is not over-enthusiastic about young widows. They are talkative and meddlesome; let them marry again, it says, and have children!

A true widow must be at least sixty; she has been married only once and is known for her helpfulness to the Christians. She should not have the care of children or of grandchildren [54]. They were recognizable by their widow's weeds. "By taking on the dress of a widow", writes Deborah Sawyer, "a woman gained the ability to move freely within the public sphere, protected from sexual harassment or assault. The guise of widowhood was a means of bypassing the norms of patriarchy, and allowing for an alternative form of existence for women" [55].

c. Female celibacy

Although widows were highly honoured - quite different from their forlorn situation in the pagan world -, it can, of course, not be said that they had chosen their non-married privileged status of their own volition. This was different with those women who remained unmarried 'because of the Kingdom of Heaven'. It is possible, as scholars think, that the wish to remain single had something to do with the Second Coming which was thought to be imminent in the ancient Church. However, male and female celibacy was a thing that proved to be permanent. Just as male celibacy was related to the fact that Jesus had remained unmarried, female virginity doubtless had a connection with the position of Mary, the mother of Jesus.

Deborah Sawyer points out [56] that there are 'three types of argument in Christian theology regarding Eve'. The first says that women are the second sex, because Adam was created first and Eve only after him; this does not necessarily mean that women are inferior to men. The second argument is that it was Eve who caused the Fall; it was she who brought sin into the world. But the third argument is typologically linked to Mary. Without her sin there would have been no redemption, no Redeemer. 'O felix culpa!', the great Preface of the Easter Vigil states boldly - in which prayer, by the way, the fault is attributed to Adam, and not to Eve. In the story of the Fall, God says to the snake : "I shall put enmity between your seed and her seed; he [her seed] shall bruise your head, and you shall bruise his heel" [57]. This is usually seen as the first Messianic promise, the Proto-Evangelium : if it is true that Eve has sinned, it is also true that it will be her progeny that will triumph over Evil.

Just as in biblical typology Jesus becomes the second Adam, Mary becomes the second Eve. The link was not laid immediately; the New Testament does not do it. It was Justin the Martyr who, around A.D. 150, was the first to make the connection. A few decades later Irenaeus of Lyons pointed out that, while Eve was still a virgin when she sinned, although she had a husband, Mary, who was also married, remained a virgin when she bore her son [58]. This means that, in every sense, virginity was seen as something of a primary nature, something more essential or necessary than marriage. The raison d'être for virginity was given in this way.

It cannot be expected that there were convents for women in the centuries before Constantine; such concentrations of religious persons would have attracted unfavourable attention from the pagan authorities. But there were diaconesses, and the diaconess is probably the forerunner of the nun. We find already women serving Jesus [59]. The early Church had diaconesses, originally perhaps widows, but later also younger unmarried women. Virginity seems to have been a condition. They fulfilled several functions; theirs was a honoured status [60]. This institution was replaced by convents for women soon after the liberation of the Church in the beginning of the fourth century. This century saw a proliferation of nunneries in the eastern as well in the western halves of the Roman Empire.

4. Men, women, and the priesthood

a. Why women were not permitted the priesthood

It will be evident that the early Church, as an institution, did not despise women. They played an important part in the propagation of the faith, to the point of not shunning martyrdom. They were present where the males could not come and cared for many groups of Christians. The Church of the first centuries would have been more impoverished without them and would have progressed at a much slower rate [61].

But, one will ask and not necessarily a feminist, if the Church had such a high regard for women, why then were they not allowed to become priests? For there is not the slightest indication in the New Testament, in the Fathers, and in the practice of the ancient Church, that there have indeed ever been priestesses. As everybody knows, the Church has barred the road to the priesthood of women ever since and does so today. Is this not a purely dualistic vision of womanhood and are women not considered and despised as utterly inferior to the male sex? Whereas the man stands at the altar performing the sacral acts, the woman sits in the pew muttering prayers.

The question why women may not become priests is hard to answer. The modern climate is favourable to them; inquiries among Roman Catholics in western countries show that a considerable percentage of them would welcome woman-priests. The Churches of the Reformation are often quoted as having female clerics who functioned well. But they are not priests in the proper sense of the word; it also took several centuries after Luther and Calvin before the first female minister appeared. The Church of England recently enabled women to become parsons. Why does the Roman Catholic Church not follow suit, since this seems to be the modern trend?

The main Church did not exclude the female half of its faithful, simply because it was woman-unfriendly; as we saw, this was absolutely not the case. The present Pope, John Paul II, is fond of advancing the argument that Jesus, the High Priest of the New Covenant, was a man who chose men as his first priests. It could be countered that little else was to be expected in the

Jewish context; Judaism too had no priestesses. But this objection does only shift the argument. For why could Jewish women not become priests? There were prophetesses in Israel but no priestesses. In Volume IV, I demonstrated that Jewish society was not woman-unfriendly at all [62]. If their women were not admitted to the priesthood, this was not because they were despised or held in contempt or considered inferior. Modern argument on this point often takes the form of a petitio principii : a. Women may not become priests; b. the only reason for this is that they are the inferior sort; c. because they are considered inferior, they cannot become priests. The possibility that there some other reason might exist is simply ruled out.

First of all, there is a manifest connection beween religion and sex. Sexuality has a religious, a sacral colouring in many pagan religions, while religious transport was thought to be akin to sexual ecstasy. We know of the 'hieros gamos', the sacred marriage in which a descending god has sexual intercourse with a woman, usually the High Priestess; it could also be the king who mated with a goddess [63]. We also know of the wide-spread institution of temple prostitution.

In Israel temple prostitution was expressly forbidden [64]. The notion that a connection might exist between sex and religious practice or liturgy is most studiously avoided. "You (the priest) must not mount up to my altar by steps, in case your private parts are exposed over against it" [65]. Circumcision, the ritual act through which a young male Jew was made a member of the Covenant, is performed on the eighth day after the child is born. In many other tribes it takes place at the age of puberty and signifies the ritual preparation of the boy for sexual life - an impression that Israel wished to avoid. By excluding women from the priestly functions Israel stressed its firm resolve to keep religious practice and sex as far apart as possible.

But there is more to it than this alone. If we could draw a vertical line dividing men from women, and two other lines going out from the basis on which that vertical line stands, one line crossing the male quadrant and the other the female one, we would then see the line in the female section slanting somewhat towards life, and that in the male section deviating somewhat towards death. In other words, and looking at it from an anthropological perspective, women are somewhat more oriented towards life and men somewhat more towards death. I am not contending that all men are potential killers nor that all women would be peacemakers. I took care to use the word 'somewhat'. Most men would not hurt a fly, whereas there are female professional killers. And did not Sophocles say that "in women too the war-god lives" [66]?

The difference in tendencies is indicated already in the story of the Fall. To the woman it is said that she will bear children with great labour, but she remains what she fundamentally is, 'the mother of all living beings' [67]. The man, however, is condemned to hard work; he must fight the earth to make it yield something [68]. He has to be aggressive in order to live. Regarding history from an anthropological viewpoint, we detect how apt this description is. Always and everywhere it is the men who march out to fight the wars; even in those countries where women have to do military service, they do not fight in the front lines. The bloody work in the slaughter-houses is without exception done by men. Undertaking too is the work of men. I am old enough to have seen a great number of coffins carried to their graves, but I have never seen a woman among the pall bearers.

And so it was also in ancient Israel. We must imagine the Temple in Jerusalem as a big slaughterhouse. Day after day large numbers of animals were sacrificed within the Temple precincts. The ones who did the butchering were, although priests, by the same token learned butchers, for they had not only to dispose of the victims but also to dissect them. All these priestly butchers were men. No woman was ever present. It is also true that the great majority of the sacrificial animals were male, in particular the larger ones, the bulls, the rams, the billy-goats.

Christianity, that had its origin in Judaism, did not take a different view of things. Its priests had to be exclusively male, not only, not even in the first place, to avoid any notion that religious ritual might have anything to do with sex. How easily this notion crops up is proved by the fact that sex invariably rears its head in the so-called 'Black Masses'. What the Roman Catholic priest first and foremost is is a sacrificer. According to Roman Catholic theology, the Mass is the unbloody repetition of Christ's sacrificing himself at Calvary for the redemption of mankind. Since what is involved is the act of somebody voluntarily sacrificing himself, the one who ritually repeats this sacrifice, has to be male, just as the Jewish sacrificers were exclusively male. This is the deepest, the most fundamental reason why the Roman Catholic priesthood is reserved for men. There is no dualistic depreciation of women in this. Rather the contrary. For what is most joyous in life, the bearing of children, the tending of them, the caring for them, is the lot of woman [69].

b. Why priests are not allowed to marry

There is yet another question : why have Roman Catholic priests to remain celibate? Inquiries held in western countries show that a substantial majority of the faithful are in favour of married priests. It is pointed out that in the Churches of the Reformation and in the Church of England clerics, even bishops, may marry. It is also argued that the orthodox Churches of the East have married priests. True, but it is conveniently overlooked that in the East a single man, once ordained, may not marry - in other words, in the East too priests are not allowed to marry, although men already married may become priests -, and also that all monks and bishops have to be celibate. These Churches have their own rules of celibacy.

A first question that must be answered is whether the Church was the only institution in Antiquity to prescribe the celibate state to religious persons. The pagan Greco-Roman world did not possess an institutional priesthood; its priests were men with other, mainly public functions who occasionally performed ritual acts. What comes to mind in this context are the Vestal Virgins. In the Forum stood the small round temple of Vesta, the goddess of the hearth; here the eternal fire was kept that was said to have brought there from Troy, even before Rome had been founded. This fire was tended by the Vestales, the Virgines Vestae. They were six in number and chosen from the most prominent families. They entered the Vestal college still very young, as pre-menstrual girls, and had no say in their choice. Since every Roman woman was under the tutelage of some man, either father or brother or husband, these virgins were under the guardianship of the Pontifex

Maximus, the High Priest. They lived together in a kind of monastery, the Atrium Vestae. They served for thirty years; after this they were freed of their obligations, could return to society, and were allowed to marry. It is a curious comment on their virginal state that among 'the sacred things' they had to tend in the inner sanctuary, things 'that may not be divulged', was the 'fascinum', the 'erect phallus', which was thought to avert evil from Rome. Imagine such a thing in a nunnery!

If a Vestalis became 'impure', that is, had sex, the fire would die of itself, which spelled disaster for Rome. The reverse was also true : if the fire went out, this could only mean that one of the women had become 'impure'. The fate of Rome was dependent on their strictly maintaining their celibate state. There is an evident dualistic element in this, a clearcut opposition of a catastrophic character between having sex and abstaining from it. This situation of 'apartheid' becomes also apparent from the fact that they were not allowed to use the water from the mains; they had their own source. Using the public waterworks would evidently bring them down to the level of the lay-people. The punishment of sinning virgins was in accordance with this dualism : they were entombed alive. We know of two occasions that this really happened : in 113 B.C. and then again under Domitian in A.D. 89 [70].

Does the Roman Catholic rule of clerical celibacy (it applies to nuns too) have its raison d'être in a dualistic contempt of sex, as this became apparent in the case of the Vestal Virgins? Must priests and nuns abstain from sexual intercourse because sex is viewed as dirty, defiling, and bad? The prototype of sacerdotal celibacy is Jesus Christ himself. But he never spoke of sex - at the rare occasions that he did speak of it - as something negative. I refer once again to that passage in the Gospels where Jesus characterized marriage as a temporary institution and that other one in which he praised people who remained single for religious reasons, people who made themselves 'eunuchs' because of the Kingdom of heaven. He did not mean, of course, that men should castrate themselves in order to remain 'religiously pure'; to the Jewish mind this would amount to blasphemy. It signifies that some people will remain unmarried for religious reasons. In this way, he introduced something that was virtually new to Antiquity, namely, religious celibacy. There is no dualism in this. Clerical celibacy is not the absolute opposite of marriage with its sexual implications; both, clerical celibacy and Christian marriage are branches on the same tree, that of chastity. Celibates may sin, but if they do, the world will be not destroyed. But it forcefully expresses that sex is not the most important thing in life; it is a sign of the world to come where we will not marry nor be given in marriage.

c. Married and unmarried clerics

Clerical celibacy was not an obligation from the very beginning. But the college of the apostles consisted of unmarried men, in all probability; not a single a wife is mentioned. Close reading is helpful here. When Peter and his brother Andrew are called by Jesus, it is said that "they left the boat and followed him" [71]; there is no mention of wives or families. In this respect it is very telling that it is the mother of John and James who asks Jesus to reserve the highest functions in the coming Kingdom for her sons [72]. Is it conceivable that we are dealing here with married men since they are led by their mother as though they were still schoolboys [73]. If it is correct that the apostle college consisted of unmarried men, then we have here the beginnings of an institution. Paul is the next great instance of celibacy.

There were in these early times men and women or small groups of them who remained unmarried for religious reasons; the men were not necessarily priests. Sacerdotal celibacy was not obligatory for clerics; many priests and even bishops were married. The First Letter to Timothy only says that a bishop should be the husband of only one wife [74]. This does not mean preventing him from living in bigamy, of course, but only that a remarried man could not become a bishop neither might a bishop remarry when he had lost his wife. This rule also seems to have prevailed for ordinary priests.

But notwithstanding this, the celibate state was held in high honour. Later it was understood that monks had to be and to remain unmarried. Arguing around 200 against second and third marriages, Tertullian praises those priests who were married only once and more in particular those who "sanctify themselves by virginity" [75]. Already then there must have been celibate priests. "How many of them", writes Tertullian, "do we see in the sacred orders, men who chose to remain chaste, preferring to be married to God" [76]. This author makes it clear that such men remained unmarried for a higher ideal, not from hatred or fear of sexuality. Around 320 Eusebius of Caesarea exhorts those who are in the service of the Lord to have no commerce with a wife [77]. This probably means that married priests should abstain from having intercourse with their wives; other ecclesiastical authors express themselves in the same vein.

But Tertullian was not sure that married priests who had committed themselves to abstinence would always be strong enough to live up to their promise, so that they would sin secretly [78]. Writing of women who had committed themselves to living as virgins, but who were found out to have carnal relations with men, Cyprian of Carthage, an advocate of virginity, if there ever was one, stated bluntly that, if they were unable to live a chaste life, they should renounce their vows and contract a lawful marriage [79]. This same bishop of Carthage spoke indignantly of holy virgins who frequented the mixed baths where men and women were all naked and where the women exposed themselves to the lecherous eyes of the males [80]. Promiscuous bathing in the nude was of course a source of irregularities. The Apostolic Constitution forbade all Christian women to take part in them [81]. This shows how hard a task the Church had in persuading its faithful, even those in religion, to abstain from their ingrained pagan customs and to lead decent Christian lives.

d. The development of the obligation of celibacy

Given the weakness of the human nature, stricter disciplinary measures became necessary. The first injunction of this kind was issued by the Synod of Elvira in Spain in 305; it stated clearly that bishops, priests, and deacons should refrain from sexual intercourse with their wives and not have children with them; those who sinned against this would lose their clerical function. It was also stipulated that no bishop or cleric should have a woman dwelling with him, not even a sister or daughter dedicated to virginity [82]. Although this council was only a provincial one and although it did not make clerical celibacy obligatory, it shows clearly in which direction the wind was blowing.

During the first ecumenical Council, that of Nicaea in 325, some bishops proposed to forbid all sexual relations between those in orders and their wives. But the Egyptian bishop Paphnutius raised his voice against this proposal. He judged that it would lay too heavy a burden on the many priests and bishops who lived in wedlock. Paphnutius was a venerable man, a celibate himself, who had led an exemplary moral life; having been martyred during a persecution, he had lost an eye. The words of this highly respected man carried weight, and the proposal was rejected [83]. This episode may show that the ancient Christian Church was not so fanatically inimical to sex as is often thought.

The first more official pronouncement came in 386 under the pontificate of Pope Siricius. The occasion was a Roman synod, but it shows that the bishops of Rome were considering the issue. Priests and deacons were expressly forbidden to live with their wives; offenders would be punished according to the degree of their culpability. Referring to the authority of the Apostolic See, the Pope stated that offenders must be deprived of all ecclesiastical orders. That he intended this to be a general rule for the whole Church becomes apparent from the fact that he instructed bishop Himerius to communicate this to all the bishops of Africa, while he himself also wrote to the African bishops in the same vein. His opinion was that offenders should even be excommunicated. It deserves attention, however, that there was no talk of a rule of celibacy, that is, that only unmarried men could be ordained [84]. Perhaps many a cleric will have thought that they had better send away their wives, if they were not allowed to have intercourse with them, but this way-out was expressly forbidden to them by the ecclesiastical authorities. The rule that they must not have intercourse with their wives will have brought them into an awkward position, and contraventions will not have been rare.

e. The custom of the Eastern Church

The western Church fought an uphill struggle to ensure that its priests and deacons lived in continence. During the fifth century provincial synod after synod had to inculcate the rule of clerical chastity anew. What about the eastern Church, always in many respects somewhat different from its western counterpart? Celibacy as such was well-known and accepted in the East since monachism had soared high in these lands after the liberation of the Church. But for the ordinary clergy it was voluntarily; there was no imperative rule, and the injunction of Pope Siricius was little heeded. The second Ecumenical Council, held in Constantinople in 381, did not broach the subject at all; incidentally, there was only one western bishop present there.

An ascetic man like Epiphanius, writing at the end of the fourth century, although pleading that clerics should remain continent, conceded that not enough priests, steadfast in this respect, could be found to man the parishes [85]. Lea concludes that "the East preserved the tradition of earlier times ..., prohibiting marriage in orders and the ordination of digami, but imposing no compulsory separation on those who had been married previous to ordination" [86]. And although we hear a chorus of Latin and Greek Fathers of the Church - Ambrose, Augustine, Jerome, John Chrysostom - pleading for clerical virginity, the period under discussion ended with there being no general rule of celibacy in the sense that only unmarried men could become priests.

5. The early Fathers on body, sex, and marriage

In the Fathers of the first two centuries of the Chuch there is remarkably little about such subjects as body, sex, and marriage; "much of the small volume of patristic literature dealing with sexual topics is devoted to a vindication of celibacy against marriage, and of widowhood against digamy or remarriage after the death of a first partner" [87]. The Church, struggling to find an identity of its own vis-à-vis Judaism and the Gnosis, and constantly in the grip of the pagan Empire, had other preoccupations. It was, as Frank Bottomley writes, and allow me to quote him at some length, "a time of continuing crisis ... This was obviously no time for considering its attitude towards, and developing its ideas about, the human body. That body was likely to be torn to pieces at any time by the most ingenious methods of a sadistic age. Nevertheless, not only are possible growth-points preserved but some of the implications are fairly discerned : the centrality of the doctrines of the Incarnation, Resurrection and communion in the Eucharistic Body of Christ is constantly asserted, the psychosomatic unity of man is maintained against heretical distortion and there is asseveration of the dignity of the human body ... At any rate, we can assert that, in spite of persecution and confusion, the essential ingredients of a balanced yet religious attitude towards the body are preserved through this endurance" [88].

Apart from a few pious exhortations, the only notable passage is to be found in the Pastor of Hermas, a work dating from the decade 140-150. From the outset he relates how he had been the slave of a Roman lady, called Rhoda, who was a Christian or perhaps later became one. Once, when she had gone bathing in the Tiber, he had to help her out of the water, naked as she was [89]. Her radiant beauty made a deep impression on him, or as Peter Brown expresses it, the incident was not "calculated to increase the prophet's peace of mind" [90].

Later he had a vision in which Rhoda appeared to him; she reproached him that there had been lust in his heart which, she said, "is a great sin" [91]. This experience made him declare that a man should keep strictly to his own wife; he should not let any thoughts arise about another man's wife. Committing adultery is doing what the heathen are doing [92]. He is not against a second marriage after the partner had died, but it is better to remain single in that case [93]. Hermas, who was a married man himself (to a talkative woman) and had children [94], did not agitate against sexuality, only against its excesses.

6. 'The devil's gateway'?

In the course of time it became necessary to say something more definite about the subjects under discussion in this chapter. With respect to moral teaching, the Church was threatened on its left flank by paganism with its loose morals and its blatant hedonism, and on its right flank by rigoristic movements like the Gnostic sects, Encratism, and Montanism. All these movements had a very low view of human nature and above all of sexuality; 'doctrinaire teetotallars and conscientious objectors' (to sex, marriage, women, the Church, the whole world), Bottomley called them in a happy phrase [95]. It was often difficult for Christian authors, and also for ordinary Christians, to steer clear of such rigorism, while at the same time acknowledging that some measure of asceticism was necessary for the true Christian. We must not be surprised if some authors tend dangerously in the direction of rigorism, towards a dualism of the spiritual and the physical.

Tertullian is an example of this difficulty of being able to draw a straight line. He himself was not a balanced person; he shifted his religous allegiance more than once. For a time he was an orthodox Roman Catholic, but after 200 became a Montanist, until he became dissatisfied with this sect [96]. He began his career as a Christian apologist with a treatise directed against the Gnostic prophet Marcion. This man was an outright dualist to whom the worlds of the spirit and of matter were totally different and radically opposed [97]. Tertullian defended the basic orthodox position that those worlds were not opposed to each other but had been harmoniously joined in the person of Jesus Christ, the God-man. He stated categorically that "the God of man, of the Christ, of woman and the Church, of the flesh and the spirit, is the same" [98].

In his 'De Carne Christi' he argued that, although 'the flesh' could sin, it was not sinful to be 'in the flesh', to be human, to have a body (it was the Gnostic position that it is was sinful). "The flesh (= the physical nature), which is accounted the minister and the servant of the soul, also turns out to be its associate and its co-heir. And if this is so in temporal things, why not also in things eternal?" [99]. Tertullian has words of praise for the institution of marriage; after all, he was a married man himself. Polemizing against Marcion, he wrote that "we [Christians] do not reject marriage, but simply refrain from it. Nor do we prescribe sanctity [with this he means the celibate state - F.] as the rule, but only recommend it ... at the same time earnestly vindicating marriage, whenever hostile attacks are made against it, to the disparagement of the Creator" [100]. In the treatise addressed to his wife, he wrote a moving encomium of Christian marriage : "How beautiful, then, the marriage of two Christians, two who are one in hope, one in desire, one in the way of life they follow, one in the religion they practice ... Nothing divides them, either in flesh or in spirit ... They have no secrets from one another; they never shun each other's company, they never bring sorrow to each other's heart" [101]. Since we find this in a treatise written for his own wife, he must have been thinking of his own marriage. Did he not call her 'my best beloved fellow-servant in the Lord' [102]?

So far so good. But often enough this same author shows a tendency towards rigorism, a tendency that became ever fiercer. In a rather early work, directed to his wife, 'Ad uxorem', his opinions are still moderate. Christian marriage is indissoluble. He does not strictly forbid to conclude a second marriage, but this constitutes an unpleasant concession to human frailty in his view. He admonishes his wife not to do this, if he came to die. A later treatise, directed to a friend, who had recently become a widower, 'De exhortatione castitatis', shows that his position was hardening. This time he condemns second marriages as fornication. He even becomes somewhat critical about a first marriage. Later still , in his 'De monogamia', a work from his Montanist period, he states that the Holy Ghost does not tolerate second marriages. Marriage itself is no more than a concession to the weakness of human nature [103].

There may be a personal cause for this rigorism. Tertullian hints, 'somewhat morbidly', finds Bailey [104], that he had sinned before he was converted [105]. Perhaps he confesses to having committed adultery before he married [106]. He also reveals that he had been 'excessive' in his marriage; he calls these things 'frivolous and dirty' and cannot imagine that God has promised them to those who are his own [107]. The dualistic gap is evident here. Later in his life he looked back on his sexual experiences with disgust. Can it be that he had initially enjoyed having sex, but came to regret this later?

His radical, his basically dualistic disposition induced him to equate normal intercourse in wedlock with fornication [108]. In his view women were basically sexual beings. This made him utter negative words about women : they "were seductive, and Christian baptism did nothing to change this fact" [109]. For this reason he castigates the female sex in the harshest of terms. "You must know that you are Eve ...; your sex is sentenced by God in this world. You are the devil's gateway ..., you were the first to desert God's law" [110]. Poor Tertullian! It was always all or nothing for him, a true dualist [111].

7. Other opinions

We should, however, not think that Tertullian's voice reflected that of the magisterium of the Church. Not all other Fathers of the Church adopted the same vehement tone. It is remarkable that the Didachê, a book of catechical instruction, dating from the second century (its author, or rather compilator, is unknown), does not devotee a single word to the subject. In the 'Apostolic Tradition', another catechical text, dating from ca. 220 and ascribed to Hippolytus, it is explicitly stated that "one who lives in the bond of wedlock is not impure; let him not hesitate to pray" [112]. Other more or less official texts could be quoted [113]. There is a discrepancy between the attitudes of the magisterium and the utterances of ecclesiastical authors. Some of these were rabidly rigoristic and others moderate and accomodating, and still others situating themselves somewhere in between.

Bottomley concludes that the Fathers did not yield "to the thoroughgoing dualism which denounced marriage as evil". But they did not all of them really extolled and celebrated the wedded state. It brought a lot of inconveniences with it, they found. Parenthood was seldom a source of joy in their opinion. One would think that it was to be expected that celibate men would express themselves in this way, but there were some married men among them. Was Bailey wrong in stating that "patristic literature adopts a pessimistic view of matrimony even when it vindicates its goodness ... nor do they (the Fathers) show much appreciation of the family"? [114].

8. What about the vox populi?

A few comments are appropriate here. First of all - it cannot be repeated too often -the Fathers are not synonymous with the magisterium of the Church; what they express are private opinions on which they do not always agree among themselves. Nor are they the vox populi. We know next to nothing of how ordinary Christians felt about their private lives. But it is rather far-fetched to believe that all of them would find the matrimonial bond to be a burden and having children a source of constant unrest and irritation.

Secondly, a sentiment as that expressed by Bailey and other authors on this subject is coloured by our modern perspective. For us, people at the turn of the twenty-first century, privacy, personal happiness, deployment of self, a secure sense of identity, and mutual sexual fulfilment, are all-important things. But Antiquity was not a great time for privacy and the rest. People lived, and for a very long time, would continue to live, in organic communities : the polis, the village, the Church, and above all, the extended family, the clan. They did not derive their values from what we call 'personal identity' but from the life and customs of the community that they were part of. This made them set less emphasis on the values we cherish above all. But this does not mean that the people of these times were callous persons, incapable of love and gentle feelings, indifferent to one another, especially to their wives and children.

If we keep this in mind, I do not think that early Christianity cut a bad figure in these respects when compared to paganism and above all to the Gnosis. We need not speak once again of the Gnosis with its rabid, dualistic rejection of all that is physical as intrinsically evil. But I have also no doubt that families were better off in Christian surroundings than in a pagan context and were held in higher regard.

9. In defense of matrimony

On the whole the positions taken by the early Fathers of the Church caused them to perform difficult balancing acts. They of course advocated virginity as the preferable state of life, but on the other hand they knew that most Christians were married, and that marriage was a divine institution, expressly sanctioned as such by Jesus himself. So, if the married state was good, celibacy was better. Quite a number of Fathers express themselves in this vein [115]. To quote only one of them, Gregory of Nazianze : "although virginity (= celibacy) is the more honourable thing, this does not mean that matrimony is something shameful" [116]. This same author admitted that celibacy could be a difficult and dangerous state, and that marriage was the safer option [117]. Clement of Alexandria, a notoriously mild man, who loves to be on the positive side, states that a man can have no better friend than a caring and loving wife [118]; losing one's children is the greatest possible evil [119]. He even goes so far as to say that it is unmanly to avoid cohabitating with a wife and children [120]. Let me quote him literally. "A real man does not prove himself so by choosing the single life. Among men that one deserves the prize of victory in the contest whom neither joy nor sorrow throws out of his way but who goes on caring for his marriage, for the education of his children, and his household. He will remain united with God's love and will emerge victoriously from all the tribulations that will be his part through having children, a wife, and possessions. Who has no family will be spared such worries. But because he has only to look after himself, he will stay behind the one who cannot equal him in caring for his salvation but who supersedes him in caring for the well-being of his whole family. This makes him an image of true [= God's] providence" [121].

Clement does not hesitate to distance himself from Paul when the apostle says that "the unmarried man is anxious about the affairs of the Lord, how to please the Lord; but the married man is anxious about worldly affairs, how to please his wife, and his interests are divided" [122]. "How now?", Clement exclaims, "is it not possible, then, to please one's wife, exactly as God wants it, and by doing so, be grateful to the Lord? Is a married man not allowed to think of the affairs of the Lord, together with his wife?" [123].

Peter Brown thinks that Clement was aware of the fact that the survival of the ancient Church was not dependent on celibate sages (of whom there were only a few). He (Brown) calls the second-century Church "a loose confederation of believing householders. Clement tended to view the world from the perspective of these householders". 'The enduring structure of the Christian household', based on marriage as a sacred bond, was the prop and mainstay of Christianity [124].

10. Origen's sombre views

If the reader read what I wrote about Origen and his ideas in the foregoing volume of this series [125], he or she will not be surprised to see that this theologian demonstrated a rather sombre view of the body. The fact that he had himself castrated shows that he did not feel at ease with his own sexuality. In Origen's view all beings had fallen by their own free will, that is, they were less excellent than they were intended to be, angels and men alike. The only one to escape this general verdict was Jesus Christ. He (Origen) displayed a general feeling of dissatisfaction with this state of affairs; this applies especially to the body. As Brown frames it, "the body was always a limit and a source of frustration" [126]. Temptations originated from it, causing confusion. But it could be transformed and transcended, not by a stroke of the wand or by sheer will power, but in the long healing process of salvation. In the ideal human make-up sexuality was not really necessary; celibate men and women proved that they could do without it. When the final deliverance had come, there would no longer be sexuality, just as marriage and procreation would vanish [127].

Origen, who was a high-strung person, always had his eye on a higher, ideal world, a product of his own fantasy mainly. This world could be found prefigured already in the present one. The celibate, virgin state was the main element of this prefiguration. Being celibate did not primarily mean the repression of the sexual urge; this would be too negative. It was the manifestation of an essential, spiritual freedom - "a freedom so intense, a sense of identity so deeply rooted, as to cause to evaporate the normal social and physical constraints that tied the Christian to his or her gender" [128]. The principal constraint was that of having to marry and bringing forth children. Having been liberated from this constraint does not make a person turn in upon him- or herself. Quite the contrary! It made him or her more available for others.

Origen did not reject the institution of marriage. As I said already, this was a non sequitur for every Christian thinker. But he did not go farther than not rejecting it. He did not deny that the marriage bed had its delights and family life its pleasures, but remaining true to his basic idea of a fallen world, he found such joys only the echo of the rejoicing to be experienced in his higher world. Origen felt, "with the intangible certainty of a refined, almost aesthetic, spiritual sensibility, that married intercourse actually coarsened the spirit" [129] (and he was not the only one to think so). In consequence, dedicated Christians had better avoid this trap. Clement's opinion that husband and wife, by loving one another, even sexually, could ascend to God, was totally alien to Origen.

He stated in as many words that even the love husbands felt for their own wives was 'dishonest' [130]. It sets one thinking that he made this statement in a homily on the Song of Songs, which is a hymn on erotic love. He went one (decisive) step further, for he also wrote that sex in marriage was the exact opposite to the luminous, spiritual love of Christ [131]. This is dualism, no doubt. It is not radical dualism since marriage is not totally rejected, but relative dualism, because marriage, with its sexual implications, is considered an inferior thing when compared with the sublimity of spiritual love. That there is dualism in Origen's conception of these things should surprise no one. In my discussion of his theological ideas in Vol. XIII I have characterized them as dualistic [132]. It would have been a miracle if this opinion he had of marriage would have formed an exception in the totality of his ideology.

11. The pastoral care of John Chrysostom

The paganism that suffused the society of these days did not evaporate so quickly. Even in the late fourth century an austere and ascetical preacher like John Chrysostom had to deal with Christians whose customs were by no standard as Christian as they should be. It would be wrong to portray him as a cleric obsessed with sex. His great interest was the deplorable situation of the poor to which he returned time and again, exhorting his faithful to be generous towards them and castigating the egotism of the wealthy. But in a pleasure-loving city like Antioch, and confronted with faithful who happily indulged in its pleasures, he could, as a popular and forceful preacher, impossibly avoid the subject.

John, the bishop of Antioch, knew only too well what was going on in the hippodroms, the theatres, and, above all, in the public baths of this seething oriental metropolis. Not without reason he said that the devil enjoyed himself enormously in Antioch [133]. And it was equally not without reason that he admonished girls and young housewives to stay at home. "In fourth-century Antioch, as in so many late classical cities, nudity had remained a fact of life", writes Brown; "the festive life of the city demanded moments of easy-going nudity in the great public baths and frank eroticism" [134]. In these baths, which were mixed, a woman might strip herself completely bare in the presence of her (male) servants; since slaves were non-persons, they were supposed not to be affected by her naked beauty [135].

A special new feature of Antioch were the water-theatres where the spectators saw naked girls splashing around in the water. John reproached his faithful for going to see this spectacle; it was 'a snare of the devil', he said [136]. We should not think of the bishop as only an austere moralist. There was a social element in his preaching. If those of high society thought that the distance between wealthy and the destitute was so great that it could not be shameful to see one another's nudity, they were wrong. He would not hear of 'non-persons'. There was no difference between the bodies of the rich and the poor [137].

As a good pastor who was in close contact with his faithful and knew what moved them, he did not want to make their lives harder by thundering against ordinary marital intercourse. It is heretical, he found, to speak ill of marriage and of all that it implies. "Why are you ashamed of what is honourable? Why do you blush for what is immaculate? ... Love is a gift of God, for it is the root of our existence." And he states explicitly that coition unites and brings together the bodies of the twain and makes them one [138].

The child born from the chaste intercourse of husband and wife would unite the spouses [139]. There is nothing dirty in the conjunction of the bodies; the evil comes from free will and bad thoughts [140]. In his catalogue of sins covetousness and avarice are far worse moral transgressions than fornication, because the sexual urge is a natural thing, which cannot be said of the lust of money [141].

He deplored the fact that Christian marriage-ceremonies differed little from those in pagan circles. The accent was not on the holy, sacramental bond of man and wife, blessed by God, but on sexual pleasure. There were bawdy songs and suggestive dances, even in the public streets [142]. All this shows how far the Antioch of the late fourth century was from being a truly Christian society. The allegiances of its Christians were divided. They certainly wanted to be true to their baptism, but at the same time they loved to enjoy the pleasures of this frolicking Hellenistic town - a town that in John's view was hardly more than a big rubbish heap, the devil's playground.

What he wanted was to replace this doomed city with a truly Christian one. The construction of such a society had to begin with the foundation of the Christian household, so that Antioch would become "a conglomeration of believing households, joined by a common meeting-place within the courtyards of the Great Church" [143]. It is here that his vision becomes dualistic. There was no compromise possible - as so many of his faithful believed - between this profoundly pagan city and the authentically Christian way of life. This implies that he was by no means against marriage and sexuality : the family was to be the prop and mainstay of the coming society. What was condemnable was not marriage but fornication and adultery; wedlock was a remedy against these evils [144]. John knew very well that, with respect to his ideal of a Christian society, he had nothing to expect from the pagan authorities and public opinion. "The man who blasphemes God will not be indicted by the public lawgivers. And if a man who, having a wife, treats her like a servant, this, so it seems, is nothing at all on account of public law or for the multitude" [145].

12. Jerome the moralist

Times were beginning to change. At the turn of the fifth and fourth centuries, one did not need a penetrating eye to see the Roman Empire tottering on its foundations. In 410 the Eternal City was stormed and thoroughly plundered by Alaric's Visigoths. The din reached the ears of a hermit living in a cave near Bethlehem. "I was so stupefied and dismayed', he wrote, "that, day and night, I could think of nothing else but the welfare of the Roman community" [146]. The catastrophe staggered belief : "The bright light of the whole world had been quenched, or rather that the Roman Empire had lost its head, and that the whole world had perished in one city [147] ... The city which had taken the whole world was itself taken" [148].

The man who wrote this knew perfectly well why all those horrifying events had happened. "God is offended with us but we do nothing to appease him. It is by reason of our sins that the barbarians are strong; it is our vices that bring defeat to the armies of Rome". But do we wrap ourselves in sackcloth? No, we do not! "The Roman world is falling, and yet we hold our heads erect instead of bending our necks" [149]. The person we are listening to - Jerome, as the reader will have understood already - was a moralist, so much is evident.

Jerome was born in 347 or 348 in Stridon, a town in present-day Slovenia (near Ljubljana, the capital) as a son of a wealthy pagan family. He studied grammar and rhetorics in Rome, where he became a Christian at the age of twenty. He travelled a lot and changed his dwelling-place often; we find him in Constantinople, Jerusalem, Antioch, and once again in Rome. Jerome was a gifted but highly irascible man, a pastmaster in the gentle art of making enemies, as his ferocious campaign against (the long deceased) Origen and John, the then bishop of Jerusalem, sufficiently proves [150].

Having since long shown a predilection for an ascetical life, he became a hermit in 386, where he lived in that cave near Bethlehem which I mentioned already; this was his abode until his death in 420. He was by no means cut off from the world there, maintaining as he did a vast correspondence with many persons. It was there that he made his famous translation of the Bible into Latin, the so-called 'Vulgata'.

Jerome never minced his words when speaking of moral matters. He knew, of course, that many priests were married, and he realized that he had to tolerate this since there were not yet enough celibate priests. But in his eyes it was an abuse. A former monk, a certain Jovinian, was active in Rome in 393, where he created a great stir with a treatise in which he stated, among other things, that the married and celibate states were equally good and meritorious; he was solemnly condemned for this by Pope Siricius. The Pope spoke of an execrable text, a 'scriptura horrifica'. Eight adherents of Jovinian were condemned along with him [151]. This is one of the extremely rare cases in which the magisterium pronounced itself on matters of this kind.

There seems, by the way, to have been some sort of offensive against exaggerated notions of virginity; Jovinian was not the only one to express himself on this point. A Latin author whose book is lost, Helvidius, arguing that Mary had not remained a virgin, concluded that this meant that marriage and celibacy were equally good. Another westerner, Vigilantius, was a Luther avant la lettre with his vigorous attacks on the veneration of relics, on too great a merit attached to almsgiving, and on the arrogance of people in religion. He advocated a married clergy and found that the option for celibacy often was the result of a lack of responsibility [152].

All three of them incurred the wrath of Jerome. We know their opinions only through him, in fact; it is impossible to say whether or not he misrepresented them. Against Helvidius he defended the perpetual virginity of Mary; this treatise was relatively short and mild, although he began with calling his opponent a boor, a barely literate man, and a turbulent fellow [153]. He defended clerical celibacy against Vigilantius whom he showered with invectives [154]. But his principal target was Jovinian. The fact that his opponent had already been excommunicated, and that Ambrose, the authoritative bishop of Milan, had already entered the lists with him, did not prevent Jerome from attacking Jovinian in a long treatise [155].

His choice of words was so coarse that it provoked indignation. A friend, Pammachius, asked him to withdraw the treatise; with his characteristic lack of self-knowledge its author asserted that he had written it 'prudenter', with prudence [156]. In a long defensive letter he toned it down somewhat [157], but convinced of being in the right, he never became truly repentant. An anonymous monk polemized against him; he retorted by calling this man a newsmonger, a pettifogger, an artful fellow [158]. But he spoiled his own cause by contemptuously declaring that he did "not condemn wedlock. Indeed, - and this I say to make my meaning quite clear to him [the monk in question] -, I should like to take everyone a wife who cannot manage to sleep alone because he gets frightened at night" [159].

There were also persons who welcomed Jerome's radical stance. In a long letter on chastity, ascribed to Pelagius, but in all probability not written by himself, Paul's dictum is quoted that "it is better to marry than to burn" [160]; consequently, the author calls marriage 'a questionable good', if the choice is between marrying and burning [161].

13. More positive opinions

There can be no doubt that Jerome's attitude to marriage was dualistic. He remained just within the margin of relative dualism (since he could not condemn it, because it is a biblical institution), but he came within an inch of totally rejecting it. It is evident that the question of celibacy and marriage was quite an issue in the Church of the late fourth century. Were they or were they not dualistically opposed? Jerome's viewpoint must have made married couples feel confused and disturbed. But well-meaning authors came forward to remove their worries.

We possess a delightful treatise addressed to a certain Gregoria, obviously a Christian lady of Roman high society. Its anonymous author was a good judge of people, for he knew that a woman, while remaining submissive to her husband, could have her own way in the household. A woman may hold sway over her husband by sharing with him the pleasures of the nuptial bed; if she does so, he will certainly let her have her way in religious matters [162]. I feel that the author is portraying Gregoria on the model of the housewife in Proverbs [163] : as the head of a large Roman household with many servants who are all treated well and all behave in an exemplary fashion [164]. We are here miles away from Jerome's caricature.

14. Augustine the good pastor

a. A man of a radical nature

It cannot be denied that Saint Augustine had a propensity towards radicalism. Earlier we saw that his personal stance in matters of grace and free will was more strict than that of the magisterium [165]. He was also the only Christian authority who was not averse to invoking the help of the secular arm against heretics (although he never did so himself in practice) [166]. It has also been suggested that his alleged puritanism was a hangover from his days with the Manichaeans [167], but it could just as well be the other way round, namely, that having a radical disposition, he felt attracted to persons of the same ilk. Respecting the influence Manichaeism may have had on him, it should be remembered that he never was an elect but only an auditor; only the elect had to renounce all forms of sexuality. He felt this was too much for him; he certainly wanted chastity, 'but not now' [168].

b. Was Augustine a dualist?

The question whether this Father of the Church was a dualist brings us in medias res. Did he put the spirit on one side and the body on the other, totally opposing them, which enabled him to utterly condemn sex, even in marriage? Some caution is needed here. "There is", says the Dutch author Van Bavel, "no worse term of abuse than the word dualism. If it is said of something that it is dualistic, then everybody believes that matter to have been classsified." And he significantly adds : "Do not all of us have something of the great-inquisitor in our blood?" [169]. Dubbing Saint Augustine a dualist in matters of sex means accusing him of condemning people to a life of bleak puritanism, always fearing that they are sinning. From the outset it must be admitted that there are a few utterances in Augustine's works that seem to underpin this accusation. The problem is how they must be interpreted.

As a young student of philosophy Augustine had been a fervent Platonist. And Plato was an outspoken dualist; he acknowledged two opposed worlds, a higher and a lower one. But once he had become a Christian, Augustine could impossibly remain true to this Platonic dualism. The coming of God's Son signified that the two worlds had been joined together; creation was the work of God, sanctified by the person of Jesus Christ. The human body was not something to be discarded like a cloak, to be left behind when the spirit soared up. This is the Christian conviction that the convert came wholeheartedly to share. If he did not remain a Manichaean dualist, he also did not remain a Platonic one.

But if he was not a dualist, was he then perhaps a pessimist, a hypochondric, "always looking on the dark side and in his gloomy imagination seeing disaster lurk everywhere"? [170] It is true that he occasionally may seem to give this impression. In his Confessions he relates how he, together with some other boys, late in the evening stole pears from a tree standing near the family's vineyard; he rightly deplored this, but he speaks of it as if he had committed the great train robbery [171]. But on the whole he enjoyed the goodness of life, admiring the beauty of nature and being delighted with the joys of love and friendship. To him creation was God's handiwork and, therefore, eminently good. He was not an ascetic; he loved good food, a glass of wine, and music; neither did he ever shun human company. The body too was good. He combated Porphyry who, in a truly dualistic style, had declared that "all that is bodily should be fled" [172].

Augustine was a realist, "regarding the world as it is, unbemused either by romantic or scientific optimism" [173], nor, may we add, unduly bothered by gloom or pessimism. It was part of this realism to view sex, not as a necessary evil but as a necessary good, as a function of the body that "was made for the service of a rational soul" [174].

c. Was Augustine sex-obsessed?

Was he perhaps obsessed by sex, as not rarely is supposed? A few remarks should be made. Augustine was a temperamental, sometimes even passionate man to whom love and friendship meant a great deal. Sex too had played a considerable role in his life, and he had found it hard to renounce it once and for all. He had become a priest and later the bishop of a large and difficult diocese, Hippo, in what is now Algeria. His administrative and pastoral tasks took up most of his time; he preached hundreds of sermons in his cathedral church. And all that he further did was writing, writing, writing, day and night.

He wrote volume after volume to combat all kinds of heresies, he explained Scripture in numerous treatises, he composed essay after essay on the most diverse subjects, on music, on fasting, on friendship, on lying, to quote only a few titles, he wrote his great seminal work, 'The City of God'. And if this were not already enough, he maintained a vast correspondence with innumerable persons. What I am trying to convey is that this man simply had no time to be 'sex-obsessed'. References to questions of sexuality are relatively rare in his enormous oeuvre. The most explicit he is in his spiritual autobiography, the 'Confessions', the first great ego-document of world-history.

d. Augustine as an almost married man

As a young man, still an adolescent, he came to know a girl, probably an African, with who he lived for thirteen years, without being married to her. There can be no doubt that he enjoyed sleeping with her; it was not a slip of his pen when he spoke of the 'sweet joys' of sex [175]. Later he called their companionship 'a pact of libidinous love'; that a child was born of it (only one in thirteen years) was obviously against his intentions [176]. For he fathered, perhaps unintentionally, a son, Adeodatus. Although his father called him 'the child of my sin' [177], he never repudiated him. On the contrary, he was proud of this precocious and intelligent boy, who figures in several of his works. He was baptized in 387, together with his father, but he died very young, not much more than fifteen or sixteen years old [178].

It was in 384, when Augustine was thirty years old, that his mother Monica found that he must marry; he was a rhetor now in Milan, and on the verge of a brilliant career. His girl-friend was obviously not good enough; remaining for always anonymous, she returned to Africa. He broke with her, not without heart-felt grief [179]. This is not the most honourable episode of Augustine's life. A prospective bride was found, a girl from a well-to-do family, but she was still too young to marry. Unable to remain celibate, the bridegroom in spe took another concubine with whom he lived for two years; her name is also unknown. So Augustine had fifteen years in all of sexual experience behind him. But when he became a priest, he no longer had a son and had severed all relations with women.

e. The break

It is a not unreasonable supposition in itself that Augustine's sexual past had something to do with his later stance in matters of sexuality. He had had such a past, and although he deplored it, he never concealed it. And it is conceivable that the reminiscence sometimes plagued him. But it is an altogether different question whether this past determined his position. There were also biblical, theological, and philosophical influences, to say nothing of his pastoral experiences.

Although probably long prepared in foro interno, the break in Augustine's life occurred rather suddenly. He converted to Christianity in 386 and was baptized a year later, after which he became a priest and in 391 the bishop of Hippo. Ambrose, the bishop of Milan, played a role in this turn-about; the spirituality of this holy man profoundly impressed him. In the summer of 386 Augustine read the Neoplatonic authors Plotinus and Porphyry who convinced him that the delights of pure spirituality were far to be preferred above erotic pleasures. He never was one to combine the one with the other; it was the one or the other. As a result, he decided to live in abstinence.

f. Augustine's basic position on sex, women, and the body

Augustine wrote on marriage and on virginity. Just like all other Fathers, he rated celibacy higher than marriage. But this does not mean that he denigrated marriage or that he found sexuality dirty, evil, or inferior. To those who considered women to be the source of all evil, he said : "The sex of a woman is not vice but nature" [180]. And to those who believed that the body was deeply inferior to the soul, he had this response that "it is not the body but the corruptibility of the body which is a burden to the soul" [181]. With 'corruptibility' he meant that our bodies are not only subject to illness, ageing, and decay, but above all, to death. Augustine's greatest problem was not what is called his 'obsession with sex' but that human beings are destined to die [182]. Along this road we come to his doctrine of the Fall.

g. The effects of the Fall

That men and women are sexually differentiated beings was not the deplorable result of the Fall in Augustine's opinion. If the first couple would not have sinned and would have stayed in the Garden of Eden in consequence, they would, thought Augustine, have founded a family; they would have had their children by mating sexually. But they would have done so without lust. It would have been friendship that brought them together [183]. It was not the necessity of sexual intercourse for the continuation of mankind that bothered Augustine, but the fact that chaste desire could so easily become lust, and by lust he understood an inordinate craving for sexual satisfaction. In Paradise the will and the desire would have been congruous, but since the Fall this was no longer so. If sex had existed in Paradise, it would have been 'innocent', he found, that is, free from lust, but through the Fall 'concupiscentia' had come to it, which made sex unruly. As Peter Brown expresses it : "The disjunction between conscious will and sexual feeling seemed to betray a dislocation of the human person" [184].

Something had gone wrong with sexuality through the Fall, which made him call it a 'discordiosum malum' [185], something disorderly, the result of sin, "an abiding principle of discord lodged in the human person since the Fall" [186]. It was not sex itself that was evil - for it was a gift of God -, but the fact that it causes confusion and disorderliness. To Augustine it was reason that made human beings fully human. The principal fruit of reason is order. He saw that marvellous expression of socio-political order, the Roman Empire, go to pieces before his eyes. In his own life, in the personal sphere, he had experienced how sex can be a source of disorderliness. This prevented him from singing the praise of sex, although he knew quite well that it brings 'sweet joys'.

A sexually aroused person is unable to reason. "So possessing is this pleasure that, at the time in which it reaches its consummation, all mental activity is suspended" [187]. Augustine, who considered reason as the greatest of God's gifts to mankind, did not find this a good thing. Body and soul could go strangely apart in sexual matters. "Sometimes lust importunes men in spite of themselves and sometimes it fails them when they desire to feel it, so though lust rages in the mind, it does not stir in the body" [188]. Whoever wishes to see this as an autobiographical remark may do so, but I feel that any sensible man, clerical or lay, might have written this.

h. Saint Augustine speaking to married couples

It is not so difficult to put Saint Augustine in the dock on account of his depreciation of sexuality in marriage. The fact that Adam and Eve immediately covered their nakedness meant, in his view, that they suddenly realized that their genitals would behave as though they no longer belonged to them. Their privy parts had become 'disobedient' and were now 'pudenda', members to be ashamed of [189]. There is no wholesale condemnation of the sexual act as such [190]. It is good and commendable if men and women use their sexual impulses for the procreation of mankind and not for the satisfaction of their lust [191].

But is it really possible to have coitus without some degree of erotic pleasure? No, Augustine knows quite well that this is not possible; in consequence, every carnal act is somewhat tainted, although not evil in itself.

[192]. How could it be otherwise since the whole man is affected by the consequences of the Fall? Man is essentially a fallen being, incapable of performing acts that are wholly and blamelessly good; everything is morally corroded to some degree. This makes Saint Augustine say that "this is the evil of sin in which every man is born" [193].

The reasoning of our author becomes somewhat twisted at this point as if he realized that he was bringing himself into difficulties and confusing married couples. Was marriage good in itself, with sex and all, or was it evil, because its sex was morally tainted? He proclaimed that marriage was good, of course : how could he do otherwise since it is instituted by God? But he somewhat ingeniously distinguishes between matrimony itself, as a sacrament and a sacred institution, and the sexuality that goes along with it. Chastity and lust live uneasily together in marriage. "But we ought not to condemn wedlock because of the evil of lust, nor must we praise lust because of wedlock" [194].

Is it possible to remain chaste in marriage and not to fall prey to the sin of concupiscence? Surely, says Augustine, "sexual intercourse is honest and licit, but on the condition that it is not done arbitrarily [i.e. for lust - F.] but from necessity [i.e. in order to have children - F.]" [195]. If this condition is fulfilled, the act is not sinful. He explained in one of his sermons that man and wife could preserve their virginity, even if they embraced [i.e. had sex - F.], for, he added, virginity is a thing of the mind [196]. However, he remained true to his fundamental theological position that sexual intercourse is the means by which original sin is transmitted. But baptism will wash away the sinfulness of concupiscence.

So far so good. But, a married couple may ask Saint Augustine : "Holy bishop, you are speaking all the time of sexual acts specifically intended to produce offspring. May we not come together for other reasons? Because we love another? Perhaps even to enjoy erotic pleasure?" Why, yes, the bishop will have answered, though somewhat hesitatingly : "You may since Saint Paul permits it. 'Do not deny yourselves to one another ..., do not burn with vain desire' [197]. If there is sin in it, it is only venial and pardonable".

To quote Bailey, "in other words, what is intrinsically sinful is nevertheless not imputed as sin, but receives forgiveness, as it were in the very moment of transgression; indeed, it is one of the excellencies of matrimony that it procures pardon even for those sexual acts which are in themselves culpable, in that they are aimed deliberately at the fulfilment of its primary end [i.e. procreation - F.] as defined in patristic theory" [198]. However, always remaining true to himself, Augustine does not glorify the act of sex. "Shame is very specially connected with lust, and rightly so." This shame makes people conceal their privy parts [199]. And is it not so that people perform their sexual acts in darkness and secrecy [200]? Shame always remains attached to it.

j. Augustine woman-unfriendly?

Was Augustine woman-unfriendly? As is to be expected, he said that the woman is created as a help to the man, that is, to bring forth children with him [201]. Would the main aim of femininity have been different, then God might just as well have created another man from the side of Adam to assist him [202]. That men lord it over their wives is the consequence of the Fall, but, so he adds, this was not the original nature of the woman [203]. A man should not allow his wife to dominate him. Should this happen, then woe to that house [204]!

Sometimes it seems that a wife is a hindrance to the man rather than a help, particularly in matters of spirituality. "Nothing, I feel, wil throw the spirit of man more out of its course than female caressing, without which one cannot have a wife" [205]. There is in every woman something of Eve - that is, of the seductress; for this reason a man should not cling too much to his wife or even to his mother [206]. That the mother is mentioned means that the author was not thinking of sexuality specifically but of sin in general.

Augustine's most questionable expression is probably this. "A good Christian should love in a woman the creature of God ..., but he should hate the intercourse and the copulation as corruptible and mortal. That is, love in her what is human, but hate in her what is 'uxor' [= sexual]" [207]. This is strong language indeed, and liable to misunderstandings. As it stands, it is undoubtedly dualistic : it proclaims the radical separation of two sides in a woman, of what he calls the human and the uxorial ones. But if we weigh this against other expressions, as cited above, it loses this dualistic character. What the author wanted to convey is not that being married and having sexual intercourse are two mutually exclusive things in moral respect, but that wedlock is not primarily there for the gratification of the senses. He knew that this was quite often the case in pagan and even in Christian marriages. But this expression was and is often played off against him, of course. No wonder, it is less than prudent.

k. In defence of woman

In other texts, usually overlooked by those who are out to criticize Augustine, he adopts a far milder tone. Both men and women are created in the image of God [208]. And if it is true that woman was the first cause of the Fall, it is equally true that the promise of salvation was given to her, and not to Adam. Mischief came to mankind through a woman; salvation came to mankind also through a woman. Christ wanted to be born from a woman, which demonstrated how much he commended the female sex. Women are not more sinful than men : each sex has its own honour, and each sex should confess its iniquity, and each sex should hope for its eternal salvation [209].

Both sexes experience carnal concupiscence, not only women. If a man wants his wife to be chaste, he should provide the example, and not only verbally. And although this is deplorable - since the man has to be the boss - many men are surpassed by women. "Women are faithful to the promise of chastity, but men prefer not to keep it; and inasmuch they are unfaithful to it, they pretend to be more virile" [210]. Augustine the pastor really knew his sheep! He showed his eminently practical mind by exhorting husband and wife to walk side by side in the street, so that they might be seen as equal (pariter) [211]. Who of us does not see arising before his or her mental eye the image of a Turkish couple with the man striding stately in front and the woman (with the shopping bags) walking humbly a few paces behind him?

[212] If Augustine found that the man was the head, he did not want the husbands proclaiming their superiority in this way.

1. An assessment of Augustine's attitude

I feel it is time for an assessment of the Church Father's opinions of marriage, women, and sex. It should be an assessment really starting from his own position and his own ideas, with regard to the time in which he lived and to the function he occupied, that of a bishop, that is, of a pastor of souls. Many modern authors do not do full justice to him, for although he is celebrated as one of the greatest minds of European history who profoundly influenced the Middle Ages, to say nothing of Luther and the Reformation, he is also criticized, often severely, for his view on sexual life. Held against the foil of our modern conceptions in this field, he does not pass the test. When we judge him, it is invariably assumed that we are right and that he is wrong. What we are celebrating, wittingly or unconsciously, is our newly won sexual freedom, but poor Augustine, the spoil-sport, is not admitted to the festival in honour of the goddess Aphrodite.

Must we conceive of Saint Augustine as the highly influential thinker "who in violent reaction against bodily pleasure straight-jacketed the Western Church into extreme puritanism" [213]? I am quoting Bottomley, but this is clearly not this author's personal opinion. It is, however, an opinion that is fairly common, although Saint Paul and Jerome too are made to share in the guilt. It is just as Van Bavel writes : "Augustine has become the black animal of the moralists nowadays. One can read in the papers that according to him the woman does not possess a soul, that the woman means the ruin of the man, and that the Church has been obsessed by sex since Augustine" [214]. But even this author, an Augustinian friar who is very positive about Saint Augustine, writes that sexual intercourse was often completely underrated by him [215]. Even such a moderate and well-informed scholar as Peter Brown concludes that Augustine "created a darkened humanism that linked the pre-Christian past to the Christian present in a common distrust of sexual pleasure. It was a heavy legacy to bequeath to later ages" [216].

But is it really conceivable that one man, however brilliant his mind, could influence the untold Christian masses of all later ages? Perhaps 10 % of the total population of the Roman Empire was literate. This percentage fell to a historical low during the Dark Ages; even such a great man as Charlemagne could not write and learned to read only later in his life. Must we believe that Augustine's bulky Latin volumes were read by people who could not read and, if they could, had only a smattering of Latin or none at all? I would like to see it explained in practical terms how Augustine exercized his allegedly pernicious influence on married couples and their sexual mores.

A second unproved supposition is that the Middle Ages and all later centuries were sexually repressed and that the Church was obsessed with sex. This curious idea, that is in no way corroborated by the facts, has its origin in our modern perspective of these things. We feel that we have been happily freed of the shackles of moral rigorism and puritanism; our sexual freedom becomes all the more enjoyable if we compare it with the anxiety and the restraints that (allegedly) were prevalent in all former times, for as would-be historians we love sweeping asertions.

I am convinced that a Belgian specialist of sexuology was quite right when he wrote the following. "The majority of the Christians lived till into the 15th century in a fairly lustful, pro-sexual way. They were far more impeded by superstitions and magical ideas than by the pronouncements of Augustine." And he adds that "it has never been proved that the typically western taboo on the sexual - as we find it conspicuously present in the 19th century - has a Christian origin" [217]. Let me quote, from Brown's book, only one instance of this care-free attitude to erotics. "As late as the sixth century A.D., the notables of Gerasa [now Jerash in Jordan - F.] were proud to have maintained a water festival [the idea had obviously spread from Antioch - F.] in which teams of nude girls sported in front of what was, by that time, a totally Christian populace. It was, they said, 'a most delightful spectacle'" [218]. These notables had not heard the warning voices of Augustine and John Chrysostom' or, if they had heard them, they certainly paid no heed to them.

An incident in the life of Augustine the bishop proves that he took an emninently practical view of sexual matters and was not dominated by a puritanical ideology. A youthful clergyman of his diocese stayed with a family whose daughter was a nun; she lived in her parents' home. One night he visited her in her bed, and Augustine was notified of this. He seems to have found this hardly more than a peccadillo; such a thing, he wrote, could "befall any serious and saintly person". The young priest was not defrocked or sent to a monastery in the desert. Being short of priests, the bishop could not afford to lose one. This does not mean that he condoned what this man had done. By no means! He found him guilty [219]. Brown tellingly adds : "One can imagine what Jerome would have made of the incident" [220]. But the bishop of Hippo was no extremist when it came to the guidance of his flock.

Saint Augustine is thought to have made life hard for married couples by imposing a form of chastity on them that was wholly supernatural, and, therefore, unearthly, impracticable, and unliveable. He is felt to have dualistically opposed his conception of marriage to one that was solely based on the biological difference of the sexes. In respect of sexual morality, this led to an exaggeratedly rigoristic moralism [221]. But if we find expressions in Augustine's treatises which seem to be or which really are disparaging of sexuality, we should not forget that he had to fight on two fronts. On one side there was the Manichaean and Encratite rejection of sex and procreation, and also the heavy accent laid on spirituality by Stoic and Neoplatonic authors like Plotinus and Porphyry. And on the other there was the rampant eroticism of his times to which his own faithful were not immune; as a good bishop, he had to be solicitous about them. He felt it his duty not to glorify sex, but rather to remain prudently reserved about it [222].

At the centre of Augustine's thought, with regard to the relations of men and women, was not sex but marriage. It is exactly in this field that he became the prophet of a brand new conception of marriage. Pagan marriages were civil contracts, very often arranged by the respective families without the declared consent of the spouses. This does not mean that the spouses never came to love one another; we know they did. But our idea that being in love was a prerequisite for marrying was totally absent. In a Roman civil marriage the man was the dominating party; men entered into wedlock in order to have children, preferably male ones, and for their sexual satisfaction. This satisfaction could also be obtained in many other ways, with the female servants, with prostitutes, and in occasional liaisons. It would have been surprising if new Christians, solely by being baptized, adopted a totally different, more lofty view of the marriage bond. Pagan conceptions persisted for a long time.

Augustine's idea of marriage and sexuality was a theological and biblical one, mainly based on the creation stories in Genesis. Created in God's image and likeness, man and woman were essentially equal and destined to live in wedlock. In Paradise they were married people already who would have intercourse and begot children, but they would have this intercourse without experiencing lust (concupiscentia). How Augustine imagined this we do not know; probably he did not know himself. It is an idealized picture. Then came the Fall and everything was tainted. Especially sexuality, as a very sensitive element of human intercourse, underwent the Fall's unruly effects.

Augustine was not against sexual intercourse in marriage and less still against marriage as an institution; what he deplored was that sex was so unmanageable, so contrary to reason. He saw sexual lust (as distinct from sexuality as an anthropological element), 'concupiscentia' in his terms, as irrational, as something not fully human. Could this defective situation be overcome and remedied? Educated pagans thought this was possible by human means. "[They] viewed the act of intercourse as one of the many aspects of their life that they could bring under their control through good sense and breeding ... Intercourse was a matter which the alert gentleman felt he could control" [223].

Augustine found this to be a pipe-dream. He found it nonsensical to think that good sense and breeding would be sufficient to bring the sexual urge under control, to say nothing of the arrogant idea that only 'alert gentlemen' were capable of performing this trick. The overwhelming majority of his faithful were not gentlemen at all, whether alert or not. But he would not leave them to themselves to cope with the problems of their marital life. I feel he would have been surprised and also indignant to hear that later authors would accuse him of having steered Christianity on a course of arid puritanism, thus depriving married couples of the joys of their love. Had he not comforted Christian couples with a treatise on the goodness of marriage [224]? I can discover nothing that would justify calling him a dualist in sexual or marital matters. He was no Gnostic, no Manichee, but a genuine admirer of God's creation, of the beauty of the body, and of the friendship and conjunction of men and women.

True to orthodox Christian teaching, Augustine did not believe that the defects caused by the Fall could be remedied on this earth. Paradise could not be regained, not before the end of times. But this does not alter the fact that the conditio humana could be made much better and more tolerable. In baptism Christian people had received an unfailing stock of grace on which they could draw. Émile Schmitt speaks of "the sacramental dynamism of baptismal grace as a source of the progressive renovation of the couples, in the context of a libido that was still marked by original sin" [225]. What this gradual renovation would lead to was that the couples would learn to evaluate their union as something higher than the purely sexual and procreational.

Time and again Augustine points to love and affection as the foundation of marriage [226]. He states literally that marriage does not only exist for the bringing forth of children, but also because of the natural bringing together of the sexes, that is, because of mutual love. For this reason older couples or those who are incapable of begetting offspring are really and fully married (with sexual intercourse and all, is the tacit implication) [227]. I may not withhold a remarkable passage from the reader who is still thinking that the bishop abhorred sex. He is speaking there of 'the realm of mutual delight' and of its beauty - of the beauty of sexual intercourse, that is. True enough, he finds this beauty of a lower order (ima), but this is, he adds, because it is 'subjected to corruption' (as a result of the Fall). "Were this not so, it would be held to be of the highest order" [228].

To conclude, Augustine did not believe in sexual repression. Man is a whole; chase out the devil of libido through the front door, another demon will enter by the backdoor. "It is often so that carnal desire, prevented from the pleasure of sexual intercourse, instead turns itself, and all the more vehemently, into an appetite for money. Having become averse of sex, it goes after money with a still more fanatical drive" [229].

15. An overall assessment

The great question dominating the discussion throughout this chapter is : was the attitude of the Christian Chuch of the first centuries with regard to marriage and sexuality dualistic or was it not? If we mean by 'the Church' the magisterium - what we now use to call 'Rome' or 'the Vatican' -, we are left with very little. No infallible pronouncements, no authoritative encyclicals referring to these matters derived from it. The only instance I know is the declaration by Pope Siricius that virginity (celibacy for religious reasons) and marriage are both good, but that virginity is better. It seems that the magisterium in this period was occupied with other, more pressing matters. Regulating the sexual behaviour and marital life of the faithful did not figure high on its agenda, or rather hardly at all.

In his valuable work on the man-woman relation in Christian perspective Bailey stated peremptorily that that "the Christian Church found it necessary ... to regulate the sexual relationships and behaviour of its members" [230]. This conjures up the unpleasant notion of a celibate clergy meddling in the private life of the faithful, not even respecting the privacy of their bedrooms. But he contradicts himself almost in the same breath by telling us that "during the first centuries ... there was little positive legislation to this end".

What we have of this kind of legislation originated in the course of the fourth and fifth centuries, that is, after the liberation of the Church; it was not promulgated by the magisterium but came from councils and synods and consists of canons and decrees. Since almost all these synods were provincial ones, there is very little that was binding for the whole of Christianity. Once again contradicting himself, Bailey writes that "it was not their object to regulate in any minute detail the private intimacies of married life" [231]. We possess very little material enlightening us on the ideas of the leading circles of the Church regarding sexual mores, so little that we are unable to answer the question whether this attitude was dualistic in the affirmative. The lack of interest shown by these circles may lead to the conclusion that it was not dualistic.

The chief interest of these synods did not go out to married lay-people but to the clergy the majority of whom were married. From the beginning of the fourth century provincial synods were laying down the rule that clerics, from bishops to deacons, should not sleep with their wives in case they were married. So many synods legislated to this effect that during the fifth century it had become a more or less general rule, at least in the West [232].

We know precious little of the sexual mores of the faithful of these times. But the little we know of it shows that they were certainly not inimical to sex. As is born out by the sermons of the Fathers, their mores did not often differ significantly from those of their pagan contemporaries. Allowance must be made, however, that moralizing preachers tend to exaggerate somewhat. For it is also true that many men and women were ready to embrace the celibate state and renounce all forms of sexuality. This would not have been possible if Christian households had not had standards of behaviour that were stricter than those of the pagans.

The great mass of information that we have about these matters comes from the Fathers. If we have the impression that they spent most of their time with writing about these subjects, we would be very wrong. Only a small part of their enormous output was devoted to such topics. And within this small volume we find only a limited range of subjects that they are interested in; they mainly attempt to demonstrate that religious virginity ranks higher than marriage, while remarriage after the death of the first partner was often not favourably looked upon [233]. This does not mean, however, that this opinion originated in a dualistic abhorrence of marriage. To quote Bailey : "By means of the convenient distinction of the good and the better, the Fathers contrived to uphold the superiority of the virgin state and the higher merit of continence without yielding to the thoroughgoing dualism which denounced marriage as evil" [234].

But Bailey cannot stop contradicting himself. While admitting, somewhat reluctantly, that the general attitude of the Fathers regarding the matters under discussion is not dualistic, he nonetheless, so it seems, wants to see them in the dock. "The Fathers do not usually explain their antipathy to coitus and the venereal ... It is clear that its proximate source is the oriental-hellenistic dualism in which the age was steeped" [235]. Does this stem from the need to formulate general, all-embracing solutions?

It is, however, a very glib statement, for it rests on two premises which are both highly conjectural. The first is that the age was really 'steeped in in oriental-hellenistic dualism'. But both Judaism and Christianity are fundamentally non-dualistic religions. Once again Bailey lands himself in difficulties, because he added that this dualism "had infected Christian thought [i.e. in matters of sexuality - F.] even while under condemnation by the Church for its heretical influence in other directions" [236]. Is this not rather curious? This author is stating, without batting an eye, that the Church was anti-dualistic, but by the same token made an exception for her opinion on sexuality. Am I over-suspicious if I feel that Bailey, like so many authors on these subjects, is unable to resist the temptation to point an accusing finger at the Church?

The second premise is that 'the Fathers' had an antipathy to 'coitus and the venereal'. But has the reader who has followed me throughout this chapter, also reached this same global conclusion? We should not speak of 'the Fathers' in this context; we must study each Father individually. What all Fathers have in common is that they rate virginity higher than marriage, but none of them condemns marriage, with procreation, as something that is evil. We also saw that some Christian authors were quite ready to judge them equally good.

I began my disquisition on the opinions and attitudes of the Fathers with Clement of Alexandria, a man who was precisely the opposite of being antipathetic to marriage and sexuality. Tertullian began by being rather positive about the matters in hand, but later in his life he glided off to an ever more negative conception which may finally be called dualistic. The next Father I wrote of was Origen. He saw fit to say some very unpleasant things of sex and marriage. With regard to him, I have arrived at the conclusion that there is dualism indeed in his opinions on sex. But even he did not condemn the institution as such. Then came John Chrysostom who, in his sermons, spoke of marriage (and all that it implies) in a positive sense; he even found it 'heretical' to speak ill of it. Jerome was just as negative as Origen, but he far surpassed him in coarseness. But then we have the charming treatise addressed to Gregoria, an effusion that is just as positive as the sombre duo Origen and Jerome are negative.

Finally, there is Augustine. This is an author who calls for selective reading. His total literary output counts eight thousand pages in the Patrologia latina. Not even the greatest expert on this Father of the Church will have read all these pages. But selective reading can mean biased reading, and I have the impression that many choices of texts are ideologically determined. It is true, under the spotlight of our modern opinions not every text of Augustine will stand the test, our test, that is. But then we start from the premise that our ideas are infallible. Are they really?

Within the frame of his own time and circumstances, Augustine must be seen as positive on the subjects of marriage and sex; he wished to be helpful to Christian couples, not wanting to make life harder for them. But he realized that it would make life more difficult for them if they relied too much on the blessings of sex. Therefore, he carefully refrained from extolling it.

NOTES TO CHAPTER III

1. Gen.2:25.
2. Vol. X, Ch. II, § 3a.
3. Vol. IV, Ch. II, § 12j-n.
4. See Vol. XI, Ch. IV, Part III, § 2.
5. Brown, Body and Society 26.
6. Plut., De sanitate 131 B 17.
7. Epictetus, Enchir. 8.
8. Cic., Pro Caelio 28.
9. Brown, Body and Society 29.
10. Foucault, Hist. de la sex. 3, 21/22.
11. Artemidorus 1.75-80. Festugière translates, resp. : 'conformes à la loi, contraires à la loi, contraires à la nature'.
12. Artemidorus 1.78. Foucault, Hist. de la sex. 3, 30-32.
13. Artemidorus 1.78.

14. Artemidorus 1.78.
15. Artemidorus 1.79.
16. Foucault, Hist. de la sex. 3, 36.
17. Artemidorus 1.80.
18. Foucault, Hist. de la sex. 3, 43.
19. Foucault, Hist. de la sex. 3, 36.
20. Foucault, Hist. de la sex., 3, 48.
21. Dodds, Pagan and Christian 32.
22. Dodds, Pagan and Christian 35/36.
23. Bailey, Man-Woman Relation 4.
24. Foucault, Hist. de la sex., 3, 53.
25. Aretaeus, Causes and signs 2.5.
26. Aretaeus, Causes and signs 2.12.
27. Rufus d'Éphèse, Fragments 60. Livre III, Ch. VIII Sur les rapports sexuels.
28. Oribasius III, Livres incertains 8.
29. Oribasius III, Livres incertains 8.
30. Brown, Body & Society 17, quoting from Galen, De usu partium 14.9.
31. Soranus, Maladies des femmes 1.30, 32 = 1.9.
32. Rousselle, Porneia 27.
33. Jo. 20:11-17.
34. Mt. 22:23-33; Mc. 12:18-27; Lc. 20:27-40.
35. Mt. 19:1-12; Mc. 10:2-12.
36. Mt. 5:28.
37. Mc. 7:21; Mt. 15:19.
38. Driver did this in an article entitled 'Sexuality and Jesus', first published in the 'Union Seminary Quarterly Review' and reprinted by M.E. Marty and D.G. Peerman in 'New Theology', No. 3, 118-132 (New York, 1966). No Dutch library is in the possession of this volume. I am referring to what Blenkinsopp, Sexuality (see Bibliography), had to report of it.
39. For Dutch readers : Gerardjan Rijnders.
40. See Vol. XII, Ch. IV, Part III, 2 and 4.
41. Preisker, Christentum und Ehe, 23.

42. 1Cor.5:1.
43. 1Cor.7:1-8.
44. 1Cor.11:8-12.
45. Eph.5:22; Col. 3:18.
46. Eph. 5:22-23.
47. Col.3:19.
48. Col.3:20; Eph.6:4.
49. I fundamentally disagree with Preisker's conclusion in his 'Christentum und Ehe' which results from a partial reading of the Pauline texts. He judges that to Paul marriage was something morally inferior; marriage was nothing but a sexual relationship and not a spiritual community, pp. 126/127.
50. Bottomley, Attitudes 54.
51. For Encratism and Tatian see Vol. XIII, Ch. V, §§ 1-3.
52. Brown, Body 55.
53. Clem.Al., Strom. 3.12.
54. 1Tim.5:3-16.
55. Sawyer, Women and Religion 146/147.
56. Sawyer, Women and religion 149 sqq.
57. Gen. 3:15.
58. Ir., Adv.haer. 3.22.4.
59. Lc.8:2-3; Mt.27:55-56.
60. See Paul Philippi s.v. 'Diakonie I.3.3. Der Anteil der Frauen'. TRE VIII (1981).
61. Hoffman, Status of women 79 : "The early orthodox view of women stands in sharp contrast to the Gnostic characterization of women and femininity ... Women in second century orthodox groups were more highly regarded than in the corresponding Gnostic groups". He combats Elaine Pagels who, in her 'The Gnostic Gospels' (London, 1979), had little good to say of the attitude of the early Church with regard to women. "By the late second century, the orthodox community came to accept the domination of men over women as the divinely ordained order, not only for social and family life, but also for the Christian churches (p. 66) ... Their consensus (i.e. of the Fathers) ... has continued to dominate the majority of Christian churches" (p. 69). But Hoffman finds her documentation defective : "Pagels' assumption that apart from Clement of Alexandria other second and early third century writers were unanimous in degrading women does not take into account contrary

literary, artistic, and epigraphic evidence" (Hoffman, p. 80). Women, he says, "held several types of leadership positions in church groups and were regarded with esteem by orthodox writers in this era ... Women were considered ontologically equal with men and were praised for their faithfulness and spiritual and intellectual discernment in various places in the works of these writers" (p. 113).

62. Vol. IV, Ch. II, §12m.
63. See for instance Vol. IV, Ch. III, § 9c.
64. Dt.23:18-19.
65. Ex.20:26; this prescription dates from an early period when the priestly vestment was still very short.
66. Soph., Elektra 1293.
67. Gen.3:20.
68. Gen.3:16-19.
69. I have been using here, although not verbally repeated, the arguments, I used already in Vol. IV, Ch. II, § 12j-n.
70. The cult was abolished in 394. Could it be that the curious story of the entombment of a living nun goes back to this custom? Every year in the dogdays the story pops up of some tourists who had stayed behind in a cathedral in some Spanish town after closing time. They saw a procession enter, led by a bishop. The floor of the sanctuary was opened, a nun was lowered into the tomb underneath, and then the opening was closed again, while all the time sombre dirges were sung. I have heard this story related more than once, sworn to be absolutely true. But nobody had actually witnessed this scene. The spokesman or -woman knew people who knew people who ...
Deborah Sawyer, Women and Religion 126-128, remarks that the accent has been placed too much on the virginity of the Vestales. "They are taken out of society before they are women, as premenstrual girls of 6, and remain sexually inactive on pain of death ... The Vestal Virgins are an example of a male-defined idealized womanhood which disempowers women according to their nature, and empowers them according to male social values. They exist because of male interest and initiative, and any advantage they may have in comparison with other women in that society is a by-product rather than a reason for the institution itself." These advantages were very real indeed : "They had social and political freedoms normally only available to men, and only to men of high social status." But "ultimately, men remained in control of these women, which is more clearly illustrated in the account of the horrible and fatal retribution which awaited any Vestal Virgin who might ... engage in sexual relations; ... the explanation of the existence and centrality of the Vestae Virgines within Roman state religion can be understood as male appropriation of female powers of regeneration to channel them for the regeneration of Rome and the Empire."

71. Mt.4:18-22; Mc.1:16-20.
72. Mt.20:20.
73. It is, of course, postulated that Peter, who was probably older than the others, was a married man, since his mother-in-law is mentioned. But the curious thing is that this woman, once cured of an illness by Jesus, "got up and attended to their needs", Mt.8:14-15, Mc.1:31, Lc.4:39. Was there no wife then to serve them? The nearest guess is that Peter was a widower.
74. 1Tim.3:2.
75. Tert., De exhort.cast. 11.
76. Tert., De exhort.cast. 13.ert
77. Eus., Demonstr.evang. 1.9.33.
78. Tert., De virg.cel. 15.
79. Cyprian, Ep. 62 ad Pomponium.
80. Cyprian, De habitu virg. 19.
81. Const.Apost. 1.9.
82. Mansi 2, Concilium Eliberitanum, canons 33 and 27.
83. Soc., HE 1.11; Sozom. HE 1.22. See for this subject Lea, Hist. of Sacerd. celib., Vol. I. London 1907. This is still an informative book, in spite of its blatant anti-Catholic bias.
84. Codex canonum 29 and 62. Lea, Sacerd.celib. 62 is not correct when he writes that no sanctions were intended. Indeed the Roman synod did not speak of them, but Siricius did.
85. Epiph., Haer. 59.4.
86. Lea, Sacerd/celib. 91.
87. Bailey, Man-Woman Relation 20.
88. Bottomley, Attitudes 57/58.
89. Hermas, Pastor, vis. 1.1.3.
90. Brown, Body and Society 70.
91. Hermas, Pastor, vis. 1.1.8.
92. Hermas, Pastor, mand. 4.1.
93. Hermas, Pastor, mand. 4.4.
94. Hermas, Pastor, vis. 2.2.3.
95. Bottomley, Attitudes 61.
96. See also Vol. XIII, Ch. V, § 8.

97. See Vol. IX, Ch. II.
98. Tert., Adv.Marc. 5.18.
99. Tert., De carne 7.
100. Tert., Adv.Marc. 1.29.
101. Tert., De uxore 2.8).
102. Tert., De uxore 1.1
103. Rambaux, Tertullien 219 : "Every time, in fact, that the moralist presents marriage as good, he hastens to add, in the next phrase or the same one, that this good is of a pitiful quality ... (227) Marriage and sexual desire did no longer appear as essential to human nature such as it was created by God; they were no more than unpleasant accidents, consequence of the Fall, exactly like divorce, polygamy, and evil in general, even if they were not just as condemnable".
104. Bailey, Man-woman relation 49.
105. Tert., De poen. 4.
106. Tert., De poen. 59.
107. Tert., Ad uxorem 1.1.
108. Tert., De exhort.cast. 9.
109. Brown, Man and society 81. Was Tertullian a misogynist? Hoffman, Status of women 147, would not dub Tertullian a misogynist. "Tertullian's views towards women have been characterized as those of an 'extreme misogynist', a classic representative of the repressive attitude of orthodoxy towards women ... (p. 148) Tertullian's views towards women, when considered within his own cultural and theological context, were not unusually negative, but were relatively positive ... Even his infamous comparison of women to Eve as the 'devil's gateway', when seen in the context of his rhetorical language and his similar condemnation of men in Adam, will not support the characterization of him as a radical misogynist". It is true that he (p. 159) calls Adam 'the originator of our race and our sin' (Tert., Exh.castit. 2). We must also take into account the genre to which the tract in question, 'De cultu feminarum' (On the dress of women) belongs. It has been characterized as a 'pamphlet', not meant as a scholarly treatise; it is a diatribe against the way Christian women adorn themselves and as such it is composed according to the art of rhetorics - which means that not every expression in it has to be taken at its face-value. Slider, Rhetoric 120, calls it 'an exhibition piece that at the same time carries an honest exhortatory purpose'. The aim of the author was not to utterly condemn the female race but to castigate them for their propensity to emulate pagan women in dress and make-up. Heathen women are not chaste which they express by their immoderate dress. If Christian women dress themselves in the same way, they give the devil his

opportunity. Hence the inglorious comparison to 'the devil's gateway'. But it is doubtless true that this expression can easily give rise to the suspicion that Tertullian really was a misogynist. It must be correct what De Vries, Psychologie 31, says, namely that the mocking tone of the treatise betrays a sense of superiority.

110. Tert., De cultu femin. 1.1.
111. Tertullian had a single-track mind, says De Vries, Psychologie 73 : "He is self-assured, he never hesitates". And he adds that he is not one for subtleties; he is not subtle himself nor does he have an eye for the subtlety of problems.
112. Hipp., Trad.apost. 41.
113. Bailey, Man-woman relation 46, note 4.
114. Bailey, Man-woman relation 24.
115. Bailey, Man-woman relation 22.
116. Greg.Naz., Or. 40 in sanctum baptisma 18.
117. Greg.Naz., Or. 8 in laudem sororis suae Gorgoniae 8.
118. Clem.Al., Strom. 2.23 (140.2).
119. Clem.Al., Strom. 2.23 (142.2).
120. Clem.Al., Strom. 2.23 (142.1).
121. Clem.Al., 7.12 (70.7-8).
122. 1Cor.7:32-34.
123. Clem.Al., Strom. 3.12 (88.2).
124. Brown, Body & Society 135/136.
125. See Vol. XIII, Ch. III, §§ 4-9.
126. Brown, Body & Society 164.
127. Brown, Body & Society 168.
128. Brown, Body & Society 171.
129. Brown, Body & Society 173.
130. Orig., Hom. in Cant.Cant. 2.1.
131. Orig., Fragm. on I Cor. 39 (p. 510 Jenkins).
132. Vol. XIII, Ch. III, § 9a.
133. John Chrys., Hom. 12 in Ep. 1 ad Cor. 7.
134. Brown, Body & Society 315.
135. Brown, Body & Society 315.

136. John Chrys., Hom. 7 in Matth. 6.
137. John Chrys., Hom. 6 in Matth. 8.
138. Jo. Chrys., Hom. 12 in Ep. ad Col. 4, 5-6.
139. Jo.Chrys., Hom. 12 in Ep. ad Col. cap. 4, 5.
140. Jo.Chrys., Hom. in Ep. I ad Cor. 19.
141. Jo.Chrys., In Ep. ad Titum 5.3.
142. Jo.Chrys., Hom. propter fornicationes (193) 2.
143. Brown, Body & Society 313.
144. Jo.Chrys., Hom. propter fornicationes (193) 2.
145. Jo.Chrys., Hom. 12 in Ep. ad Cor. 5.
146. Hier., Comm. in Ez. 1.1-2.
147. Hier., Comm. in Ez. 1.3.
148. Hier., Ep. 127.12; I took the translations from Bottomley, Attitudes 79/80.
149. Hier., Ep. 60.17.
150. I refer the reader for this to Vol. XIII, Ch. III, § 10.
151. Epistula Siricii Papae adversus Jovinianum haereticum. Mansi 3, 663/664.
152. Bailey, Man-Woman Relation 27.
153. Hier., De perp.virg. 1 (205).
154. Hier., Contra Vigil.
155. Hier., Adv. Jovin.
156. Hier., Ep. 49.2.
157. Hier., Ep. 48.
158. Hier., Ep. 50.1.
159. Hier., Ep, 50.5; translation found in Bailey, Man-Woman Relation 28.
160. 1Cor.7:9.
161. Ep. de castitate 10.
162. Liber ad Gregoriam 8.
163. Prov. 31.
164. Liber ad Gregoriam 18-19.
165. See Vol. XIII, Ch. VIII, § 15.

166. See Vol. XIII, Ch. II, 8.
167. This especially by Alfaric in his 'L'évolution intellectuelle' (see Bibliography).
168. Aug., Conf. 8.7.17.
169. Van Bavel, Augustinus 49.
170. Bottomley, Attitudes 87.
171. Aug., Conf. 4.9-5.10.
172. Aug. Retract. 1.4.3.
173. Bottomley, Attitudes 87.
174. Aug., Civ.Dei 22.24.
175. Aug., Conf. 8.11.26.
176. Aug., Conf. 4.2.2; De bono 5.5.
177. Aug., Conf. 9.16.14.
178. Aug. Audollent s.v. 'Adeodatus', Dict. d'hist. et geogr. eccl. 1, 547/548. Paris, 1912.
179. Aug., Conf. 6.15.
180. Aug., Civ.Dei 22.17.
181. Aug., Civ.Dei 13.16.
182. Arendt, Love 11 : "Life on earth is a living death, mors vitalis, or vita mortalis. It is altogether determined by death; indeed it is more properly called death.For the constant fear that rules it prevents living, unless one equates living with being afraid. This basic fear guides all our fears of specific evils ... (13) There can be no doubt that death, and not just fear of death, was the most crucial experience in Augustine's life."
183. Aug., De bono 1.1 and 8.8.
184. Brown, Body & Society 407.
185. Aug., Contra Jul. 4.49.
186. Brown, Body & Society 408.
187. Aug., Civ.Dei 14.16.
188. Aug., Civ.Dei 14.16.
189. Aug., Civ.Dei 13.13.
190. Ladomérszky, Saint Augustin 154/155 : "En lui même, l'acte conjugal est exempt de tout péché : il est utile et honnête. Même s'il entraîne accidentellement quelque excès de passion, la faute ne sera pas grave; car la fidélité conjugale en diminue la malice."

191. Aug., De pecc.mer. 1.29 (57).

192. Aug., De nuptiis 1.24 (27).

193. Aug., De pecc. 1.29 (57).

194. Aug., De nuptiis 1.7 (8). Ladomérszky, Saint Augustin 157 : "Le mariage est honnête par sa nature, et ni les excès de la concupiscence, ni les abus des conjoints ne sauraient nuire à l'essentielle 'bonté' qu'il tient du Créateur."

195. Aug., De nuptiis 1.8 (9).

196. Aug., Sermo 351.4 (5).

197. 1Cor.7.5 and 9.

198. Bailey, Man-Woman Relation 57.

199. Aug., Civ.Dei 14.17.

200. Aug., Civ.Dei 14.18.

201. Aug., De gen. ad lit. 9.3 (5).

202. Aug., De gen. ad lit. 9.5 (9).

203. Aug., De gen. ad lit. 11.37 (50).

204. Aug., Contra Manich. 2.11 (15).

205. Aug., Soliloquia 1.32.10 (17).

206. Aug., Ep. 243.10.

207. Aug., De sermone domini in monte 1.14.

208. Aug., De Trin. 12.7.9-10.

209. Aug., Sermo 51.2 (3).

210. Aug., Sermo 132.2 (2).

211. Aug., De bono 1.1.

212. Turks themselves would remark that the man walks in front in order to defend his wife against possible dangers.

213. Bottomley, Attitudes 81/82.

214. Van Bavel, Augustinus 55.

215. Van Bavel, Augustinus 56.

216. Brown, Body & Society 426.

217. Van Ussel, Christendom 658.

218. Brown, Body & Society 24.

219. Aug., Ep. 13 and 18.

220. Brown. Body & Society 397.
221. I am paraphrasing Schmitt, Mariage chrétien 283/284. I was alas unable to lay my hands on the work of Elizabeth A. Clark, St. Augustine on marriage and sexuality. Washington D.C., 1996; this book contains a useful collection of Augustinian texts referring to these matters.
222. Schmitt, Mariage chrétien 285.
223. Brown, Body & Society 19/20.
224. Aug., De bono conjugali.
225. Schmitt, Mariage chrétien 15.
226. Van Bavel, Augustinus 58.
227. Aug., De bono 3.3.
228. Aug., De vera rel. 40.74.
229. Aug., De bono viduitatis 21.26.
230. Bailey, Man-Woman Relation 69.
231. Bailey, Man-Woman Relation 74.
232. Bailey, Man-Woman Relation 30.
233. Bailey, Man-Woman Relation 20.
234. Bailey, Man-Woman-Relation 22/23.
235. Bailey, Man-Woman Relation 48.
236. Bailey, Man-Woman Relation 48.

CHAPTER IV

CHRISTIANITY AND CLASSICAL CULTURE : REJECTION OR ACCEPTANCE?

1. An issue that hung in the balance

The question now confronting us is of the greatest, even of decisive importance for the future of European culture : would early Christianity be prepared to adopt classical culture, with or without modifications or adaptations? The answer to this question will conclude not only this volume but also that part of this series - fourteen volumes in all -that is devoted to the ancient world, and at the same time serve as the transition to the volumes on the Middle Ages that I am planning. On the face of it it would have been more than conceivable that the early Christians would have rejected classical culture as being pagan and perhaps have attempted to substitute a purely Christian one for it.

The fact that I attended a Roman Catholic grammar-school where we were taught Greek and Latin by teachers some of whom were priests proves that this rejection did not take place. The Graeco-Roman cultural heritage is just as much essential to our own culture as the Judaeo-Christian patrimony. However, the issue hung in the balance for some time in those early days; there were influential Christian thinkers who found the pagan culture wholly objectionable. Christian thought about this culture developed in about the same way as Christian thinking about the Roman Empire. At first, many saw this as an instrument of the devil, but it later came to be accepted, albeit never really wholeheartedly, as the great guarantee of law and order [1]. A specific point in the acceptance of classical culture by the Christian community was the question of whether it could be cleansed of what was objectionable in it without making it lose its identity. Or in other words, could the Graeco-Roman heritage be christianized without becoming unrecognizable?

2. The great flourishing of Roman culture

Roman culture was flourishing at that time. A plethora of great names can be cited, Cicero, to whom the Roman language owed so much, Virgil, the 'Roman Homer', Horace and Ovid, the poets, Livy, Tacitus, and Sallust, the historians, to mention the greater names only, but there were also many lesser known names. And there was the influx of Greek philosophy and literature with which western culture gradually became suffused. It would be hard for early Christianity to claim all this as worthless pagan nonsense and to sweep it under the carpet. A specific problem for the Christians, especially for the educated élite, was that they had been born and reared in this pagan culture. Many of them were not even cradle-Catholics but had been baptized as adults. They had heard the Homeric tales at their mother's knee, had attended pagan schools, and were steeped in Latin rhetorics and Greek philosophy. It would not be easy to shed all this and start anew with something authentically Christian.

3. What to start with?

And what would they start with? Upon which elements could a new culture be built? The foundation of Christian life was the Bible. The Old Testament was a book written in Hebrew by Semitic authors; as such it had remained largely unknown in the pagan world. However, there existed, as is well-known, a Greek translation of the Old Testament, the so-called 'Septuagint', made in the centuries before Christ. We know that some pagan authors quoted from it [2], but its use seems to have been restricted to non-Hebrew speaking Jews (like Philo), mainly in Egypt. Latin translations of the Old Testament began to circulate in the West from the second century A.D., but they were found to be dissatisfactory since they were based on the Septuaginta instead of the original Hebrew. Around 400 Jerome produced a good Latin translation of the

Hebrew text, called the 'Vulgata', the 'People's Bible'. It became the standard Latin version for the Roman Catholic Church.

The New Testament already shows signs of adaptation since it was written in Greek, although it is possible that the oldest Gospel texts were in Aramaic, equally a Semitic language. It seems that those responsible for the final redaction of the New Testament texts have realized that it would enormously hinder the spread of the new faith if the message was published in a non-Greek and non-Roman language. Knowledge of Greek was not widespread in the western world, especially not among the popular classes. A Latin translation of the New Testament was therefore needed. Since the second century the early Church had had one in the form of Vetus latina, which we know only fragmentarily.

For the time being there was little else. The texts of the Apostolic Fathers, the letters of Clement of Rome, Ignatius and Polycarp to Christian communities, written around the turn of the first and second centuries A.D. would probably not have struck educated pagans as being important contributions to classical culture. Only later in the second century Christian authors such as Hermas, Justin the Martyr, and Irenaeus began to write somewhat more convincingly. In the decade 170-180 A.D. Celsus, a pagan philosopher, wrote a book against Christianity [3]. He had a low opinion of Christians and his tone was contemptuous, but his work also demonstrated that he took Christianity seriously enough to polemize against it. More than a century later Origen found it still worthwhile to refute Celsus at great length in his 'Contra Celsum'. Christian and pagan standpoints had begun to clash.

4. The Christians and the pagan Empire

Christianity began making its way into the Graeco-Roman world exactly at a time when the prospects of Roman society had got considerably brighter. The horrible days of the civil wars of the last century B.C. were over, and with the rise to power of Octavian-Augustus an era of peace and prosperity had begun, which was to continue under his successors, the Julian and Flavian Emperors. The fact that the position of the imperial rulers became ever stronger, ever more self-evident, entailed a great risk for the Christians. A process of imperial deification began, bringing about the greatest difficulties since, even if they acknowledged the Emperor as their lawful ruler, they were unable to venerate him as a god.

It is no wonder that the early Christians found accepting the idea of a pagan Empire and its culture problematic. Some of their rulers, the first being Nero and the last Diocletian and Licinius, persecuted them in the most bloody way; the faithful of the first three centuries never knew where the axe would fall. The Empire was the great frame within which classical culture functioned; at the same time it was part of that culture itself. The most vociferous of those authors who expressed their aversion of the Empire and all that it represented was Tertullian. "I owe no obligation to Forum, campus, or Senate. I stay awake for no public function; I make no effort to monopolize the platform, I pay no heed to any adminstrative duty, I shun the voter's booth, the juryman's bench ... I serve neither as magistrate nor soldier, I have withdrawn from the life of secular society" [4]. His conclusion is unambiguous : "It is impossible to serve two masters, God and Caesar." [5] Nothing could be more un-Roman, for every well-educated Roman citizen hat to be ready to accept a public function.

Yet it was not only the Empire to which he objected; he rejected every form of secular power. "All secular powers are not merely alien from, but hostile to God" [6]. This is a dualistic viewpoint. But was it influential? Harnack thought not [7]; in his opinion Tertullian provided an exceptional example of rigorism and severity rather than typically representing the Christian attitude. Harnack was not wholly correct on this point, for in 248 Origen wrote that "we [the Christians] do not fight under the Emperor, even though he would command it" [8].

5. The Christians and military service

Linked to the attitude of the Christians to the Empire was the question whether they could serve in the imperial armies with a clear conscience [9]. The problem was not only whether it was permissible to assist a pagan ruler in his war efforts but still more whether a Christian should not rather be a principal pacifist and abstain from every form of violence, especially from fighting in wars. Celsus reproached the Christians for their unwillingness to become soldiers. "If everybody acted like you, nobody could guard the Emperor from utter solitude and loneliness, and the dominion of the Empire would fall into the hands of the most wild and lawless barbarians" [10]. If he thought that there were no Christian legionaries at all, he was wrong. We know that in the year 173 A.D. Christians served in the Legio XII fulminata [11]. Tertullian mentioned the presence of Christians in the army in 197 [12]; he did not approve of this [13]. We also know of Christian soldiers who became martyrs.

There were legionaries who left the service after their conversion [14] and even of a young Christian who was executed because he refused to enlist [15]. If the Christian Church had objections to Christians serving as legionaries, the imperial government too was far from pleased about their presence in the army. Towards the end of the persecution period its aversion to Christian legionaries reached a culmination point. Eusebius reports that the last great persecution, that of Diocletian, began as an action against the Christians in the army. "First of all, the persecution was directed against Christians serving as soldiers" [16], for, he thought, "once he [the Emperor] would have triumphed over them, he could easily bring down the rest". Given the choice to either participate in sacrifice or leave the army, most Christians preferred the latter option [17].

It was not really Diocletian himself who initiated these measures, but his co-emperor Galerius. He though that the gods were angry because there were Christians in the army; this would lead to defeats. Lactantius who relates this, says that Christian officers partook in the sacrifices, but not without making the sign of the cross; this made the demons powerless [18].

Were the Christian soldiers numerous [19]? In the first two centuries certainly not; later there were more of them. Bainton thinks that resistance to the military profession was strongest in the Hellenistic East, but far less in the frontier regions where the barbarian menace was felt [20]. There were several reasons for sincere Christians to stay away from the army. First of all, there was the pacifism that was thought to be congenial to the Christian mind; Christians referred to this saying of Jesus : "Who does take up the sword will perish by it" [21]. Then there was the obligation of taking an oath of fidelity to the Emperor, the pagan ruler, who at any time could become a persecutor of the Christians. Soldiers had to attend the religious services of the regiment, a duty that could not easily be dodged. Finally, the barracks were not a place of high morality; dirty jokes were told and bawdy songs sung.

But there is another side to the question. It was hard for citizens and inhabitants of the Empire, whether pagans or Christians, to totally repudiate that great political entity in which they lived [22]. The Christians knew quite well that the *Pax Romana* also favoured them, that the Emperor was their lawful ruler, and that the legions also served for their protection. Of course, they knew themselves to be citizens of the heavenly city, but the reality in which they lived was that of another civitas. We find this expressed by Clement of Alexandria who speaks of Christ's army that does not shed blood, but on the other hand contents himself with quoting John the Baptist's injunction to the (Christian) soldiers that they should refrain from robbery and extortion [23]. John did not say 'stop being soldiers'. It should not be overlooked that it was perfectly possible to serve many years as a legionary without ever seeing action; we should think here, for instance, of the men who spent their time of service in garrisons or who fulfilled police functions only [24].

Many scholars are of the opinion that the early Church was decidedly and principally pacifist; I am thinking here of Harnack and Cadoux, for instance. But this does not wholly tally with the facts. The magisterium of the Church never forbade Christians to serve as soldiers. If it is true that before 179/180 A.D. we never hear of Christians in the army, it is also true that after that there were Christian legionaries. Not all Christian authors were so mordicus against this as Tertullian and Origen. There was no uniform opinion on this point, but on the whole we may say that the Church remained reserved about Christians serving in the army.

In 314 the Synod of Arles stipulated in its canon 3 that those "who throw away their arms in time of peace must be excluded from the communion" [25]. This can hardly mean anything else than that Christians might serve as garrison soldiers or in police functions, but should not take part in the actual fighting. A refusal to serve in time of peace was obviously found to be un-Christian. Harnack's conclusion is that "herewith from the side of the Church complete concord of state and Emperor on the one hand and of Christianity and Church on the other in the field of army organization was proclaimed" [26].

This is really going too far! This Synod did in fact nothing else but approve of a situation that had long since existed. But it is true that it went a step further by declaring that it was unpermissible to quit the servive in peacetime. A certain shift in the Christian attitude was coming to the fore. If, however, Harnack categorically states that "in any case the Church by this decision thoroughly revised the theoretical position with respect to the army and war it had taken so far" [27], we might object, first that the Synod did not revise the ecclesiastical attitude to warfare, and secondly, that a provincial Synod is not 'the Church'. That there was no rapid change is proved by the fact that Martin of Tours remained a soldier after his conversion, but left the army two years later, in 336, when there was a battle expected [28].

There are texts in the Fathers that seem to concur with Harnack. Athanasius found that, although "murder is not permitted, killing opponents in war is lawful as well as praiseworthy" [29]. Ambrose too praises those who defend the fatherland against the barbarians and protect the weak [30]. Somewhat later Augustine became an advocate of the idea of the 'just war' that would play such a great role in the Christian discussion. Roman soldiers, he found, when conducting war, in fact served the cause of peace and of general well-being [31].

This led the Dutch theologian Heering to speak of a 'radical change of Christianity respecting such an important thing as warfare'. He did not hesitate to call this a 'Fall', a fall into sin, so that Christendom became 'degenerate' on this point. And if other opinions became audible, they were repressed by the Church [32]. A few remarks are necessary. When Augustine was writing, the barbarians were pounding on the Empire from all sides; the Visigoths were in Rome in 410, and the dying bishop saw the Vandals laying siege to his own Hippo. Was it not very difficult in these circumstances to tell the Christians to stay at home with their arms crossed?

Secondly, several oriental Fathers, John Chrysostom and Basil the Great among them, remained just as averse to military exploits as pre-Constantinian authors. And they were not repressed by the Church. We have not a few ecclesiastical rulings, even from the period after the liberation of the Church, to the effect that soldiers about to receive baptism should leave the service, or that they might continue to serve on the condition they would never kill. Cadoux concludes that this is "conclusive proof that in large sections of the Christian community, the decisions taken by official Christendom, as seen for instance in the Canons of the Synod of Arelate, were not accepted ... It is evident that in many quarters the settlement was accepted only gradually and with an uneasy conscience" [33].

Author after author takes it for granted that such a 'settlement' (between Church and state) really existed. But I should like to be informed when and where and by whom it was concluded. When speaking of the allegedly enthusiastic and whole-hearted acceptance of the Empire by the Christian Church, even to the point of concluding some sort of alliance, we should not let it escape our attention that Augustine, for one, was not uncritical of the Christian Empire; perhaps he did not admire it at all. His City of God is not identical to that Empire by any measure. In his eyes there was no essential difference between the pagan and the Christian Empires. The most that could be said was that the Empire would be better off with a Christian than with a pagan ruler, but this only on the condition that this ruler was a good Christian. Augustine had no high idea of the Christian value of most of the rulers [34].

6. First contacts between pagan and Christian culture

The very first contacts between the young Christianity and pagan culture took place at almost the earliest possible date. When Paul was in Athens, he used to have discussions on the agora with Epicurean and Stoic philosophers. They listened with interest to him, but when he began to speak of the resurrection of the dead, they shrugged their shoulders and went their own way. In his speech on the Areopagus Paul demonstrated that he was acquainted with Greek literature, for he quoted from a Greek poem [35].

7. Opponents of classical culture

There can be no doubt, however, that in the first centuries of the Church we find in many Christian authors a wholesale rejection of pagan culture, especially in its philosophical aspects, but as Danny Praet states, this was more common in the Latin West than in the Hellenistic East [36]. There was a real possibility of a dualistic split in culture, with the pagan culture doomed to slowly wither away. The Didascalia, a catechical handbook of the first quarter of the fourth century, exhorts its readers to set aside all those 'strange and demonical books' [37]. In an earlier volume I related with how much venom Tatian spoke of Greek culture [38]. And who never heard the famous words of Tertullian, spoken around A.D. 200 : "Quid Athenae Hierosolymis?", what has Athens to do with Jerusalem, the Academy with the Church? 'Athens' stands here for the totality of pagan culture, 'Jerusalem' for Christianity. And he goes on to state that "we [the Christians] have no curiosity since Jesus Christ, not for inquiry since the Gospel". Pagan philosophy is nothing but 'idle speculation, useless affectation of a fastidious curiosity' [39].

"What is there in common", he asks, "between the philosopher and the Christian, the pupil of Hellas and the pupil of Heaven, the worker for reputation and that for salvation, the manufacturer of words and of deeds, the interpolator of error and the artificer of truth, the thief of truth and its custodian?" [40]. This is the sheerest dualism [41] which is completed with yet another opposition, that of "the simple and uncultivated soul, such as they have who have nothing else, whose whole experience has been gleaned on street-corners and crossroads and in the industrial plant [and] the soul [of the pagan] which, formed in the schools, trained in the libraries, belches forth a fund of academic wisdom" [42]. This is not only dualism, it is also undiluted obscurantism [43].

A few remarks may be made to exculpate Tertullian to a certain extent. He was a fanatic who used to express himself in extravagant terms. It should also not be forgotten that he was a rhetor which signifies that not everything he said should be taken literally. It belonged to the art of the rhetor to oppose and to vilify. Moreover it is also true that the pagan opponents of Christianity often would express themselves in the most vehement terms. Tertullian paid them back in kind. Even two centuries later Jerome, another author who did not mince his words, asked rhetorically : "What has Horace [= pagan culture] to do with the Psalter [= the Christian faith]? What Maro [= Virgil] with the Gospel? What Cicero with the apostle?" [44].

8. The true philosophy

Christian intellectuals opposed biblical teaching to pagan thought as the true philosophy. As far as I know, this term was coined by Augustine. "Can paganism, I ask you, produce anything equal to ours, the one true philosophy [vera philosophia]?" [45]. The problem was that educated Christians, trained as they were in the art of rhetorics, were not charmed by the way biblical authors expressed themselves : 'sermo piscatoria', they found it, a fisherman's mode of speaking [46]. Augustine himself relates how he, as a nineteen-year old adolescent, opened the Bible, in all probability for the first time, found it not to his taste, and laid it away [47]. The line of defence Christians took was that the truth presented in the Bible was so sublime that it needed no rhetorical embellishment. To Basil Scripture was like a fresh young girl in her natural beauty, and pagan rhetoric like a painted old whore. Yet another line of defence was that the biblical message was couched in simple terms in order to make it accessible to uneducated people [48].

Piety, however, is a very good thing, but in a discussion with opponents of the Christian faith it does not carry much weight. Even the severest critics of pagan culture realized that Christians needed schooling, and no other schooling was to be had but that offered by pagan institutes. Nobody ever forbade Christian adolescents to study there. Not even the sour Tertullian did this. He too found that young Christians needed education; they would get nowhere in daily life without it. At a certain moment he even forgot himself so far that he discovered something good in pagan philosophy [49]. With these concessions he distanced himself from such truly obscurantist authors like Epiphanius and Lucifer of Calaris who would have absolutely nothing to do with pagan culture. "[Their] opinions are most violent; [both were] stylistically considered, very indifferent authors, and as thinkers not even in the second rank" [50].

9. Evidence of a change to the positive

Evidence of a change in the Christian appreciation of classical culture are discernible at a very early date [51]. Around A.D. 170 Justin the Martyr had some praise to spare for pagan thinkers, especially Socrates; he remained true to the Platonic line by castigating Homer and other poets who had a bad influence because they had introduced evil demons [52]. There was an institution where pagan thought played a constitutive role within a Christian context, namely the catechetical school of Alexandria. The word 'school' does not refer to a building, for the instruction was given in private homes. It was made famous by its third headmaster, Origen, around 200. Origen, the son of a father who had fallen victim to pagan persecution, was very well versed in pagan literature and possessed a large library of it. But he sold all his books because he found their contents incompatible with his Christian convictions. He had second thoughts, however, when he saw that not only Christian youth but also pagans and heretics came to hear him. He then realized that the study of pagan philosophy was a must if Christian culture wanted to become the equal of its heathen counterpart or even to replace it.

Yet reconciling purely pagan thought and Christian orthodoxy is a very hard task and perhaps even impossible. The scholar who attempts to combine them in a coherent system runs the risk of gliding away in the one or the other direction. An early example of this are the writings of Philo, the Jewish Alexandrian scholar, who, perhaps unwittingly, favoured the Hellenistic philosophy of his days far more than biblical theology [53]. It is the same with Origen who more often than once came dangerously close to heresy [54]. The great protestant scholar Harnack even accused him of having 'hellenized' Christian thought and of having steered it in the wrong direction.

Origen's teacher and contemporary was Clement of Alexandria; he too was no enemy of non-Christian thought [55]. Knowledge was important for him, the knowledge that in Greek is called 'Gnosis', with a capital. In Gnostic thinking, Gnosis is the absolute opposite of 'Pistis' = Faith; one should not have faith but knowledge. But to Clement, Gnosis was the corrolary of Pistis; faith, consecrated in baptism, would lead to knowledge, to a deeper and fuller understanding of what faith implies. This comprehension did not end with a broad understanding of theological and biblical tenets but would also involve, so to speak, the things of this world, in particular philosophy.

Clement found it a dangerous thing that so many Christians, even educated ones, rejected all that was pagan. In his opinion there was much that was good and positive in pagan thinking. In order to convince his co-religionists he wrote his 'Paedagogus'. How must a Christian live in a society that is still fundamentally marked by paganism?, that is the leading theme of this book. Its author knew quite well that the heathen life-style was thoroughly un-Christian, and he duly warned his readers against its excesses. But he also found that Christians who wanted to pass for educated persons, should have more than a vague (and negative) notion of pagan philosophy. There was in his view no real opposition between its best products and biblical teaching.

10. Between two worlds

However, the writings of Clement and Origen "did not yet spell the completion of the process of accomodation" [56]. Authors writing in this vein were often viewed with mistrust. In the eyes of many a Christian they were too ready to lend an ear to pagan opinion. As Cochrane states, "Clement's scheme of Christian propaedeusis [was] obviously based on Neopythagorean-Platonic practice" [57].

The situation did not become significantly better after the liberation of the Church. In the second half of the fourth century we see John Chrysostom hovering between two extremes. Even in his days, the wild cry 'away with pagan education!' was still heard. But with John it fell on deaf ears. "'Shall we raze the [pagan] schools to the ground?', this is not what I am saying". But pagan education must not be injurious to Christian virtue [58]. John poked fun at pagan philosophers with their long beards, but he himself had studied with the great pagan rhetor Libanius at Antioch, and he honoured his teacher by becoming a great orator who could express himself in perfect Greek. He clearly was a product of both worlds.

We see the same in Basil the Great, a Cappadocian, born a pagan, who had studied (Neoplatonic) philosophy in Athens, thought of a career in rhetorics or philosophy, but became a convert to Christianity, and ended as a bishop in his native Cappadocia and as an influential ecclesiastical author - a career that bears a great resemblance to that of Augustine. In spite of his philosophical training, or perhaps because of it, Basil remained somewhat distrustful of the pagan intellectual inheritance.

But other authors, like Eusebius of Caesarea or Gregory of Nazianzus, argued rather in the line of Clement and Origen. Gregory was definitely positive with regard to pagan education. "The first of our advantages is education, and not only this more noble form of it [=Christian teaching] ... but even that pagan culture which many Christians spit upon, as treacherous and dangerous and keeping us from God." It will be remarked that this author, although defending pagan culture, does not put it on a par with Christian culture, for this is 'more noble'. But we must "reap what advantage we can from them [the pagan authors] for our life and enjoyment, while we avoid their dangers ... From secular science we have received principles of inquiry and speculation, while we have rejected their idolatry, terror, and pit of destruction." What the Christians should adopt from pagan education is method rather than contents. And Gregory concludes : "We must not then dishonour [pagan] education, because some people are pleased to do so, but rather suppose such men to be boorish and uneducated" [59].

11. The problem of Augustine

Laistner concludes : "The continuity in respect to literature and scholarship between Antiquity and the Middle Ages was never broken" [60]. In the long perspective this was true, but Augustine presents us with a problem. As a young man he was raised and reared in the truest classical tradition. Before his conversion he planned to make a career as a Latin rhetor. That he became a Christian and a priest made no difference to his attachment to this culture, at least not at first. For a long time he remained favourably disposed to Greek philosophy, especially to Platonism; he was certain then that the truth could be found not only by faith but also by understanding.

But as he grew older, his attitude changed [61]. The quotations from pagan authors, at first so abundant, dwindled [62]. In his Confessions he showed himself averse to reading heathen authors in school [63]. Even rhetoric was now dubbed 'nundinae loquacitatis', a loquacity fair, fit only to make young people mendacious [64]. Even the greatest Latin poet, Virgil, comes in for a very unfavourable judgment, for this poet did no more than sell words [65].

The Swedish scholar Harald Hagendahl concludes that "as a man of the Church Augustine came to regard differently the literary heritage under whose influence he had lived and worked. There is no doubt that he was strongly influenced by the old Christian prejudice against it and more and more felt its incomptability with the new religion. The Confessions represent the climax of an attitude of unconcern, aversion, even hostility that subsisted, though occasionally less austerely, to the end of his life" [66].

12. Conquest or fusion?

Praet's comment on the situation discussed in this chapter is that "just as the triumphant Romans were 'conquered' by the older Greek culture, Christendom was 'conquered' by the Graeco-Roman synthesis [67]. This sweeping statement is built on two untenable premises. The first is that such a thing as a 'Graeco-Roman synthesis' really existed. In Vol. XI, Ch. VI, I demonstrated that this was far from being the case. It is equally untrue that Christianity was 'conquered' by that synthesis. The Bible, for instance, is not a product of Graeco-Roman culture, while Roman Catholic liturgy, the Eucharist above all, has its roots in Judaism. I therefore do not think that the two cultures fused in the works of Saint Augustine. I even ask myself whether they ever fused [68]. Speaking of classical culture and Christian culture means speaking of two very unequal things.

Around 400 there was not yet much of a Christian culture. Pagan culture was still in control of all the elements that make a culture, while Christians still had very little to offer in the way of philosophy, poetry, historiography, art and architecture. The renowned Christian authors, like Tertullian, Jerome, Ambrose, Augustine, the Cappadocian theologians, all took the style of the great pagan authors as their model. What Christianity had was an enormous volume of theology, which it bequeathed to later ages.

The encounter of pagan philosophy and Christian theology was fraught with dangers. Tertullian was aware of this, but Origen was not, and he almost succumbed to the song of the heathen siren. Even those theologians who were most positive with regard to classical culture in its pagan form and particularly to its philosophy, always remained somewhat reticent in their appraisal and ambivalent in their attitude. This becomes especially evident in the works of the three great Cappadocians, or four if we include Macrina, the sister of Gregory of Nyssa and Basil the Great, the fourth then being Gregory of Nazianzus. Jaroslav Pelikan devoted a brilliant book to their encounter of natural theology with Hellenism [69].

'Natural theology' can best be described as that knowledge and understanding of God and things divine that can be attained by means of our reason, that is, without the help of biblical revelation. It still is an object of study. In 1881 Adam Lord Gifford founded an annual series of lectures at the University of Aberdeen in Scotland - called after him 'the Gifford Lectures' - for 'promoting, advancing, teaching, and diffusing the study of natural theology'. Since then these lectures have been delivered by such worthies as Étienne Gilson, Karl Barth, Stanley L. Jaki, Werner Jaeger, and Arthur Darby Nock. But curiously enough, Newman was never invited.

In the early stages of the development of a Christian theology natural theology "tended to present itself as an alternative - or even as an antidote - to the cultic practices and sacred narratives of traditional religious observance". Its students were not "the priests of the cult but lay philosophers and apologists, and sometimes opponents and critics who were sceptics or agnostics and even atheists" [70]. The thesis of Pelikan's book is that "at the hands of such thinkers as the Cappadocians [who were both philosophers and priests] natural theology underwent a fundamental *metamorphosis*. It became not only an apologetic but a presupposition for systematic dogmatic theology" [71].

The Cappadocian Fathers - I already described Gregory of Nazianzus' attitude to pagan education - were positively disposed towards the classical heritage. There already existed a kind of 'alliance between Christianity and classical culture', when the Emperor Julian the Apostate (361-363) attempted to break it up. He forbade Christian teachers to use the pagan authors in their lessons, because he feared that they would treat the (pagan) religion with contempt. And why should they teach ideas in which they themselves did not believe? There was by no means general rejoicing among the Christians that they were now rid of that burden. Rather the contrary! Gregory of Nazianzus protested in a long treatise. He accused the Emperor of attempting to introduce pagan teachers of philosophy into the school curriculum as the only valuable ones [72].

That part of classical culture that was most dear to the Cappadocian Fathers was the Greek language of which they were all pastmasters. More specifically it was the art of rhetoric that they loved. They held Greek poetry in high esteem, but were at the same time critical of it, for they found many unpalatable myths therein. Pelikan describes their attitude to classical thought as 'ambivalent' [73]. They saw the origin of heresy mainly in the circumstance that Christian thinkers indebted themselves too much to pagan philosophy. Gregory of Nyssa spoke of 'the foolish beliefs of the Greeks' [74]. As Pelikan wrote, "each of the three (or four) Cappadocians stood squarely in the tradition of Classical Greek culture, and was at the same time intensely critical of it. Each was in constant intellectual interchange, and in no less constant controversy, with the monuments of that culture and with contemporary expositions of the monuments" [75].

That natural theology now became the presupposition for dogmatic, orthodox Christian theology may be seen as an infrastructure and a superstructure. Since the rational infrastructure contained many pagan, mainly Hellenic elements, it would not be suprising if these too found their way into the superstructure. The result of this encounter was not the harmonious fusion of two sets of thought. The cohabitation of Hellenism and Christian doctrine in the minds of the Cappadocians remained somewhat uncomfortable. Gregory of Nyssa used a revealing metaphor to defend his use of pagan ideas that was criticized by some. He referred for this to God's command to the Israelites to plunder the possessions of the Egyptians, when they were fleeing Egypt [76]. He seems to have had an inkling of how arduous their task was. "We must fit together according to the explanation of Scripture and to that derived from reasoning statements that seem, by a kind of necessary sequence, to be opposed, so that our whole subject may be consistent in train of thought and order" [77].

13. Was the Christian attitude to classical culture dualistic?

How must we characterize the attitude of the Christian community towards classical, that is, to pagan culture. As dualistic? First of all, there is no authoritative pronouncement from the side of the magisterium on the study of pagan authors and their use in schools. It was, therefore, not forbidden. We know nothing at all of the attitude of the Christian masses . But the great majority could neither write nor read, so we may assume that the question was of no consequence to them. We are entirely dependent on those Christians who expressed themselves in writing. There can be no doubt that some of them were so fiercely opposed to the pagan authors that we must speak of radical dualism. If their views had triumphed, a definite break in culture would have occurred; European civilization would have developed in a manner that we can simply not imagine.

What saved the classical heritage from total destruction was, on the one hand, the inner force of that tradition, on the other, the unshakeable position it had in the Graeco-Roman world. To do away with it would have been an impossible task. The effect of this situation was that the rejection of that culture was never as radical as it looks on paper. From the later second century onwards Christian authors were more ready to accept classical culture, at least to a certain extent. Some of them remained radical opponents on paper; we may think here of Tertullian and Augustine. But even those who were more positive always kept their reservations; they had their problems with the frivolous parts of pagan poetry and with the deism, pantheism, and atheism of pagan philosophy. I feel that Christian theologians would have protested if we could have spoken to them about a fusion. The pagan intellectual heritage was valuable to them, but in the last resort it was no more than a presupposition. They worked with certain principles, methods, and ideas that they borrowed from pagan thinkers, but they used them to construct something quite different.

14. The chasm remains

My conclusion is that educated Christians never wholeheartedly accepted the pagan heritage. Although they were citizens of the Roman Empire, and although they were tributary to its civilization, they lived in a different mental world. In this respect it did not greatly matter whether this Empire was pagan or Christian. We should, I think, speak of relative dualism here. Cases of radical rejection were rare, cases of total acceptance were non-existent. Great Christian minds borrowed freely from pagan philosophy, but they found it inferior to Christian doctrine, which was the 'true philosophy'.

I wonder whether this changed very much over the centuries. In the time when I attended a Roman Catholic grammar school, the situation was not really different. We were thoroughly grounded in the Greek and Latin languages for which I remain grateful to the present day. But the school was elective with regard to the authors we read. We did not read philosophers, with the exception of Plato's Apology. Instead, we read the *Octavius* by

Minucius Felix. We also studied Ovid, but not his Ars amatoria; I did not even know then that it existed. We equally did not become acquainted with the bawdy parts of Horace's poetry. It was out of the question that we should have read such a charming book as Longus's Daphnis and Chloe. I remember quite well a comic incident that happened when we, as fourteen-year-olds began to read Homer's Iliad. On its very first page it is related that the captured girl Briseis shared Achilles' bed. We virtuously translated 'who approached his bed' to which our teacher (a layman) hastily added : 'to make it'. And we accepted this without a snigger. Of course, I am speaking of how it was more than sixty years ago. Perhaps things are different now. But then there was still a line of fracture visible.

NOTES TO CHAPTER IV

1. See for this subject more extensively Vol. XII, Ch. I, Part III, §§ 2-6.
2. See Vol. XI, Ch. V, Part IV.
3. See Vol. XII, Ch. I, Part II, § 10.
4. Tert., De pallio 5. I take the translation from Cochrane, Christianity.
5. Tert., De idol. 19.
6. Tert., De idol. 18.
7. Harnack, Mil.Chr. 68.
8. Orig., Contra Cels. 8.73. For Origen's opinions see Harnack, Mil.Chr. 70-72. Cadoux, Christian attitude 49-57, quotes all early Christian authors who condemned warfare.
9. Harnack, Mil.Chr. 47/48, sums up eight reasons why they could not.
10. Orig., Contra Cels. 8.68-69.
11. Bainton, Frühe Kirche 190.
12. Tert., Apol. 37.
13. Tert., De corona 11.
14. Tert., De corona 11.
15. Bainton, Frühe Kirche 192.
16. Eus., HE 8.17.
17. Eus., HE 8.4.

18. Lact., De morte persec. 10. See Harnack, Mil.Chr. 80-82.
19. See Cadoux, Attitude 228-243.
20. Bainton, Frühe Kirche 191/192.
21. Mt.26:52.
22. For a more extensive treatment see Grant, Early Christianity, Ch. IV Christian Devotion to the Monarchy (see Bibliography).
23. Lc. 3:14. Quotation from Clement in Harnack, Mil.Chr. 23 and 58.
24. Bainton, Frühe Kirche 197/198.
25. Harnack, Mil.Chr. 87.
26. Harnack, Mil.Chr. 88.
27. Harnack, Mil.Chr. 88.
28. Sulp.Sev., Vita Mart. 1.1-4.
29. Athan., Ep. ad Ammonium.
30. Ambr., De off. 1.27 (219).
31. August., Contra Faust. 22.75.
32. Heering, Zondeval 46/47.
33. Cadoux, Attitude 259-261.
34. See more extensively Vol. XII, Ch. I, Part III, § 6.
35. Acts 17:16-33. It is usually assumed that this quotation came from Cleanthes's Hymn to Zeus, but it is also possible that the source was the 'Phaenomena' by Aratus of Soli, see Sordi, Christians 158.
36. Praet, God der goden 109.
37. Did. 2.6.
38. Vol. XIII, Ch. V, § 3b.
39. Tert., De praescr.haer. 7.
40. Tert., Apol. 46.
41. Armstrong/Markus, Christian Faith 139 speak here of 'an uncompromising opposition to pagan philosophy'.
42. Tert., De test.an. 10.
43. I am utterly astonished to read in Bailey, who is a well-informed scholar, Man-Woman Relation 223/224, about "the notorious credo quia absurdum [I believe because it is absurd] which, by asserting the shameful, the silly, and the impossible, as against the evidences of good taste, probability, and reason itself [yet another dualism! - F.], hurls a defiant challenge in the face of the classical world". Another reputable

scholar who should know better, Henry Chadwick, Early Christian Thought 2, wrote 'of the grinding paradox' of Tertullian : "I believe because it is absurd", referring to Tertullian's De carne Christi 5. I do not know how many times I have found this quoted as an authoritative statement of the medieval mode of thought. Most of the time the quotation is given without any indication of author and work as though it were typical for all ancient and medieval theologians. Fredouille, Tertullien 326, comments : "Ce mot, sous cette forme inexacte ['credo quia absurdum'], a néanmoins assuré une gloire certaine à Tertullien, devenu, par le fait, comme le symbole de l'antirationalisme, l'incarnation d'une certaine attitude religieuse typique à l'égard de l'intelligence".

It will be clear why this phrase is so popular. If believing would really be absurd, we had, as sensible people, rather not believe. And with this, as an orthodox Roman Catholic, I heartily concur. In letters to leading Dutch newspapers I offered a prize for the person who could tell me who said this and where and in which context. The money is still in my pocket, and for an obvious reason : no ancient or medieval author ever said this. A phrase 'credo quia absurdum' simply does not exist. The closest guess is a text by Tertullian in De carne Christ, 5 (28) where he writes about the death on the cross of the Son of God : "prorsus credibile est quia ineptum", it is altogher believable because it lacks sense. It is inadmissible that Bailey and others turn this into 'credo quia absurdum'.

This is yet another instance of Tertullian's predilection to express himself in terms of opposition, a usual style figure with him : 'credibile-ineptum'. It must be admitted that he is not very prudent expressing himself in this way, because it may cause misunderstandings. But all he wanted to say that, although it is contrary to reason that God would die, we have to accept it because it is a fact. He certainly did not want to say that believing is good exactly because it is absurd. Fredouille, Tertullien 373 : "L'attitude antirationaliste consiste à 'croire contre la raison' : elle n'est pas celle de Tertullien, ni ici ni ailleurs".

It is also necessary to realize that in 'De carne' its author is not polemizing against the pagans but against Marcion, the Gnostic, who denied the reality of Jesus's conception and birth; he found such biological events undignified for God's Son. Tertullian retorts with a strong rhetorical paradox : you may find it impossible or undignified or whatever you like, but it is a fact that he died, physically. It should not be overlooked that there is a strong element of rhetoric in his expression, Fredouille, Tertullien 335-337.

Let us conclude with quoting Fredouille again, Tertullien 337 : "Les considérations critiques ou passionées auxquelles a donné lieu le credibile est quia ineptum, paraissent, donc, en définitive, bien fragiles".

44. Hier., Ep. 22.29.7. For this passage see Praet, God der goden 109.

45. Aug., Contra Jul. 4.14 (72).

46. Praet, God der goden 111.

47. Aug., Conf. 3.4-6 and 5.9.
48. Praet, God der goden 111, with the quotation from Basil.
49. Tert., De idol. 10; De anima 2.
50. Laistner, Christianity 51.
51. Armstrong/Markus, Christian Faith 136/137 : "How did Christian thinkers put together this twofold insistence of St. Paul's : the insistence, on one hand, on the the radical novelty of faith in Christ, its unattainability by human initiative, and the insistence, on the other hand, that somehow human speculation could find a home within faith? The process of reconciling these two positions within Christian thinking was gradual."
52. Just., Apol. 1.46 and 2.8. See for Justin more extensively Chadwick, Early Christian Thought 10-22.
53. For Philo see Vol. VIII. Ch. I.
54. For this see Vol. XIII, Ch. III, §§ 5-9.
55. For Clement see Chadwick, Early Christian Thought, Ch 2 The liberal puritan.
56. Praet, God der goden 114.
57. Cochran, Christianity 226.
58. Jo.Chryst., Adv.opp. 2.5 and 2.11. PG 47.
59. Greg.Naz., Or. 43.11. PG 36.
60. Laistner, Christianity 72.
61. Callahan, Augustine 93-95.
62. With exception of 'De civitate Dei'.
63. Aug., Conf. 1.16.26.
64. Aug., Conf. 9.2.2.
65. Aug., Sermo 105.8. PL 38.
66. See for this passage Hagendahl, Augustine and the Latin Classics. Vol. II, Ch. X, § 4 Augustine's attitude : changes and tendencies. Marrou, Saint Augustin 541-545, does not see Augustine as a typical representative of the classical culture; he is rather a man still standing with one leg in that culture, with the other already in the Middle Ages. We see the transition where he breaks with the art of rhetoric and devotes himself to the 'sacred science' of the Bible and the Christian faith. Marrou remarks that Augustine never was a philosopher, let alone a good one. Although he admired the Platonists, he had read very little of Plato and also of Aristotle. In this respect he surely did not transmit the classical heritage to later times.

67. Praet, God der goden 115.
68. That such a fusion really took place is the thesis of Combès, Saint Augustine, Ch. III.
69. Pelikan, Christianity and Classical Culture (see Bibliography).
70. Pelikan, Christianity 38.
71. Pelikan, Christianity 38.
72. Pelikan, Christianity 12.
73. Pelikan, Christianity 17.
74. Greg.Nyss., Contra Eunomium 3.2.35.
75. Pelikan, Christianity 10.
76. Greg.Nyss., Vita Moysis 2 (300).
77. Greg.Nyss., De hominis opificio. Praef.

BIBLIOGRAPHY

I ORIGINAL SOURCES

A COLLECTIONS

CODEX CANONUM ECCLESIAE ET CONSTITUTORUM S. SEDIS APOSTOLICAE. PL 56. (Paris, 1846).

CORPUS MEDICORUM GRAECORUM. Berlin.

CORPUS INSCRIPTIONUM LATINARUM (quoted as CIL). Berlin, 1863-1936.

CORPUS MEDICORUM GRAECORUM II. Berlin, 1958.

CORPUS SCRIPTORUM CHRISTIANORUM. Pars latina. Turnholti.

CORPUS SCRIPTORUM CHRISTIANORUM ORIENTALIUM. Louvain.

CORPUS SCRIPTORUM ECCLESIASTICORUM LATINORUM. Vienna. (Quoted as CSEL).

DIE GRIECHISCHEN CHRISTLICHEN SCHRIFTSTELLER DER ERSTEN DREI JAHRHUNDERTE. Leipzig.

PATROLOGIA GRAECA (PG).

PATROLOGIA LATINA (PL).

SACRORUM CONCILIORUM COLLECTIO. Ed. J.D. Mansi. Florence. (Quoted as Mansi.)

STOBAEUS
   Ioannis Stobaei Anthologium. Vol. I. Ed. Curtius Wachsmuth. Berolini, 1884.

SOURCES CHRÉTIENNES. Paris.

B INDIVIDUAL AUTHORS

AELIUS LAMPRIDIUS
Severus Alexander. Scriptores Historiae Augustae. Ed. David Magie. Loeb Classical Library 140. Oxford/Cambridge (Ms), 1924.

ALCINOUS
Didaskalia. Ed. John Whittaker, Alcinoos, Enseignement des doctrines de Platon. Traduction Pierre Louis. Collection 'Budé'. Paris, 1990.

AMBROSIUS
De officiis. PL 16. Paris, 1845.

APPIAN
Appianus, Romaika. Roman History. Edited and translated by Horace White. Loeb Classical Library. London/Cambridge (Ms), 1958 (1912[1]).

APULEIUS, Lucius
1. The Golden Ass, being the metamorphoses of --. Translated by W. Adlington (1566). Revised by S. Gaselee. Loeb Classical Library. London/Cambridge (Ms), 1958.
2. Metamorphoses. Les Métamorphoses. T. III. Collection Budé. Paris, 1956.

ARETAEUS
On the causes and signs of chronic illnesses. Ed. Carolus Hude. Corpus medicorum graecorum II. Berlin, 1958. Die auf uns gekommenen Schriften des Kappociers Aretaeus aus dem griechischen übersetzt von Dr. Amann. Halle, 1858.

ARTEMIDORUS
Onirocriticon. Ed. Roger A. Pack. Leipzig, 1963. Artémidore, La clef des songes. Traduit et annoté par A.-J. Festugière. Paris, 1975.

ATHANASIUS
Epistola ad Ammonium episcopum de fuga sua sub Juliano. PG 26. Paris, 1857.

ATTICUS
Fragments. Ed. Édouard des Places. Collection 'Budé'. Paris, 1977.

AUGUSTINUS
1. De bono conjugali. PL 40. Paris, 1861.
2. De bono viduitatis. PL 40. Paris, 1861.
3. De civitate Dei contra paganos. The City of God agaianst the Pagans. Loeb Classical Library. 7 vols. Cambridge (Ms)/London.

4. Confessiones. Eds. E. Tréhorel et G. Bouissiou (Latin text with French translation). Bibliothèque augustinienne. Oeuvres de Saint Augustin, vols. 13 and 14. Louvain, 1962.
5. Epistulae. Ed. J. Divjak. CSEL 88. Vienna, 1981.
6. Contra Faustum Manichaeum. PL 42. Paris, 1861.
7. De Genesi ad literam. PL 24. Paris, 1845.
8. Contra Julianum. PL 44. Paris, 1845.
9. Contra Manichaeos. PL 34. Paris, 1845.
10. De nuptiis et concupiscentia. PL 10. Paris, 1845.
11. De peccatorum meritis et remissione. PL 10. Paris, 1845.
12. Retractationes. PL 32. Paris, 1845.
13. De sermone Domini in monte. PL 34. Paris, 1845.
14. Sermones. PL 38. Paris, 1861.
15. Soliloquium. PL 32. Paris, 1845.
16. De Trinitate. PL 42. Paris, 1862.
17. De vera religione. PL 24. Paris, 1845.

CICERO
1. Academica. Ed. H. Rackham. Loeb Classical Library 268. Oxford/Cambridge (Ms), 1961.
2. Academica posteriora. Ed. Michel Ruch. Collection 'Érasme'. Paris, 1970.
3. Brutus. Ed. G.L. Hendrickson. Loeb Classical Library 342. Oxford/Cambridge (Ms), 1939.
4. Pro M. Caelio. Ed. R.G. Austin. Oxford, 1952^2 (1933^1).
5. De finibus bonorum et malorum. Ed. Jules Martha. Collection 'Budé'. Paris, 1928.
6. De natura deorum. Ed. H. Rackham. Loeb Classical Library 268. Oxford/Cambridge (Ms), 1961.
7. De oratore. Ed. H. Rackham. Loeb Classical Library 349. Oxford/Cambridge (Ms), 1960.
8. Timaeus. M. Tullius Ciceronis scripta quae mansuerint omnia. Fasc. 46. Ed. Otto Plasberg. Recognovit W.A. Wax. Stuttgart, 1965 (editio stereotypa editionis primae 1938).
9. Tusculanae disputationes. Ed. Jules Fohlen and Jules Humbert. Collection 'Budé'. Paris, 1931.
10. Scholia in Ciceronis Orationes Bobiensia. Ed. Paulus Hildebrandt. Leipzig, 1907.

CLEMENS ALEXANDRINUS
Stromateis. Les Stromates. Texte et traduction de Marcel Caster et autres. Série : Sources chrétiennes 38, 278. 279. Paris, 1954-1981.

CONSTITUTIO APOSTOLICA. PG 1. Paris, 1857.

CYPRIANUS CARTHAGIENSIS
1. Epistolae. PL 4. Paris, 1844.
2. De habitu virginum. PL 4. Paris, 1844.

DAMASCIUS
Traité des principes. Ed. L.G. Westerink, traduction Joseph Combes. Collection 'Budé'. Paris. 1991.

THE DIDASCALIA APOSTOLORUM IN SYRIAC.
Ed. Arthur Vööbus. Corpus Scriptorum Christianorum Orientalium, Vols. 406, 407 and 408. Scriptores Syri, T. 175, 176, 179 and 180. Louvain, 1979.

DIO
Dio Cassius Cocceianus, Roman History. 9 vols. Ed. Earnest Clary. Loeb Classical Library. Oxford/Cambridge (Ms), 1954 (1916[1]).

EPICTETUS
1. Diatribai. Discourses. Ed. W.A. Oldfather. Loeb Classical Library 131. Oxford/Cambridge (Ms), 1925.
2. Encheiridion. Ed. W.A. Oldfather. Loeb Classical Library 218. Oxford/Cambridge (Ms), 1928.

EPIPHANIUS
Panarion haeresium alias Haeresium fabularum compendium. Die griechischen christlichen Schriftsteller der ersten drei Jahrhunderte. Herausgegeben von Karl Holl. Leipzig, 1915. Also PG 41. Paris, 1863.

EUNAPIUS
Lives of the Philosophers. Philostratus and Eunapius. Lives of the Sophists. Ed. Wilmer C. Wright. Loeb Classical Library 134. Oxford/Cambridge (Ms), 1921. Iamblichi Chaldicensis in Platonis Dialogos commentarii fragmenta. Ed. John M. Dillon. Philosophia antiqua. Vol. XXIII. Leiden, 1973[3].

EUSEBIUS CAESARIENSIS
1. Demonstratio evangelica. PG 22. Paris, 1857.
2. Historia ecclesiastica (quoted as HE). Die griechischen christlichen Schrifsteller der ersten drei Jahrhunderte. Eusebius II,1. Herausgegeben von Eduard Schwartz. Leipzig, 1903.

GREGORIUS NAZIANZUS
1. Oratio in sanctum baptisma. PG 36. Paris, 1858.
2. Oratio contra Julianum. PG 36. Paris, 1858.
3. Oratio 43 in laudem Basilii Magni. PG 36. Paris, 1858.
4. Oratio in laudem sororis suae Gorgoniae. PG 35. Paris, 1858.

GREGORY NYSSENUS
1. Contra Eunomium. Gregorii Nysseni Opera. Ed. Werner Jaeger. Vol. II. Leiden, 1960.
2. De hominis officio. PG 44. Paris, 1863.
3. De Vita Moysis. Gregorii Nysseni Opera. Ed. Werner Jaeger. Vol. II. Leiden, 1960.

HERMAS
Pastor. The Shepherd. With an English translation by Kirsopp Lake. Loeb Classical Library 25. Cambridge (Ms)/London (1970, 1913[1]).

HIERONYMUS
1. Commentarium in Ezechielem prophetam. PL 5. Paris, 1845.
2. Epistolae. PL 5. Paris, 1822.
3. Epistola de castitate. PL Supplementum 1. Paris, 1958.
4. Libri duo adversus Jovinianum. PL 23. Paris, 1845.
5. De perpetua virginitate. Adversus Helvidium. PL 23. Paris, 1845.
6. Contra Vigilantium. PL 23. Paris, 1845.

HIPPOLYTUS
Hippolyte de Rome, La tradition apostolique d'après les anciennes versions. Ed. Bernard Motte. Sources chrétiennes 11bis. Paris, 1968[2].

HOMER
The Iliad (quoted as Il.). Translated by A.J. Murray. Loeb Classical Library 170 qnd 171. London/Cambridge (ms), 1924[1].

IAMBLICHUS
De mysteriis liber. Ed. Gustavus Parthy. Amsterdam, 1965 (photostatic reprint of the original edition Berlin, 1857.)

JOHANNES CHRYSOSTOMUS
1. Homiliae in Epistolam ad Colossenses. PG 62. Paris, 1862.
2. Homiliae in Epistolam I ad Corinthios. PG 62. Paris, 1862.
3. Homiliae propter fornicationes. PG 51. Paris, 1862.
4. Homiliae ad Matthaeum. PG 58. Paris, 1862.
5. Homiliae in Epistolam ad Titum. PG 62. Paris, 1862.
6. Adverus oppugnatores eorum qui ad vitam monasticam inducunt. PG 47. Paris, 1863.

JUSTINUS MARTYR
Apologia 1. PL 6. Paris, 1857.

LACTANTIUS
De mortibus persecutorum. PL 7. Paris, 1844.

LIBER AD GREGORIAM. PL Supplementum 3. Paris, 1963.

LIVIUS, TITUS
Livy. 14 volumes. Loeb Classical Library. London/Cambridge (Ms).

LUCIANUS
Menippus or the Descent into Hades. Ed. A.M. Harmon. Loeb Classical Library. Cambridge (Ms)/London, 1953.

LUCRETIUS
De rerum natura. Ed. W.H.D. Rouse, revision by Martin F. Smith. Loeb Classical Library 181. Oxford/Cambridge (Ms), 1975.

MARCUS AURELIUS
Meditations. Ed. C.R. Haines. Loeb Classical Library 58. Oxford/Cambridge)Ms), 1930 (revised edition).

MARINUS
The Life of Proclus. Marinos of Neapolis, The Extant Works. Ed. Al. N. Oikonomides. Chicago, 1977.

NUMENIUS
Fragments. Ed. Édouard des Places. Collection Budé. Paris, 1973.

OLYMPIODORUS
Olympiodori philosophi in Platonis Phaedonem commentaria. Ed. William Norvin. Hildesheim, 1968 (photostatic reprint of the original edition Berlin, 1913.)

ORIBASIUS
Oeuvres d'Oribase en grec et en français. Eds. Bussemaker et Ch. Daremberg. Paris, 1858.

ORIGENES
1. Contra Celsum. PG 11. Paris, 1857.
2. Fragments on I Corinthians. Ed. E.C. Jenkins in Journal of theological Studies, Vol. 9 (1907/1908).
3. Homiliae in Canticum canticorum. PG 13. Paris, 1857.

PHILOSTRATUS
The Life of Apollonius of Tyana. Ed. F.C. Conybeare. Loeb Classical Library 16-17. Oxford/Cambridge (Ms), 1912.

PLOTINUS
Enneades. Plotinus, The Enneads, translated by Stephen Mackenna, revised by B.S. Page. London (1964[4], 1917-1930[1]). Plotini opera. 3 vols. Eds. Paul Henry and Hans-Rudolf Schwyzer. Scriptorum classicorum bibliotheca oxoniensis. Oxford, 1964-1982. Plotinus. 6 vols. Ed. A.H. Armstrong. Loeb Classical Library 440-445. Oxford/Cambridge (Ms). Plotin et la quête de l'une. Présentation, choix et traduction des textes, bibliographie par Pierre-Jean About. Série : Philosophie de tout le temps. Paris, 1973

PLUTARCHUS
1. De animae procreatione in Timaeo. On the generation of souls in the Timaeus. Platonic Essays. Ed. Harold Cherniss. Moralia XIII, Part I. Loeb Classical Library 427. Oxford/Cambridge (Ms), 1976.

2. Consolation to his wife. Moralia VII. Eds. Phillip H. de Lacy and Benedict Einarson. Loeb Classical Library 405. London/Cambridge (Ms), 1959.
3. De defectu oraculorum. Moralia V. On the obsolescence of oracles. Ed. Frank Cole Babbitt. Loeb Classical Library 306. Oxford/Cambridge (Ms), 1967.
4. E apud Delphos. Moralia V. The E at Delphi. Ed. Frank Cole Babbitt. Loeb Classical Library 306. Oxford/Cambridge (Ms), 1967.
5. De facie quae in orbe lunae apparet. Moralia XII. Concerning the face which appears in the orb of the moon. Eds. Harold Cherniss and William C. Helmbold. Loeb Classical Library 406. Oxford/Cambridge (Ms), 1957.
6. De genio Socratis. Moralia VII. On the Sign of Socrates. Eds. Phillip de Lacy and Benedict Einarson. Loeb Classical Library 405. Oxford/Cambridge (Ms), 1959.
7. De Iside et Osiride. Moralia V. Isis and Osiris. Ed. Frank Cole Babbitt. Loeb Classical Library 306. Oxford/Cambridge (Ms), 1967. Plutarch's De Iside et Osiride. Ed. J. Gwyn Griffiths. University of Wales Press, 1970.
8. Pompeius. Pompey. Translated by B. Perrin. The Parallel Lives, Vol. V. Loeb Classical Library, 87. London/Cambridge (Ms), 1917.
9. Questiones platonicae. Platonic Questions. Platonic Essays. Ed. Harold Cherniss. Moralia XIII, Part I. Loeb Classical Library 427. Oxford/Cambridge (Ms), 1976.
10. De sanitate tuenda. Advice about keeping well. Moralia II. Loeb Classical Library 222. London/Cambridge (Ms), 1956.
11. De sera numinis vindicta. On the Delays of the Divine Vengeance. Eds. Phillip H. De Lacy and Benedict Einarson. Loeb Classical Library 405. Oxford/Cambridge (Ms), 1959.

PORPHYRIUS
1. De abstinentia. De l'abstinence. Ed. Jean Bouffartique. Collection 'Budé'. Paris, 1977-1979.
2. On the cave of the nymphs. Translation by Robert Lamberton. Barrytown, NY (1983).
3. Sententiae ad intelligibilia ducentes. Ed. Erich Lambertz. Bibliotheca Teubneriana. Leipzig, 1975.
4. Vita Plotini. Plotinus I. Ed. A.H. Armstrong. Loeb Classical Library. Oxford/Cambridge (Ms), 1966.

PROCLUS
1. Proclus, The Elements of Theology. A revised Text with Translation, Introduction and Commentary. Ed. E.R. Dodds. Oxford, 1963^2 (1933^1.)
2. De malorum subsistentia. Über die Existenz des Bösen. Übersetzt und erläutert von Michael Erler. Beiträge zur klassischen Philoge. Heft 102. Meisenheim am Glan (1978.)
3. Commentarium in Platonis Parmenidem. Procli philosophi opera inedita. Ed. Victor Cousin. Frankfurt am Main, 1962 (photostatic reprint of the original edition Paris, 1864.) Proclus' commentary on Plato's Parmenides. Translation by Glenn R. Morsch and John M. Dillon. Introduction and Notes by John M. Dillon. Princeton, 1987.

4. Procli Diadochi in Platonis Timaeum commentaria. Ed. Ernestus Diehl. Amsterdam, 1965 (photostatic reprint of the original edition Leipzig, 1903-1906.) Proclus, Commentaire sur le Timée. Traduction et notes par A.J. Festugières. Paris, 1966-1968. Proclus, Théologie platonicienne. Eds. H.D. Saffrey and L.G. Westerink. Collection 'Budé'. Paris, 1978.

RUFUS EPHESIUS
Rufus d'Ephèse, Fragments extraits d'Aétius. Oeuvres, ed. Ch. Daremberg et Émile Ruelle. Amsterdam, 1963. (Réimpression anastatique de l'édition Paris, 1879.)

SENECA
1. De beneficiis. Ed. John W. Basore. Loeb Classical Library 310. Oxford/Cambridge (Ms), 1935.
2. Epistolae ad Lucilium. Collection'Budé'. Paris, 1957.
3. Naturales quaestiones. Ed. Thomas H. Corcoran. Loeb Classical Library 77. Oxford/Cambridge (Ms), 1971-1972.
4. Phaedra. Ed. Frank J. Miller. Loeb Classical Library 62. Oxford/Cambridge (Ms), 1917.
5. De providentia. L. Annaeus Seneca, Philosophische Schriften Lateinisch und Deutsch. 1.Bd. Ed. Manfred Rosenbach. Darmstadt, 1969.

SEXTUS EMPIRICUS
Against the Physicists. Ed. R.G. Bury. Loeb Classical Library 311. Oxford/Cambridge (Ms), 1936.

SIRICIUS
Epistola Siricii Papae adversus Jovinianum haereticum. Mansi 3.

SOCRATES
Historia ecclesiastica. PG 64. Paris, 1867.

SOPHOCLES
Elektra. Ed. and translated by F. Storr. Loeb Classical Library 21. Cambridge (Ms)/London, 1928 (1913[1].

SORANUS
Soranos d'Ephèse, Maladies des femmes. Eds. Paul Burgière, Danielle Gourevitch et Yves Malinas. Collection Belles Lettres. Paris, 1988.

SUETONIUS
1. Augustus. The Lives of the Caesars. Translated by J.C. Rolfe. Loeb Classical Library. London/Cambridge (Ms). 1960 (1913[1]).
2. Tiberius. The Lives of the Caesars. Translated by J.C. Rolfe. Loeb Classical Library. London/Cambridge (Ms), 1914.

SULPICIUS SEVERUS
Vita Martini. CSEL 1. Vienna, 1866.

SYRIANUS
In metaphysica commentaria. Ed. G. Kroll. *Commentaria in Aristotlem graeca*. Vol. VI. Berlin, 1902.

TERTULLIANUS
1. De anima. PL 2. Paris, 1844.
2. Apologeticus adversus gentes pro Christianis. PL 1. Paris, 1844.
3. De baptismo. PL 1. Paris, 1844.
4. De carne Christi. PL 2. Paris, 1844.
5. De corona. PL 2. Paris, 1844.
6. De cultu feminarum. PL 1. Paris, 1844.
7. De exhortatione castitatis. PL 2. Paris, 1844.
8. De idolatria. Tertulliani Opera Pars II. Corpus Scriptorum Christianorum. Pars Latina. Turnholti, 1954.
9. Adversus Marcionem. PL 2. Paris, 1844.
10. Ad nationes. PL 2. Paris, 1844.
11. De pallio. PL 2. Paris, 1844.
12. De poenitentia. PL 2. Paris, 1844.
13. De praescriptionibus adversus haereticos. PL 1. Paris, 1844.
14. De testimonio animae. PL 1. Paris, 1844.
15. Ad uxorem. PL 1. Paris, 1844.
16. De virginibus celandis. PL 1. Paris, 1844.

VALERIUS MAXIMUS
Valerii Maximi factorum et dictorum memorabilium libri novem. Rec. Carolus Kempf. Leipzig, 1888.

II SECONDARY WORKS

A WORKS OF REFERENCE

AUSFÜHRLICHES LEXIKON DER GRIECHISCHEN UND RÖMISCHEN MYTHOLOGIE. Herausg. W.H. Roscher. Leipzig/Berlin, 1924-1937.

DICTIONNAIRE D'HISTOIRE ET DE GÉOGRAPHIE ECCLÉSIASTIQUE. Paris.

THE ENCYCLOPEDIA OF PHILOSOPHY. New York/London.

OXFORD CLASSICAL DICTIONARY. Oxford, 1996.

DER KLEINE PAULY. Stuttgart/Weimar.

PAULYS REAL-ENCYCLOPÄDIE DER CLASSISCHEN ALTERTUMSWISSENSCHAFT. Neue Bearbeitung von Georg Wissowa. Stuttgart (cited as PW).

THEOLOGISCHE REALENZYKLOPÄDIE (quoted as TRE).

B   COLLECTIONS

L'ASSOCIATION DIONYSIAQUE DANS LES SOCIÉTÉS ANCIENNES. Actes de la table ronde organisée par l'École française de Rome, 1986.

AUFSTIEG UND NIEDERGANG DER RÖMISCHEN WELT (Cited as ANRW). Geschichte und Kultur Roms im Spiegel der neueren Forschung. Berlin/New York.

ÉTUDES MITHRAIQUES. Actes du 2e Congrès International des --, Téhéran, du 1er au 8ième Septembre 1975. Acta Iranica 17. Première série, Actes de congrès. Téhéran-Liège, 1978.

MITHRAIC STUDIES. Proceedings of the First International Congress of Mithraic Studies. Vol. I and II, Ed. John R. Hinnells. Manchester University Press, 1975 and 1986.

MITHRAISM IN OSTIA. Mystery Religion and Christianity in the ancient Port of Rome. Ed. Samuel Laeuchli (1967).

DER MITTELPLATONISMUS. Herausg. Clemens Zintzen. Wege der Forschung. Bd. LXX. Darmstadt, 1981.

PLOTINUS AMID GNOSTICS AND CHRISTIANS. Ed. David T. Runia. Papers presented at the Plotinus Symposium held at the Free University, Amsterdam, on January 1984. Amsterdam, 1984.

C   MONOGRAPHS

ACKERMANN, Erich,   Lukrez and der Mythos. Reihe : Palingenesia. Monographien und Texte zur klassischen Altertumswissenschaft. Bd. XIII. Wiesbaden, 1979.

ALFARIC, Prosper,   L'évolution intellectuelle de Saint Augustin. Du Manichéisme au Néoplatonisme. Paris, 1918.

ALT, Karin, Weltflucht und Weltbejahung. Zur Frage des Dualismus bei Plutarch, Numenios, Plotin. Akademie der Wissenschaften und der Literatur - Mainz. Abhandlungen des geistes- en sozialwissenschaftlichen Klasse. Jhrg. 1993, nr. 8. Mainz, 1993.

ARENDT, Hannah,   Love and Saint Augustine. University of Chicago Press, 1996. (Translation and revision of 'Liebesbegriff bei Augustin'. 1929. Doct. thesis).

ARMSTRONG, A.H.,   Dualism Platonic, Gnostic, and Christian. in : Plotinus amid Gnostics and Christians.

ARMSTRONG, A.H. and MARKUS, R.A., Christian Faith and Greek Philosophy. London (1964², 1960¹).

ARNOU, René, Le désir de Dieu dans la philosophie de Plotin. Rome, 1967, deuxième édition revue et corrigée (1921¹).

AUTRAN, Charles, Mithra, Zoroastre et la préhistoire aryenne du Christianisme. Paris, 1935.

BAILEY, Derrick Sherman, The Man-Woman Relation in Christian Thought. London, 1959.

BAINTON, Ronald H., Der frühe Kirche und der Krieg. Wege der Forschung. Bd. CCLXVII. Darmstadt, 1971. (Translation of 'The early Church and the war.' Harvard Theological Review 39 (1946)).

BALADI, Naguib, La pensée de Plotin. Series : Initiation philosophique. Paris, 1970.

BALTES, Matthias, Die Weltentstehung des platonischen Timaios nach den antiken Interpreten. Philosophia antiqua, Vol. XXX, Teil I. Leipzig, 1976.

BASTID, Paul, Proclus et le crépuscule de la pensée grecque. Paris, 1969.

BAVEL, T.J. van, Augustinus. Van liefde en vriendschap. Baarn (1970).

BECK, Roger,
1. Mithraism since Franz Cumont. ANRW 2.17.4. 1986.
2. Planetary gods and planetary orders in the mysteries of Mithras. Leiden, 1988.

BEIERWALTES, Werner, Proklos Grundzüge seiner Metaphysik. Reihe : Philosophische Abhandlungen. Bd. XXIV. Frankfurt am Main (1965).

BESKOW, Per, The routes of early Mithraism. In : Études mithraiques.

BIANCHI, Ugo,
1. Plutarch und der Dualismus. in : ANRW 2.36.1. Berlin/New York, 1987.
2. Tipologia storica dei misteri di Mithra. ANRW 2.17.4, 1984.

BLENKINSSOP, Joseph, Sexuality and the Christian tradition. London/Sydney, 1970.

BONFANTE, G., The Name of Mithra. In : Études mithraiques.

BONHÖFFER, Adolf, Epiktet und das Neue Testament. Religionsgeschichtliche Versuche und Vorarbeite. 10. Bd. Berlin, 1964 (photostatic reprint of the original edition Gießen, 1911.)

BOTTOMLEY, Frank, Attitudes to the Body in Western Christendom. London (1979).

BOWIE, Ewan Lyall, Apollonius of Tyana : Tradition and Reality. In : ANRW II.16.2. Berlin/New York, 1978.

BOYCE, M., Mihragan among the Irani Zoroastrians. in : Mithraic Studies I.

BROWN, Peter, The Body and Society. Men, Women and Sexual Renunciation in Early Christianity. London/Boston (1988).

CADOUX, Cecil John, The Early Christian Attitude to War. A contribution to the history of Christian ethics. London, 1919.

CALLAHAN, John F., Augustine and the Greek Philosophers. The Saint Augustine Lectures Series. Saint Augustine and the Augustinian Tradition, 1964. Villanova University Press, 1967.

CAZANOVE, Olivier de, De quelques théories modernes sur l'association dionysiaque. In : L'association dionysiaque.

CHADWICK, Henry, Early Christian Thought and the Classical Tradition. Studies in Justin, Clement, and Origen. Oxford, 1966.

CLAUSS, Manfred, Cultus Mithrae. Die Anhängerschaft des Mithras-Kultes. Stuttgart, 1992.

COCHRANE, Charles Norris, Christianity and Classical Culture. A Study of Thought and Action from Augustus to Augustine. A Galaxy Book. New York, 1957^3 (1939^1).

COLPE, Carssen, Mithra-Verehrung, Mithras-Kult und die Existenz iranischer Mysterien. in : Mithraic Studies II.

COMBèS, Gustave, Saint Augustin et la culture classique. Paris, 1927.

COPLESTON, Frederick, A History of Philosophy. Vol. I, Greece and Rome. Part II. New revised edition. Garden City N.Y. (1962, 1946^1).

CUMONT, Franz, Les mystères de Mithra. Bruxelles, 1913^3 (1899^1).

DABBAD TRABULSI, José Antonio, Dionysisme. Pouvoir et société en Grèce jusqu'à la fin de l'époque classique. Centre de Recherches d'Histoire ancienne (Université de Besançon), 95. Paris, 1990.

DANIELS, C.M., The Roman army and the spread of Mithraism. In : Mithraic Studies I.

DETIENNE, Marcel, Dionysos et ses parousies. in : L'association dionysiaque.

DEUSE, Werner, Untersuchungen zur mittelplatonischen und neuplatonischen Seelenlehre. Akademie der Wissenschaften und der Literatur - Mainz. Abhandlungen der geistes- und sozialwissenschaftlichen Klasse. Einzelveröffentlichung 3. Wiesbaden (1983).

DILLON, John, The Middle Platonists. A Study of Platonism 80 B.C.-A.D. 220. London (1977).

DODDS, E.R., Pagan and Christian in an age of anxiety. Some aspects of religious experience from Marcus Aurelius to Constantine. The Wiles Lectures given at Queen's University Belfast, 1973. Cambridge, 1965.

DUNAND, Françoise, Le culte d'Isis dans le bassin oriental de la Méditerranée. Série : Études préliminaires aux religions orientales dans l'Empire romain. Tome 26. Leiden, 1973.

EMILLSON, Eyolfur, Plotinus' soul-body dualism. In : Psychology. Companions in ancient thought. Ed. Stephen Everson. Cambridge, 1991.

FELLIN, Armando, Lucrezio, Della natura.. A cura di --. Classici latini 18. Torino (1969).

FERGUSON, John H., Epicureanism under the Roman Empire. Revised and supplemented by Jackson P. Herschbell. in : ANRW, Bd. 36, 4. Teilband. 1990.

FOUCAULT, Michel, Histoire de la sexualité. 3 Le souci de soi. Paris, 1984.

FREDE, Michael, Numenius. ANRW II.36.2. Berlin/New York, 1987.

FREDOUILLE, Jean-Claude, Tertullien et la conversion de la culture antique. Paris, 1972.

FREUDENTHAL, J., Der Platoniker Albinos und der falsche Alkinoos. Hellenistische Studien III. Berlin, 1879.

GAWLICK, Günther and GÖRLER, Waldemar, Cicero. Grundriss der Philosophie. Philosophie der Antike, Bd. 4 Die hellenistische Philosophie. Basel, 1994.

GERNET, Louis, Anthropologie de la Grèce antique. Paris (1982).

GERSH, S.E., Kinêsis akinêsis. A study of spirit and motion in the philosophy of Proclus. Series : Philosophia antiqua. Bd. XXVI. Leiden, 1973.

GERSON, Lloyd P., Plotinus. London/New York, 1994.

GÖRANSSON, Tryggve, Albinus, Alcinous, Arius Didymus. Acta universitatis gothoburgensia. Studia graeca et latina gothoburgensia. Göteborg, 1995.

GORDON, R.L., Cumont. In : Mithraic Studies I.

GRANT, Robert M., Early Christianity and Society. Seven Studies. London (1978², 1977¹).

GROH, Dennis, The Ostian Mithraeum. In : Mithraism in Ostia.

HAGENDAHL, Harald, Augustine and the Latin Classics. Vol. II. Studia graeca et latina gothoburgensia XX:1. Acta Universitatis Gothoburgensis (1967).

HALFWASSEN, Jens, Der Aufstieg zum Einen. Beiträge zur Altertumskunde. Bd. 9. Stuttgart, 1992.

HAMDORF, Friedrich Wilhelm, Dionysos/Bacchus. Kult und Wandlungen des Weingottes. München, 1980.

HARNACK, Adolf von, Militia Christi. Die christliche Religion und der Soldatenstand in den ersten drei Jahrhunderten. Darmstadt, 1963 (photomechanischer Nachdruck von Tübingen, 1905).

HEERING, Gerrit Jan, De zondeval van het Christendom (The Fall of Christianity). Een studie over Christendom, staat en oorlog. Collectie 'Labyrinth'. Utrecht, 1981⁵ (1928¹).

HEYOB, Sharon Kelly, The Cult of Isis among Women in the Graeco-Roman World. Études préliminaires aux religions orientales dans l'Empire romain. T. 51. Leiden, 1975.

HOFFMAN, Daniel L., The Status of Women and Gnosticism in Irenaeus and Tertullian. Series : Studies in Women and Religion. Vol. 36. Lewiston/Queenston/Lampeter (1995).

JARAFEY, A.A., Mithra. Lord of Lands. Mithraic Studies I.

JEANMAIRE, H., Dionysos. Histoire du culte de Bacchus. Paris, 1959.

JONES, P., Plutarch and Rome. Oxford, 1971.

KRISTENSEN, W.B., Het mysterie van Mithra. Mededeelingen der Koninklijke Nederlandsche Akademie van Wetenschappen, afd. Letterkunde. Nieuwe Reeks, deel 9, no. 3. Amsterdam, 1946.

LADOMèRSKY, Nicolas, Saint Augustin, docteur du mariage chrétien. Étude dogmatique sur les biens du mariage. Série : Urbaniana V. Roma, 1942.

LAEUCHLI, Samuel, Mithraic Dualism. In : Mithraism in Ostia.

LAISTNER, M.L.W., Christianity and Pagan Culture. In : The Later Roman Empire. Cornell Paperbacks. Ithaca and London. 1978 (1951[1]).

LAMBRECHTS, P., Augustus en de Egyptische godsdienst (avec un résumé français). Brussel, 1956.

LEA, Henry C., History of sacerdotal celibacy in the Christian Church. Vol. I. London, 1907.

LECLANT, J., Inventaire bibliographique des Isiaca. 3 Tomes (= A-Q, T. III avec G. Clerc). Série : Études préliminaires aux religions orientales dans l'Empire romain. Leiden, 1972-1985.

LE CORSU, France,
1. Isis. Mythe et mystères. Collection d'études mythologiques. Paris, 1977.
2. Plutarque et les femmes dans les Vies parallèles. Paris, 1981.

LLOYD, A.C., The Anatomy of Neoplatonism. Oxford, 1990.

LUCK, Georg, Der Akademiker Antiochos. Inaugural-Dissertation Bern. Bern, 1953.

LUEDER, Annemarie, Die philosophische Persönlichkeit des Antiochos von Askalon. Inaugural-Dissertation Göttingen. Göttingen, 1940.

MACMULLEN, Ramsay, Enemies of the Roman Order. Treason, Unrest, and Alienation in the Empire. Cambridge (Ms), 1966.

MARROU, Henri-Irenée, Saint Augustin et la fin de la culture antique. Paris (1958[4]).

MAYRHOFER, Manfred, Die bisher vorgeschlagenen Etymologien und die ältesten Bezeugungen des Mithra-Namens. In : Études mithraiques.

MERCKELBACH, Reinhold, Mithras. Ein persisch-römischer Mysterienkult. Weinheim, 1994² (Königstein, Taunus, 1984[1]).

MICHEL, Wilhelm, Apollon und Dionysos. Dualistische Streifzüge. Stuttgart, 1904.

MORESCHINI, Claudio, Attico : una figura singolare del Medioplatonismo. In : ANRW 2.36.1. Berlin/New York, 1987.

NILSSON, Martin P., The Dionysiac Mysteries of the Hellenistic and Roman Age. Lund, 1957.

O'BRIEN, Dennis, Plotinus on the origin of matter. An exercise in the interpretation of the Enneads. Series : Collana di testi e studi sul pensiero antico. XXIII (1991).

PAILLER, Jean-Marie, Bacchanalia. La répression de 186 av. J.C. à Rome et en Italie : vestiges, images, tradition. Bibliothèque des Écoles françaises de Athènes et de Rome, fasc. 270. Rome, 1988.

PELIKAN, Jaroslav, Christianity and Classical Culture. The Metamorphosis of Natural Theology in the Christian Encounter with Hellenism. Gifford Lectures at Aberdeen 1992-1193. Yale University Press (1993).

PERELLI, Luciano, Lucrezio porta dell' angoscia. Firenze (1969).

POHLENZ, Max, Die Stoa. I. Göttingen, 1978[5], 1959[1]).

PRAET, Danny, De God der goden. De christianisering van het Romeine Rijk. Serie : Mens en tijd. Kapellen (B)/Kampen (NL), 1997[2] (1995[1]).

PREISKER, Herbert, Christentum und Ehe in den ersten drei Jahrhunderten. Eine Studie zur Kulturgeschichte der Theologie und der Kirche. Aalen, 1979 (Neudruck der Ausgabe Berlin, 1927.)

PUECH, Henri-Charles, Numenios von Apamea und die orientalischen Theologen im 2. Jh. n. Chr. Translation of Numénius d'Apamée et les théologiens orientales au seconde siècle, 1934. In : Der Mittelplatonismus.

RAMBAUD, Claude, Tertullien face aux morales des trois premiers siècles. Collection d'études anciennes. Paris, 1979.

RIèS, Julien, Plutarque historien et théologien des doctrines dualistes. Gnosticisme et monde hellénistique. Actes du colloque de Louvain-la-Neuve (11-14 mars 1980). Publications de l'Institut orientaliste de Louvain 27. Ed. Julien Riès. Louvain, 1982.

ROSáN, Laurence Jay, The Philosophy of Proclus. The Final Phase of Ancient Thought. New York, 1949.

ROUSSELLE, Aline, Porneia. De la maîtrise du corps à la privation sensorielle, IIe-IVe siècle de l'ère chrétienne. Série : Les chemins de l'Histoire. Paris, 1983.

ROZELAAR, Marc, Seneca. Eine Gesamtdarstellung. Amsterdam, 1976.

SAWYER, Deborah F., Women and Religion in the First Christian Centuries. Series : Religion in the First Christian Centuries. New York, 1996.

SCARPAT, Giuseppe, Il pensiero religioso di Seneca e l'ambiente ebraico e cristiano. Brescia (1977).

SCHMITT, Émile, Le mariage chrétien dans l'oeuvre de Saint Augustin. Une théologie baptismale de la vie conjugale. Paris, 1983.

SCHRIJVERS, P.H., Horror ac divina voluptas. Études sur la poétique et la poésie de Lucrèce. Amsterdam, 1970.

SLIDER, Robert Dick, Ancient Rhetoric and the Art of Tertullian. Series : Oxford Theological Monographs. Oxford, 1971.

SOLMSEN, Friedrich, Isis among the Greeks and Romans. Harvard University Press, 1979.

SORDI, Marta, The Christians and the Roman Empire. Translated from the Italian by Annabel Beldini. London/Sydney (1983).

SPEIDEL, Michael P., Mithras-Orion. Greek Hero and and Roman Army God. Série : Études préliminaires aux religions orientales dans l'Empire romain. T. 81. Leiden, 1980.

STÜCKELBERGER, Alfred, Atomistik in römischer Zeit. In : ANRW. Bd. 36, 4. Teilband. 1990.

TAKACS, Sarolta A., Isis and Sarapis in the Roman World. Series : Religion in the Graeco-Roman World. Vol. 124. Leiden, 1995.

THIEME, P., The Concept of Mithra in Aryan Belief. in : Mithraic Studies.

TROUILLARD, Jean
1. La mystagogie de Proclos. Paris, 1982.
2. La procession plotinique. Bibliothèque de philosophie contemporaine. Histoire de philosophie et philosophie générale. Paris, 1955.
3. La purification plotinique. Paris, 1955.

TURCAN, Robert, Mithra et le Mithraicisme. Collection : Que sais-je? Paris, 1981.

USSEL, J. van, Het Christendom en de sexuele problematiek. In 'Kultuurleven'. Jg. 35 (1968).

VALGIGLIO, Ernesto, Divinità e religione in Plutarco. Genova (1988).

VARESSIS, Evangelia, Die Andersheit bei Plotin. Beiträge zur Altertumskunde. Bd. 78. Stuttgart/Leipzig, 1996.

VERMASEREN, M.J., De Mithrasdienst in Rome. Nijmegen, 1951.

VERSNEL, H.S., Inconcistencies in Greek and Roman Religion I. Ter unus. Isis, Dionysus, Hermes. Three Studies in Henotheism. Studies in Greek and Roman Religion, Vol. 6. Leiden, 1990.

VRIES, Gerrit Jacob de, Bijdrage tot de psychologie van Tertullianus. Doct. thesis. Utrecht, 1929.

WALLIS, R.T., Neoplatonism. London, 1972.

WASZINK, J.H., Het oude Christendom en de antieke Wijsbegeerte. In : Christendom en Oudheid. Eindhoven (NL), 1947.

WINSPEAR, Alban D., Lucretius and scientific thought. Montreal (1963).

WHITTAKER, John, Platonic Philosophy in the Early Centuries of the Empire. In : ANRW 2.36.1.

WISSOWA, Georg, Religion und Kultus der Römer. Handbuch der klassischen Altertumswissenschaft. Bd. 5, Abt. 4. München, 1912^2 (1902^1).

WITT, R.E., Isis in the Graeco-Roman World. Series : Aspects of Greek and Roman Life. London, 1971.

ZELLER, Eduard, Die Philosophie der Griechen in ihrer geschichtlichen Entwicklung. III. Teil, 2. Abteilung, 2. Hälfte. Hildesheim, 1963 (photomechanischer Nachdruck von Leipzig, 1923^5).

ZIEGLER, Konrad, Plutarchos von Chaironea. Stuttgart/Waldsee, 1949.

GENERAL INDEX

Aberdeen, University of, 253
About, Pierre-Jean, 110
Abraham, 18
Academy of Plato, 20, 25, 26, 80, 81, 91, 92
Acheron, 141
Achilles, 256
Ackermann, Erich, 5, 98, 99
Adam, 188, 216, 219, 233
Adeodatus, son of Saint Augustine, 213-214, 228
Africa(n), 196, 213, 214
Ahriman, 145
Ahura-Mazda, 144, 145, 163
Alaric, Visigoth king, 208
Albinus, 27, 105
Alcimus, a Roman, 147
Alcinous, 27-30, 106
Alexander the Great, 126, 128
Alexander Polyhistor, 17
Alexandria, 19, 45, 80, 126, 249
Alfaric, 236
Algeria, 213
Alt, Karin, 21, 22, 24, 28, 41, 59, 103, 104, 105, 106, 107, 108, 112
Ambrose, 197, 209, 214, 245, 253, 258
Amesha-Spenta, 144
Ammonius Saccas, 45
Andrew, apostle, 194

Anthropology, anthropological, 124, 148, 190, 191
Anthropomorphism, 32, 122
Anthroposophy, 124
Antioch, 45, 206, 207, 208, 221, 251
Antiochus of Ascalon, 26-27, 105
Antiquity, 121, 158
Antoninus Pius, 133
Anubis, 138, 139
Apameia (Qal't el Moudiq), town in Syria, 20, 102
Aphrodite, 52, 220
Apollo, 124, 125
Apollonius of Tyana, 18, 102
Apostolic Constitution, 195
Apostolic Fathers, 241
Apostolic Tradition, 201
Appianus, 162
Apuleius, Lucius, 136, 138, 140, 141, 142-143, 162
Aramaic, 241
Aratus of Soli, 258
Arendt, Hannah, 236, 258
Areopagus, 247
Aretaeus, Greek doctor, 179, 180, 229
Aristotelian(ism), 41
Aristotle, 8, 19, 36, 70, 81, 99, 260
Armenia, 146
Armstrong, A.H., 46, 62, 64, 103, 109, 113, 114, 258, 260
Arnou, René, 47, 48, 53, 109,

110, 111
Artemidorus, 176-178, 228, 229
Aryan, 143
Ascalon, 26
Asia Minor, 18, 80, 132, 146
Aspasia, 32
Atheism, 121
Athanasius, Father of the Church, 245, 258
Athena, 142
Athens, Athenian, 1, 26, 31, 70, 80, 91, 123, 155, 246, 247, 251
Atomism, atomistic, 2, 5
Atrium Vestae, 193
Atticus, 41-45, 108, 109
Augustine, 7, 99, 197, 211-224, 236, 237, 238, 245, 246, 248, 251, 252, 253, 256, 258, 259, 260
Augustus (Octavianus), 175, 241
Autran, Charles, 163
Avesta, 143, 163
Ayer, A.J., 81

Babylon, 146
Bacchanalia, 128, 129-131
Bacchant(s), Bacchic(s), 125, 126, 128, 129-131, 160
Bacchus see Dionysus
Bactria, 146
Bailey, Derrick, 179, 200, 201, 202, 218, 225, 226, 227, 229, 232, 234, 235, 237, 238, 258-259
Bainton, Ronald H., 243, 257, 258
Baladi, Naguib, 54, 111
Baltes, Matthias, 105, 109
Barth, Karl, 253
Basil the Great, Father of the Church, 246, 248, 251, 253, 260
Basilides, Gnostic prophet, 77
Bastid, Paul, 117, 118, 119, 120

Bavel, T.J. van, 211, 220, 236, 237, 238
Beck, Roger, 143-144, 163, 164
Beierwaltes, Werner, 88, 117, 119, 120
Belgian, 136, 221
Beskow, Per, 164
Bethlehem, 208
Beutler, Rudolf, 85, 87, 90, 94, 117, 118, 119, 120
Bianchi, Ugo, 106, 150, 164, 165
Bible, 240, 248, 253, 260
Black Mass, 191
Black Sea, 146, 147
Blenkinsopp, Joseph, 183, 229
Boethius, 6
Bonfante, G., 163
Bonhöffer, Adolf, 13, 101
Bottomley, Frank, 186, 197, 199, 201, 220, 230, 232, 235, 236, 237
Bouffartique, Jean, 115
Boyce, Mary, 164
Brahmans, 103
Briseis, Achilles' girl friend, 256
Britannia, 147, 148
Brown, Peter, 175, 180, 198, 203, 204, 206, 215, 220, 221, 222, 228, 229, 232, 233, 234, 235, 236, 238
Byblos, town in Fenicia, 34
Byrrhaena, in the Golden Ass, 142
Byzantine, 109

Cadoux, Cecil John, 244, 246, 257, 258
Caelius (Rome), 139
Caesar, Julius, 19
Caesarea (town in Palestine), 70
Calcidius, 21, 24, 103, 104
Caligula, 138
Callahan, John F., 260
Calvary, 191
Calvin, Johannes, 189
Campus Martius (in Rome), 138
Canadian, 27
Capitol (in Rome), 136, 172
Cappadocia(n)(s), 18, 251, 253, 254, 255
Caracalla, 18, 139

Carnutum (Petronell, Lower Austria), 150
Carthage, 195
Cazanove, Olivier de, 160
Celsus, pagan philosopher, 241, 243
Chadwick, Henry, 259, 260
Chaeronea, 30
Chalcis (Qinnesrin, town in Syria), 74
Charlemagne, 221
Charles X, King of France, 169
Cherniss, Harold, 37, 108
Church of England, 189, 192
Circumcision, 190
Clauss, Manfred, 147, 148, 165
Clemens Alexandrinus, 102, 186, 203-204, 205, 227, 230, 234, 244, 250, 251, 258, 260
Clemens Romanus, 241
Christian(s), 8, 13, 52, 69, 70, 71, 80, 95, 100, 123, 129, 131, 139, 154, 157, 158, 170, 172, 181-228, 233, Ch. IV passim
Christianity, 52, 68, 122, 123, 133, 154, 157-158, 174, 179, 183, 191, 202, 204, 214, 223, 225, 227, Ch. IV passim
Chronos, 124
Cicero, 5, 6, 18, 19, 26, 27, 34, 99, 102, 104, 105, 240
Cilicia, 19, 146, 164
Clark, Elisabeth A., 238
Cleanthes, 258
Cleopatra, 32, 132
Cochrane, Charles Norris, 250, 257, 260
Colpe, Carssens, 151, 166
Combès, Gustave, 261
Constantine I the Great, 188
Constantinople, 80, 208
Consul, 7

Copleston, Frederick, 7, 12, 32, 47, 68, 76, 99, 100, 101, 102, 106, 108, 111, 115, 120
Cordoba, 6
Corinth(ians), 142, 143, 184
Corrigan, Kevin, 113
Council of Constantinople, 197
Council of Nicea, 196
Cumont, Franz, 146, 148-149, 154, 161, 163, 165, 166
Cyprian of Carthage, 195

Dabbad Trabulsi, José Antonio, 160
Damascius, 116
Daniels, C.M., 165
Decius Mundus, a Roman knight, 137-138
Delphi, 31
Delta (of Egypt), 134
Demiurge, 21, 23, 24, 27, 27, 28, 43, 44, 45, 68, 76, 78, 94, 95-96
Democracies, modern, 121, 155
Democritus, 2
Des Places, Édouard, 103
Descartes, René, 12
Detienne, Marcel, 125, 160
Deuse, Werner, 35, 104, 106, 108
Diaspora, 157
Didachê, 201
Dillon, John, 22, 23, 103, 104, 105, 108, 109, 116
Dio Cassius, 102, 162
Diocletianus, 150, 242, 243
Diogenes Laertius, 17
Dione, 52
Dionysiaca see Bacchanalia
Dionysus (Bacchus), 124-133, 137, 157, 158, 160, 161
Dodds, E.R., 53, 54, 111, 112, 118, 179, 229
Domitian, 12, 193
Driver, Tom F., 183, 229
Dualism, dualistic, 4, 5, 7, 10-11, 13, 14, 15, 16, 17, 20-22, 24, 25, 26, 28, 30, 31, 32, 33, 35, 35-36, 37, 38, 39, 40, 41, 42, 43-45, 46, 50, 51, 54, 55, 56, 58, 59-60, 62,

64, 65, 68, 69, 72, 73, 77, 79, 82, 85, 86, 88, 91, 92, 93, 95, 97, 101, 104, 106, 107, 108, 112, 115, 125, 132, 135, 136, 144, 148, 150, 153-154, 166, 170, 175, 178, 181, 186, 193, 199, 200, 201, 202, 205, 211-212, 219, 225, 226, 227, 243, 247, 258
Dunand, Françoise, 161
Dutch, 183, 211, 229, 245, 259
Delphi, 124

Egypt(ian), 34, 45, 80, 103, 128, 132, 134, 135, 137, 138, 173, 182, 196, 240, 255
Eleusis, mysteries of, 123
Emanation, doctrine of, 52-53
Emillson, Eyólfur, 112
Empedocles, 91
Encratism, Encratite, 186, 197, 222, 230
Ephesus, 176
Epicureanism, Epicureans, Part I, 14, 98, 127, 245
Epictetus, 12-14, 14, 16, 101
Epicurus, 1, 3, 9
Epiphanius, 196, 232, 249
Epirus, 12, 128
Eucharist, 253
Eunapius, 116
Euripides, 125
European, 220, 239, 255
Eusebius of Caesarea, 195, 232, 243, 251, 257
Eve, 188, 216, 218, 233

Flavius Arrianus, editor of Epictetus' works, 12
Farnesina gardens (Rome), 132
Fathers of the Church, 12, 152, 154, 189, 197-198, 201, 202, 202-224, 226, 227, 230, 245, 255-257
Fayûm (in Egypt), 134
Fenicia, 34
Ferguson, John, 98
Festugière, A.-J., 228
Flavian emperors, 241
Forum, Rome, 171, 192, 242
Fotis, in the Golden Ass, 142, 143
France, 121
Foucault, Michel, 177, 178, 179, 228, 229
Frede, Michael, 102, 103
Frederick the Great, 12
Fredouille, Jean-Claude, 259
French, 138
Freudenthal, J., 27, 105
Fulvia Paulina, a Roman lady, 137-138

Galenus, 180, 229
Galerius, Roman emperor, 243
Gawlick, Günter, 99
Gaza, 26
Genesis, Book of, 53, 223
Gerasa (Jerash in Jordan), 221
German, 27, 160
Gernet, Louis, 125, 159
Gersh, S.E., 119
Gerson, Lloyd P., 109, 110, 112, 115
Gifford, Adam Lord, 253
Gilson, Étienne. 253
Gnosis, Gnostic(s), 21, 23, 29, 57, 58, 64, 68, 77, 78, 83, 96, 114, 123, 149, 173, 183, 197, 199, 202, 224, 230, 250, 259
Göransson, Tryggve, 105
Görler, Woldemar, 99
Gordianus III, Roman Emperor, 45
Gordon, R.L., 148, 161, 165
Gospels, 182-183, 193, 241, 247
Grant, Robert M., 258
Great Britain, 121
Greece, 122, 123, 124, 126, 164
Greek(s), 5, 6, 12, 15, 16, 17, 29, 30, 31, 32, 33, 65, 72, 73, 78, 89, 91, 111, 122, 124, 126, 127, 128, 135, 142, 146, 150, 156, 158, 165,

173, 176, 179, 181, 184, 185, 197, 239, 240, 241, 247, 250, 251, 252, 254, 255, 256
Gregoria, 228, Roman lady, 210
Gregorius Nazianzus, 152, 166, 203, 251, 253, 254, 260, 261
Gregorius Nyssenus, 254
Griffiths, J. Gwyn, 107
Groh, Dennis, 131, 166

Hades, 152
Hadrianus, Emperor, 12
Hagendahl, Harald, 252, 260
Halfwassen, Jens, 110
Hamdorf, Friedrich Wilhelm, 161
Harnack, Adolf von, 242, 244, 245, 250, 257, 258
Hebrew, 240, 241
Heering, Gerrit Jan, 245, 258
Hellas see Greece
Hellenic see Greek
Hellenism, Hellenistic, 1, 126, 132, 207, 243, 247, 249, 253, 255
Helvidius, Christian author, 209
Hermas, early Christian author, 241
Hesiod, 124
Heyob, Sharon, 139, 162
Hieronymus, 240, 248, 253, 259
Hieropolis, town in Phrygia, 12
Hinnells, John R., 149, 163, 165
Hippo Regius, 213, 214, 222, 246
Hippolytus (Father of the Church), 105, 201, 234
Hoffmann, 230, 231, 233
Homer, 124, 249, 256
Homosexuality, 32, 130, 174, 176, 181

Horatius, 240, 248, 256
Horus, 134

Iamblichus, 74-79, 81, 103, 109, 116
Ida, a freedwoman, 137-138
Ignatius, early Christian author, 241
India(n), 18, 45, 143
Indo-European, 143
Ioannnes Philoponus, 109
Iran(ian), 36, 45, 62, 143, 144, 145, 146, 148, 149, 163, 165
Irenaeus of Lyons, 188, 230
Isis, 34, 132, 133-143, 157, 158
Isis cult, 133-143, 162
Islamic, 121
Israel(ites), 121, 173, 182, 190, 191, 255
Italy, 5, 17, 19, 128, 130, 136, 161, 165

Jaeger, Werner, 253
Jaki, Stanley L., 253
James, apostle, 194
Jarafcy, A.A., 164
Jeanmaire, H., 127, 132, 161
Jerome, 197, 208-210, 210, 211, 220, 222, 227-228, 235
Jerusalem, 208, 247
Jesus Christ, 18, 69, 182, 183, 185, 187, 188, 189, 191, 193, 203, 205, 212, 219, 231, 243, 247
Jew(s), Jewish, 8, 20, 34, 52, 70, 95, 103, 157, 158, 170, 181, 182, 184, 190, 192, 194, 199, 204, 240, 249, 259
John, apostle, 194
John the Baptist, 244
John, bishop of Jerusalem, 208
John Chrysostom, 197, 205-207, 221, 227, 234, 235, 246, 250-251, 260
John Paul II, Pope, 189
Jones, C.P., 31, 106
Josephus, Flavius, 137-138, 162
Jovinian, a Roman monk, 209
Judaism, 21, 52, 122, 123, 133, 157, 190, 191, 197, 227, 253

Judaizers, 133
Julian emperors, 241
Julian the Apostate, 254
Julius Caesar, 132, 136, 137
Juppiter Capitolinus, 150, 157, 158, 171, 172
Justinus Martyr, 188, 241, 249, 260
Justinian I, 25

Kristensen, W.B., 163

Lactantius, Christian author, 243, 258
Ladomérszky, 236, 237
Laeuchli, Samuel, 166
Laistner, M.L.W., 260
Lambrechts, P., 136, 162
Lampridius, Aelius, 102 6, 24, 80, 157
Latin, 2, 5, 158, 197, 208, 209, 221, 239, 240, 241, 247, 252, 256
Le Corsu, France, 106, 161, 162
Lea, Henry, 197, 232
Leclant, J., 161
Letter to Timothy, First, 194
Letters of Paul, 183-186
Lepidus, Macrus Aemilius, 136
Libanius, Greek rhetor, 251
Licinius, Roman emperor, 242
Lilybaeum (town in Sicily), 70
Livius, Titus, 128, 129-130, 160, 240
Ljubljana, 208
Lloyd, A.C., 79, 92, 116, 120
Longinus (philosopher), 70
Longus, 256
Louis, Pierre, 29
Lucianus, 152, 166
Lucifer of Calaris, Christian author, 249
Lucilius, pen-friend of Seneca, 10

Lucius, in the Golden Ass, 142-143
Luck, Georg, 105
Lucretius, 2-6, 98, 99
Lucullus, Lucius Licinius, 26
Lueder, Anne-Marie, 105
Luna, 151
Luther, Martin, 189, 209, 220
Lycia, 80
Lydia, 81

Mackenna, Stephen, 54
MacMullen, Ramsay, 154, 156, 157, 166
Macrina, sister of Gregory and Basil, 253
Magna Graecia, 136
Malchus = Porphyry, 70
Manchester, 149
Manichaean(s), Manichaeism, 211, 212, 222, 224
Marcella, wife of Porphyry, 70
Marcion, Gnostic prophet, 199, 259
Marcus Aurelius, 12, 14-16, 16, 101
Marinus, bioographer of Proclus), 80, 81, 117
Mark Antony, 132, 136, 137
Markus, R.A., 258, 260
Marrou, Henri-Irenée, 260
Mars, 151
Martinus of Tours, 245
Marx, Karl, 156
Mary, mother of Jesus, 187, 188, 209
Mary Magdalen, 182, 183
Materialism, materialistic, 2, 4, 5, 8, 14, 15
Mayrhofer, Manfred, 163
Mecca, 219
Mediterranean Sea, 161
Merckelbach, Reinhold, 163, 164, 166
Mercurius, 150
Merlan, Philip, 52, 111
Metempsychosis, 29
Michel, Wilhelm, 160
Middle Ages, 12

287

Middle Kingdom (Egypt), 134
Middle Platonism, Ch. I, Part IV, 58, 105
Middle Stoa, 6
Mihragan (Mithraic festival), 144, 164
Milan, 209, 214
Milete, 17
Minturnae (Minturno), town in Middle Italy, 46, 128, 132
Minucius Felix, Christian author, 256
Mithra-Varuna, 144, 163, 163
Mithradates (Mithridates), 146
Mithraea, 152, 153
Mithras (cult), 143-153, 157, 158, 163, 164, 165
Mithridatic Wars, 17, 26
Moderatus (philosopher), 103
Monica, mother of Saint Augustine, 214
Monism, monist, 13, 14, 15, 16, 19, 21, 54, 84-85, 97, 113
Monotheism, 136
Montanism, Montanist, 199, 200
Moreschini, Claudio, 109
Moroccan, 54
Moses, 103
Mozart, Wolfgang Amadeus, 134
Mycenaean-Minoan, 124
Mysticism, 127, 139

Neoplatonism, Neoplatonic, 20, 21, 25, Ch. I Part V, 214, 222, 251
Neopythagoreanism, Neopythagoreans, Part III, 78, 102, 250
Nephthys, sister of Isis, 134
Nero, 6, 12, 157, 242
Nerva, 18
Netherlands, the, 121, 168
New Kingdom (Egypt), 134

New Testament, 13, 101, 182, 182-187, 189, 241
Newman, John Henry, 253
Nicopolis, town in Epirus, 12
Nietzsche, Friedrich, 125, 159
Nigidius Figulus, Publius, 18, 19
Nile, 34, 134, 135, 147
Nilsson, Martin P., 161
Nock, Arthur Darby, 253
Numenius, 20-25, 47, 102, 103, 104

O'Brien, Dennis, 113
Octavianus-Augustus, 132, 136, 137
Old Kingdom (Egypt), 134
Old Testament, 20, 182, 209, 240
Olympian gods, religion, 3, 4, 5, 77, 122, 123, 124, 159
Olympiodorus, 116
Oribasius, 229
Origenes, 45, 102, 103, 204-205, 208, 227, 234, 241, 242, 244, 249, 250, 253, 257
Orpheus, 18, 102
Orphism, Orphic, 17, 123, 124
Osiris, 34, 134, 135, 138
Ostia, 152
Ouranos (Heaven), 52
Ovidius, 240, 256

Paedophilia, 174
Paganism, 153, 158-159, 199, 202
Pagels, Eliane, 230
Pailler, Jean-Marie, 160
Palestine, 70
Pammachius, friend of Jerome, 209
Pamphile, in the Golden Ass, 142
Panaetius, 6
Pantheism, 9-10, 13
Paphnutius, Egyptian bishop, 196
Parkinson's Law, 77
Parmenides, 32, 52
Parthian Empire, 149
Pascal, Blaise, 12
Pastor of Hermas, 198, 232
Patillon, Michel, 115

Paul, apostle, 14, 66, 183-186, 187, 194, 203, 210, 217, 220, 230, 246-247, 260
Pax Romana, 155, 244
Pelagius, 210
Pelikan, Jaorslav, 253, 254, 261
Penteus, king of Thebes, 125
Perelli, Luciano, 98
Persia(n)(s), 21, 22, 149, 150, 152, 164 ,
Peter, apostle, 194, 231, 232
Philippi, Paul, 230
Philo, 25, 240, 249, 260
Philostratus, 18, 102, 105
Photius, Byzantine author, 105
Phrygian, 12, 124, 144
Plato, 7, 8, 16, 20, 24, 25, 28, 29, 30, 36, 37, 40, 47, 65, 80, 81, 92, 103, 108, 114, 122, 127, 212, 256, 260
Platonism, Platonist(s), Platonic, 25, 26, 27, 28, 41, 46, 55, 58, 59, 75, 80, 92, 94, 98, 108, 113, 115, 212, 249, 250, 252, 260
Plotinus, 25, 45-70, 70, 71, 74, 77, 78, 79, 81, 97, 109, 110, 111, 112, 113, 114, 115, 122, 214, 222
Plutarch (of Athens, philosopher), 81, 91, 117
Plutarch (of Chaeronea), 28, 30-41, 41, 42, 106, 107, 108, 117, 127, 135-136, 146, 160, 161, 164, 175
Pohlenz, Max, 7, 10, 15, 19, 98, 100, 101, 102
Polycarpus, early Christian author, 241
Pomerium (of Rome), 137, 138
Pompeii, 132, 136, 146, 161
Pompey, 18, 146, 164
Pontus, 146
Porphyry, 41, 46, 48, 60, 70-74, 79, 103, 104, 109, 110, 112, 116, 152, 162, 166, 212, 214, 222
Posidonius, 1, 6
Pontifex maximus, 192
Praet, Danny, 247, 258, 259, 260, 261
Praetor urbanus, 130
Praetorian Guard, 147
Preisker, Herbert, 229, 230
Proclus, 41, 43, 44, 80-98, 109, 117, 118, 119, 120
Proselytes, 133
Proserpina, 141
Proverbs, Book of, 210
Ptolemaean Pharaohs, 128
Puech, Henri-Charles, 102, 103, 116
Pythagoras, 17, 18, 65, 70, 78, 89, 91
Pythagoreanism, Greek, Pythagorean(s), 16-18, 22, 25, 33, 36, 91, 92, 93, 98, 103, 123, 142
Pythagoreanism, Roman, 18-19

Quaestor, 9
Quirinal (Rome), 139

Rambaux, 233
Reformation, Churches of the, 189, 192, 220
Rhine, 147
Rhodes, 6
Rhoda, Roman lady, 198
Riès, Julien, 32, 106
Rijnders, Gerdjan, 229
Roman(s), 1, 2, 5, 7, 10, 17, 26, 31, 46, 98, 122, 129, 131, 132, 133, 136, 137, 138, 139, 140, 146, 147, 148, 149, 150, 151, 153, 155, 156, 157, 158, 165, 171, 172, 173, 175, 177, 178, 184, 197, 208, 210, 222, 231, 232, 240, 241, 242, 245, 252
Roman Catholic, 239, 253, 255, 259
Roman Catholic Church, 89, 133, 181, 183, 186-196, 220, 221, 232, 241, 243, 244, 246, 247, 250

Roman Empire, 6, 31, 98, 123, 133, 143, 146, 147, 149, 155, 158, 164, 171, 172, 173, 176, 188, 197, 208, 210, 216, 221, 225, 227, 230, 231, 239, 242, 243, 244, 245, 246, 255
Rome (city), 1, 17, 19, 30, 31, 46, 70, 74, 128, 129, 130, 131, 136, 137, 138, 139, 140, 143, 147, 152, 154, 164, 175, 181, 183, 192, 193, 196, 208, 209, 245
Rosán, Laurence, 80, 82, 117, 118
Roscher, W.H., 107
Rostra (in Rome), 131
Rousselle, Aline, 181, 229
Rufus of Ephesus, philosopher, 181, 229

Sallustius, 240
Sarastro, 134
Sasanian Empire, Sasanians, 149, 150
Satan, 183
Sawyer, Deborah, 187, 188, 230, 231
Scarpat, Giuseppe, 100
Schmitt, Émile, 224, 238
Schoolmen, 43
Schrijvers, P.H., 99
Schwyzer, H.-J., 113
Scotland, 253
Seeck, O., 91, 120
Semitic, 240, 241
Seneca, 6-11, 16, 100, 101, 157
Senate, 129, 136, 139, 154, 160, 171, 242
Senator(s), 9, 129
Septuagint, 240
Serapis (Sarapis), 136, 138, 161
Seth, 34, 134
Severus Alexander, 18
Sextus Empiricus, 19, 102
Sexuality, Ch. III passim

Shamans, 38
Sicily, 19, 70, 71, 74, 128, 136
Siricius, Pope, 196, 197, 209, 225, 232, 235
Slider, 233
Slovenia, 208
Sociology, 148
Socrates (Church historian), 70, 213, 232
Socrates (the philosopher), 84, 91, 122, 127, 156, 249
Solmsen, Friedrich, 136, 161
Song of Songs, 174, 205
Sophocles, 191, 232
Soranus, Greek doctor, 181, 229
Sordi, Marta, 258
Sozomenos, 231
Spain, Spaniard, Spanish, 6, 195, 231
Speidel, Michael P., 165
Stoa, Stoic(s), Stoicism, 1, Ch. I, Part II, 19, 26, 100, 105, 127, 156, 222, 246
Stridon, town in Slovenia, 208
Stückelberger, Alfred, 99
Styx, 141
Suetonius, 162
Sulla, Lucius Cornelius, 25, 136
Sulpicius Severus, Christian author, 258
Swiss, 12
Syncretism, syncretistic, 159
Synod of Arles, Arelate, 244-245, 246
Synod of Elvira, 195
Syria, 20, 74
Syrianus (philosopher), 81, 91, 119

Tacitus, 240
Takacs, Sarolta A., 162
Tatianus, 186, 230, 247
Teheran, 149
Temple of Isis Campensis (in Rome), 138
Temple of Jerusalem, 191
Temple of Vesta in Rome, 192
Tertullianus, 161, 166, 194, 195, 199-201, 201, 232, 233, 234, 242,

243, 244, 247-248, 248-249, 253, 256, 257, 258, 259
Thebes (in Greece), 125
Thessaly, 142
Thieme, P., 163
Thracian, 124
Tiber, 138
Tiberius, 137, 138
Tiriolo (town in Calabria), 160
Traianus, 133, 147
Trouillard, Jean, 85, 111, 114, 117, 118
Troy, 192
Turcan, Robert-Alain, 146, 164, 166
Turkey, Turkish, Turks, 121, 219, 237
Tyana, town in Cappadocia, 18
Typhon (Seth), 34, 135
Tyre (Tyrus), 70

United States, the, 121
Ussel, van, 237

Valerius Maximus, 162
Vandals, 245
Varessis, Evangelia, 110, 113
Varro, Marcus Terentius, 26
Varuna, 163
Vedic, Vedism, 143, 144, 149, 163
Vegetarian(ism), 72, 80, 123, 140
Venus, 4, 151
Vermaseren, M.J., 147, 151, 164, 166
Versnel, H.S., 159
Vespasian, 156
Vestal Virgins, 192-193, 231
Vesuvius, 161
Vetus latina, 241
Vienna, 160
Vigilantius, Christian author, 209
Virgilius, 240, 252
Visigoths, 208, 245

Volusius, M., a Roman official, 136
Vries, de, 234
Vulgata, 209, 241

Wallis, R.T., 75, 116
Waszink, J., 104
Winspear, Alban D., 98
Whittaker, John, 27, 105
Will, E., 164
William of Moerbeke, 80
Wissowa, Georg, 139, 161, 162
Witt, R.E., 162
Wüst, Ernst, 163

York, 148

Zeller, Eduard, 17, 19, 46, 53, 74, 79, 84, 95, 102, 105, 109, 111, 116, 118, 119, 120
Zeus, 15, 52
Ziegler, Konrat, 106
Zoroaster, Zoroastrian(ism), 36, 144, 149